4

Life

SECOND EDITION

NATIONAL GEOGRAPHIC

L E A R N I N G

HELEN STEPHENSON

PAUL DUMMETT

JOHN HUGHES

Australia · Brazil · Mexico · Singapore · United Kingdom · United States

Contents

Unit	Grammar	Vocabulary	Real life (functions)	Pronunciation
1 Culture and identity pages 9–20	simple present and present continuous dynamic and stative verbs question forms: direct questions question forms: indirect questions	word focus: *love* feelings wordbuilding: adjective + noun collocations	opening and closing conversations	direct questions short questions
VIDEO: Faces of India **page 18** ▶ REVIEW **page 20**				
2 Performing pages 21–32	present perfect *already*, *just*, and *yet* present perfect and simple past	musical styles emotions word focus: *kind* describing performances	choosing an event	weak forms intonation with *really*, *absolutely*, etc.
VIDEO: Taiko master **page 30** ▶ REVIEW **page 32**				
3 Water pages 33–44	simple past and past continuous past perfect	describing experiences wordbuilding: adverbs with *-ly* word focus: *get*	telling stories	d and t after *-ed* endings *was* and *were*
VIDEO: Four women and a wild river **page 42** ▶ REVIEW **page 44**				
4 Opportunities pages 45–56	predictions future forms	word focus: *job* and *work* education wordbuilding: prefix *re-* pay and conditions job requirements	making and responding to requests	weak and strong auxiliary verbs
VIDEO: Everest tourism changed Sherpa lives **page 54** ▶ REVIEW **page 56**				
5 Well-being pages 57–68	modal verbs first conditional *when*, *as soon as*, *unless*, *until*, *before*	a healthy lifestyle word focus: *so* restaurants	describing dishes	weak forms disappearing sounds
VIDEO: Dangerous dining **page 66** ▶ REVIEW **page 68**				
6 Mysteries pages 69–80	purpose: *to*, *for*, and *so that* certainty and possibility	word focus: *long* art wordbuilding: nouns and verbs *-ly* adverbs in stories	reacting to surprising news	weak form of *have* showing interest and disbelief
VIDEO: Encounters with a sea monster **page 78** ▶ REVIEW **page 80**				

Listening	Reading	Critical thinking	Speaking	Writing
an excerpt from a TV program about Native American culture two people taking a quiz about colors and their meanings	an article about cultural identity an article about globalization	examples	getting to know you a color quiz how international you feel first impressions	text type: a business profile writing skill: criteria for writing
two people talking about arts events a man talking about his dance academy	an article about listening to music an article about performance art	balance	new releases experiences performing a survey on the arts arts events	text type: a review writing skill: linking ideas
an excerpt from a radio program about water recreation interviews about what happened next	an interview about underwater discoveries an article about an unforgettable experience	drawing conclusions	the first time What had happened? learning a lesson	text type: a blog post writing skill: interesting language
three people talking about their childhood ambitions three women talking about decisions	an article about the future of work an article about the economic boom in China	the author's view	predictions planning your calendar the perfect job requests	text type: a cover letter writing skill: formal style
an excerpt from a radio program about healthy eating two people discussing the power of the mind	a news article about traditional dishes a news article about imaginary eating an article about modern lifestyles	the writer's purpose	rules and regulations consequences modern life restaurant dishes	text type: a formal letter/email writing skill: explaining consequences
two people discussing an unusual photo a speaker at a conference talking about a puzzle an excerpt from a radio program about the Nasca lines	an article about flexible thinking an article about one of aviation's greatest mysteries	speculation or fact?	What's it for? speculating comparing ideas surprising news	text type: a news story writing skill: structuring a news story

Unit	Grammar	Vocabulary	Real life (functions)	Pronunciation	
7 Living space pages 81–92	*used to*, *would*, and simple past comparative adverbs comparative patterns	in the city wordbuilding: noun → adjective word focus: *as* and *like*	stating preferences and giving reasons	rising and falling intonation	
VIDEO: The town with no Wi-Fi **page 90** ▶ REVIEW **page 92**					
8 Travel pages 93–104	verb patterns: *-ing* form and infinitive present perfect and present perfect continuous How long?	vacation activities travel problems	dealing with problems	strong and weak forms	
VIDEO: Questions and answers **page 102** ▶ REVIEW **page 104**					
9 Shopping pages 105–116	passives articles and quantifiers	shopping wordbuilding: compound adjectives	buying things	linking silent letters	
VIDEO: Making a deal **page 114** ▶ REVIEW **page 116**					
10 No limits pages 117–128	second conditional defining relative clauses	medicine word focus: *take* injuries	talking about injuries	sentence stress *and*	
VIDEO: What does an astronaut dream about? **page 126** ▶ REVIEW **page 128**					
11 Connections pages 129–140	reported speech reporting verbs	communications technology	telephone language	contrastive stress polite requests with *can* and *could*	
VIDEO: Can you read my lips? **page 138** ▶ REVIEW **page 140**					
12 Experts pages 141–152	third conditional *should have* and *could have*	wordbuilding: prefixes *in-*, *un-*, *im-* word focus: *go*	making and accepting apologies	*should have* and *could have* sentence stress	
VIDEO: Shark vs. octopus **page 150** ▶ REVIEW **page 152**					

COMMUNICATION ACTIVITIES **page 153** ▶ GRAMMAR SUMMARY **page 156** ▶ AUDIOSCRIPTS **page 180**

Listening	Reading	Critical thinking	Speaking	Writing
three people talking about different living arrangements podcast replies about house design	an article about what New York used to be like an article about a small town in Puerto Rico	descriptions	places advice a tourist destination stating preferences	text type: a description of a place writing skill: organizing ideas
three people talking about travel tips people talking about their vacations an excerpt from a radio program about a wildlife conservationist	an article about writers returning to their roots an article about the impact of tourism	reading closely	travel companions favorite activities going green travel problems	text type: a text message writing skill: informal style
market research interviews with three people who are shopping an excerpt from a radio program about impulse buying	an article about two ways of going shopping an article about how to negotiate a price	testing a conclusion	shopping now and in the future souvenirs buying things	text type: customer reviews writing skill: clarity: pronouns
a podcast about the *Marathon des Sables* an excerpt from a TV show about bionic bodies	an article about life on another planet two stories about acts of endurance	reading between the lines	I'd love to live in … medicine inspirational people talking about injuries	text type: a personal email writing skill: linking ideas
four conversations about the news four conversations about news headlines	an article about isolated tribes an article about community journalism	opinions	news stories personal communication apps telephone messages	text type: an opinion essay writing skill: essay structure
an interview with a farmer two stories about difficult situations	a review of a book about Arctic expeditions an article about the samurai	relevance	decisions Where did I go wrong? going back in time making and accepting apologies	text type: a website article writing skill: checking your writing

Life around the world—in 12 videos

Unit 6 Encounters with a sea monster

Three people tell their stories about what they saw in the water.

Unit 12 Shark vs. octopus

What happens when a shark and an octopus meet.

Unit 2 Taiko master

The history of Taiko drumming from its origins in Japan to modern-day San Francisco.

Unit 7 The town with no Wi-Fi

Find out what life is like in the quiet zone of Green Bank.

Unit 11 Can you read my lips?

Rachel Kolb tells us about communicating as a deaf person.

Unit 8 Questions and answers

National Geographic Explorers from Spain, the UK, Peru, and other countries talk about their roles and about objects that are important to them in their work.

Canada

USA

UK

Spain

Morocco

Peru

Unit 10 What does an astronaut dream about?

British astronaut Helen Sharman describes her experience of being on the Mir space station.

Unit 3 Four women and a wild river

Amber Valenti leads a kayak trip down the Amur River in Mongolia, Russia, and China.

Russia

Unit 9 Making a deal

Learn how to bargain in Morocco.

Mongolia

Japan

China

Nepal

Unit 5 Dangerous dining

Find out why people eat the most dangerous fish on Earth—fugu.

India

Unit 1 Faces of India

Find out about Rajasthan through a focus on its people and faces.

Unit 4 Everest tourism changed Sherpa lives

Find out if Everest tourism has been a good or a bad thing for the local people.

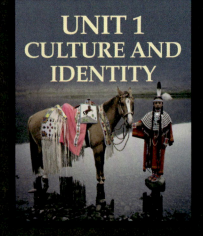

**UNIT 1
CULTURE AND IDENTITY**

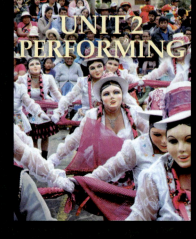

**UNIT 2
PERFORMING**

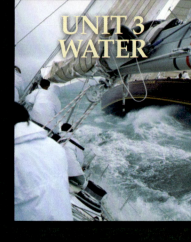

**UNIT 3
WATER**

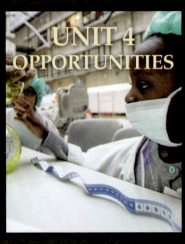

**UNIT 4
OPPORTUNITIES**

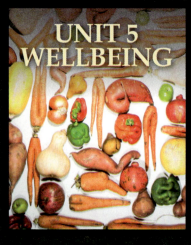

**UNIT 5
WELLBEING**

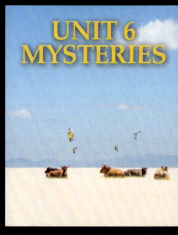

**UNIT 6
MYSTERIES**

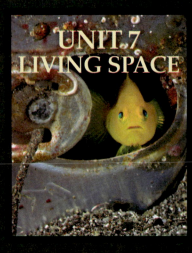

**UNIT 7
LIVING SPACE**

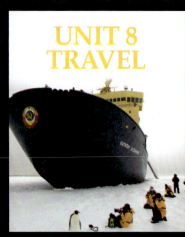

**UNIT 8
TRAVEL**

**UNIT 9
SHOPPING**

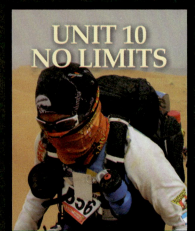

**UNIT 10
NO LIMITS**

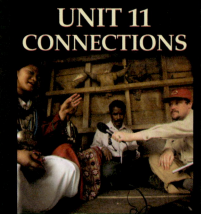

**UNIT 11
CONNECTIONS**

**UNIT 12
EXPERTS**

Unit 1 Culture and identity

Destiny Buck, of the Wanapum tribe of Native Americans, with her horse Daisy

FEATURES

10 How we see other cultures

How we think about cultural groups

12 Culture and color

Take quizzes about color

14 A world together

Find out what globalization really means

18 Faces of India

A video about the photographer Steve McCurry

1 Work in pairs. Look at the photo and the caption. Discuss the questions.

1. Where is the girl from?
2. What is she wearing?
3. The photo shows two things that are important in Native American culture. What do you think they are?

2 ▶1 Listen to an excerpt from a TV program on world cultures. Check your ideas from Exercise 1.

3 ▶1 Listen to the excerpt again. Complete the sentences.

1. People from all cultures need a sense of …
2. Many Native American children learn to ride …
3. Wearing the colors of our favorite team says: "We …"

4 Work in pairs. Do you belong to any of these groups? Tell your partner about them or any other groups you know about.

cultural societies	hobby groups
educational classes	online communities
family groups	sports clubs

1a How we see other cultures

Reading

1 Work in pairs. Look at the hats. Which part of the world do you think each one comes from?

2 Read the article and check your ideas from Exercise 1.

3 Read the article again. Find three reasons why we form general opinions of other cultural groups.

4 Work in pairs. How do movies, news reports, and TV shows influence our opinions of other cultural groups?

Grammar simple present and present continuous

> **SIMPLE PRESENT and PRESENT CONTINUOUS**
>
> **Simple present**
> It **means** that our brain doesn't work so hard.
> [...] people **put** the things they see in the world into groups.
>
> **Present continuous**
> He**'s wearing** one of those bush hats.
>
> For more information and practice, see page 156.

5 Work in pairs. Look at the grammar box. Which verb form do we use for these things?

1 things that are permanent or generally true
2 things that are temporary or in progress at the time of speaking

6 Circle the correct option to complete the sentences.

1 *I work / I'm working* for a large cultural organization. My job is usually quiet, but, at the moment, *I work / I'm working* extra hours—it's the busy season.

2 *We live / We're living* with my parents until our apartment downtown is ready. *They live / They're living* just outside the city.

3 The kids *are / are being* usually very good, but they went to bed late last night, and *they're / they're being* naughty today. Sorry!

4 I usually *find / am finding* this class easy, but *I have / I'm having* some problems this semester.

How we see other cultures

▶ 2

My neighbor recently came back from vacation. I guess he was in Australia—he's wearing one of those bush hats with corks around it everywhere he goes. I'm curious about why we identify places by things like hats. I mean, baseball caps are certainly popular in the United States, but I went to London on vacation and didn't see anyone wearing a bowler hat. And you don't see many Mexicans with sombreros or Vietnamese with straw hats in everyday life, either.

The question is, why do we think about other national groups in this way? According to psychologists, it's because people put things they see in the world into groups. We do this for several reasons. First, it means that our brain doesn't work so hard because it doesn't need to analyze every new individual thing. Another reason is that when we understand (or think we understand) something, we can make predictions about it—we know what kind of behavior to expect. Finally, it seems that we all love to feel good about ourselves and the group we belong to. This is easier when we put others into groups, too.

So is it a good thing or a bad thing to have these general opinions? Perhaps the first and more important question is to ask ourselves if the things we believe about other groups are actually true. And in the case of hats, I don't think it is!

baseball cap

straw hat

bowler hat

sombrero

bush hat

7 Complete the pairs of sentences with the simple present and present continuous forms of the verbs.

1 a He _____ (not / feel) relaxed when he flies.
  b He _____ (not / feel) very well at the moment.

2 a I _____ (come) from Scotland originally.
  b I _____ (come)—wait for me!

3 a My friend _____ (look) for a new job in a different company.
  b My friend always _____ (look) tired after she comes back from the gym.

> **▶ DYNAMIC and STATIVE VERBS**
>
> **Dynamic verbs**
> *People **put** the things they see in the world into groups.*
> *Just a minute. **I'm putting** my hat and scarf on.*
>
> **Stative verbs**
> *We **know** what kind of behavior to expect.*
> *(not are knowing)*
>
> For more information and practice, see page 156.

8 Look at the grammar box. Circle the correct option to complete the rules.

1 Dynamic verbs *are / are not* used in both the continuous and simple forms.
2 Stative verbs are not normally used in the *continuous form / simple form*.

9 Underline these stative verbs in the article.

believe	belong	mean
need	seem	understand

10 Add the stative verbs from Exercise 9 to the table. Then add these verbs.

contain	hate	love	prefer	realize
remember	like	suppose	taste	wonder

Stative verbs	
Thoughts and mental processes	know, _____, _____, _____, _____, _____, _____, _____, _____
The senses	hear, _____
Emotions	want, _____, _____, _____, _____, _____
Possession	have, _____, _____

11 Circle the correct option to complete the sentences.

1 Jake's on the phone. *He tells / He's telling* Pat about his vacation.
2 What *do you think / are you thinking* of my hat?
3 *Do you remember / Are you remembering* last summer?
4 *I hear / I'm hearing* you have a new job.
5 Maria's at the travel agency. She *asks / is asking* about the dates of the flight.
6 *I want / I'm wanting* to pass my exams the first time.
7 Sorry, *I don't know / I'm not knowing* the answer.
8 *Do you make / Are you making* coffee? Great.

Word focus *love*

12 Work in pairs. Look at this excerpt from the article. Then look at how *love* is used in the sentences. When could you use each expression?

*… we all **love** to feel good about ourselves …*

1 I'd love to! Thanks.
2 I love walking in the rain.
3 Lots of love, Jenna
4 We love the summer.
5 Please give Oscar our love.
6 The story of two strangers who fall in love
7 They are very much in love.
8 I'm loving it.

13 Work in pairs. Write short conversations using the expressions in Exercise 12. Then act out your conversations.

A: *Do you want to come over for something to eat after class?*
B: ***I'd love to!*** *Thanks.*

Speaking myLife

14 Work in pairs. Ask and answer questions using these stative verbs. Ask one follow-up question each time.

1 remember / first English class?
2 clubs / belong to?
3 hours of sleep a night / need?
4 any food / hate?
5 prefer / tea or coffee?
6 food / love?

A: ***Do you remember*** *your first English class?*
B: *No, why?* ***Do you?***

1b Culture and color

Vocabulary feelings

1 Work in pairs. How do you think the people described in sentences 1–3 feel? Choose from these adjectives.

| angry | cheerful | happy | lucky | positive | sad |

1 He's feeling kind of blue today.
2 She began to see red!
3 He's in a black mood today.

2 Circle the correct option to complete the sentences. Then ask your partner the questions.

1 What are two things that make you *happiness / happy*?
2 When was the last time you had good *luck / lucky*?
3 Can you tell me if you are *brave / bravery*?
4 What achievements are you *pride / proud* of?
5 Do you think *anger / angry* is a good thing?
6 Who do you think is the most *power / powerful* person in the world?

Listening

3 ▶ **3** Work in pairs. Take the quiz *Colors and their meaning*. Then listen and check your answers.

4 ▶ **3** Listen again and complete the table.

Color	Place	Meaning
red	Western cultures Asian cultures	1 _____ 2 _____
yellow	3 _____ 4 _____	knowledge 5 _____
6 _____	some Asian cultures	7 _____ 8 _____
9 _____	Mexico	death
green	10 _____	environmentalism

5 Work in pairs. Do these colors mean the same thing in your culture? What's your favorite color?

Colors and their meaning

1 Look at the photo. Where are the women going?
a to a birthday party
b to a wedding

2 Does red mean different things in Asian and Western cultures?
a yes   b no

3 Where does yellow mean "knowledge"?
a China   b India

4 Which color means "happiness" in some Asian cultures?
a orange   b pink

5 Do people wear blue at funerals in Mexico?
a yes   b no

6 Who uses green as their symbol?
a environmentalists
b the women's movement

Grammar question forms

6 Work in pairs. Look at the grammar box. Which type of question has the same subject–verb word order as affirmative statements?

7 Work in pairs. Look at the quiz in Exercise 3 again. Which questions are subject questions? Which are other questions?

8 Write questions for these answers. Begin with the words in parentheses.

1 People in many countries wear black at funerals. (who)
   Who wears black at funerals?
2 Yellow means happiness in Egypt. (which color)
3 Some people wear purple on International Women's Day. (what color)
4 Picasso painted a white dove as a symbol of peace. (who)
5 Red means anger in many cultures. (what)
6 The president of the United States lives in the White House. (who)

9 Pronunciation direct questions

a ▶4 Listen to the questions from Exercise 8. Does the speaker's voice rise at the end of the questions? Or does it rise, then fall?

b ▶4 Listen again and repeat the questions.

10 Work in pairs. Look at the grammar box. What is the order of the subject and verb in indirect questions?

11 Write indirect questions for these direct questions. Begin with the words in parentheses.

1 How many hours a week do you study English? (Can you tell me)
   Can you tell me how many hours a week you study English?
2 Why are you taking this course? (Can you tell me)
3 When does the course end? (Do you know)
4 How many languages does the teacher speak? (Do you know)
5 Which other courses are you taking? (Can you tell me)
6 How many students are there in this class? (Do you know)

Speaking my Life

12 Work in pairs. Ask and answer your questions from Exercise 11.

13 Complete these *blue* and *yellow* quiz questions with verbs or question words.

1 Where _____ the blue-footed booby live?
2 _____ lives in the Blue House in South Korea?
3 _____ you know the name of the country where the Blue Nile begins?
4 _____ part of the USA is famous for blues music?

1 Where _____ yellow taxi cabs from originally?
2 Which fruit _____ the California Yellow Fruit Festival celebrate?
3 _____ event gives a yellow jersey to the winner?
4 Can you tell me where the house that inspired Vincent van Gogh's "Yellow House" painting _____ ?

14 Work in two pairs within a group of four.

Pair A: Turn to page 153 and follow the instructions.

Pair B: Turn to page 154 and follow the instructions.

1c A world together

Reading

1 Complete the definition of *globalization*. Use the same word twice.

Globalization is the idea that companies are now working in many different _____ . The cultures of those _____ are also becoming more similar.

2 Read the article quickly. Work in pairs. Which paragraph(s) talk(s) about business? Which talk(s) about culture?

3 Work in pairs. Read the article again. Answer the questions.

1 Which two recent experiences demonstrated globalized culture to the author? (paragraph 1)
2 Which inventions have increased the connections between countries? (paragraph 2)
3 Which things do some people think have a negative effect on other cultures? (paragraph 3)

4 Work in pairs. Does globalization affect you or someone you know? How?

Wordbuilding adjective + noun collocations

> **WORDBUILDING adjective + noun collocations**
>
> Some adjectives and nouns often go together.
> *national identity, vegetarian food*
>
> For more practice, see Workbook page 11.

5 Look at the wordbuilding box. Complete the sentences with these words. Then find the collocations in the article and check your answers.

culture	market	view	identity

1 Television is a good example of **popular** _____ .
2 Nowadays, companies sell to a **global** _____ .
3 Watching baseball is part of the American **national** _____ .
4 I try to have a **positive** _____ of changes in my life.

6 Work in pairs. Think of at least one more collocation with each adjective in Exercise 5. Then ask and answer questions with the collocation.

*Do you like **popular music**?*

Critical thinking examples

7 Giving examples is one way of helping to make a point. Underline examples of these things in the article.

1 how popular culture moves from one country to another (paragraph 1)
2 globalization in business (paragraph 2)
3 how national cultures are strong (paragraph 3)

8 Work in pairs. How did the author's examples help you understand what globalization is?

9 Read the pairs of sentences. Underline the example sentence in each pair. Then write another example of your own for each one.

1 You can eat great international food in my town. There are lots of Thai restaurants.
2 Internet TV gives you access to shows from different countries. Brazilian soap operas are popular here now.
3 There's a lot to do at night in my area. We have a couple of great theaters.

Speaking *my* Life

10 Work in pairs to prepare a survey on how "international" other students' lives are. Use these ideas. Then work on your own and ask at least two other students your questions.

clothes	food	movies
music	sports	technology

Are any of your clothes made in other countries?
Which international foods do you eat/like?

11 Share the results of your survey with the class. Which international items are most common?

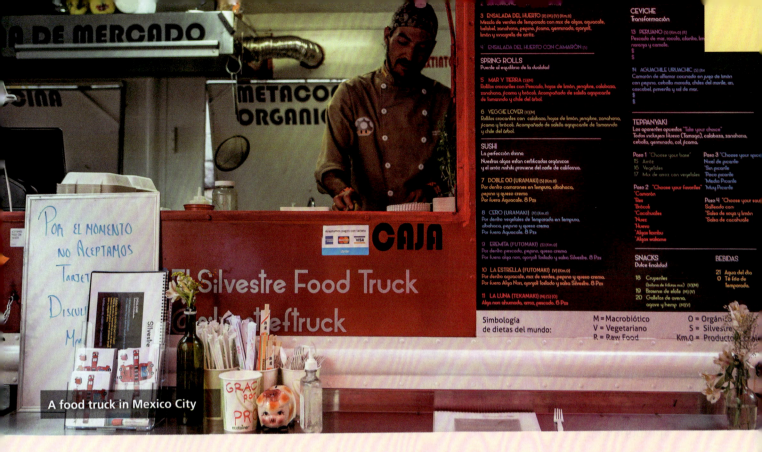

A food truck in Mexico City

A WORLD TOGETHER

BY ERLA ZWINGLE

▶ 5

1 We are in the middle of worldwide changes in culture. Popular culture is crossing from one country to another in ways we have never seen before. Let me give you some examples. One day, I'm sitting in a
5 coffee shop in London having a cup of Italian espresso served by an Algerian waiter, listening to American music playing in the background. A few days later, I'm walking down a street in Mexico—I'm eating Japanese food and listening to the music of a Filipino band. In
10 Japan, many people love flamenco. Meanwhile, in Europe, Japanese food is incredibly popular. European girls decorate their hands with henna tattoos. This is the globalization of culture.

2 The globalization of culture continues on from the
15 globalization of business. Modern industry now has a global market. Businesses make their products in one country and sell them in another. Companies employ people on one continent to answer telephone calls from customers on a different continent. It's true that
20 buying and selling goods in different countries is not new. But nowadays, everything happens faster and travels farther. In the past, there were camel trains, ships, and railways. Then planes, telephones, and television brought us closer together. Television had
25 fifty million viewers after thirteen years; the internet

had the same number after only five. Today, the internet can connect us all in real time as we watch the same news story as it happens, anywhere in the world.

30 How do people feel about globalization? It depends **3** on where they live and how much money they have. Not everyone is happy about globalization. More than a fifth of all the people in the world now speak some English. Some people believe that there is a
35 kind of "cultural attack" from the English language, social media, and McDonald's and Starbucks. But I have a more positive view. I think that cultures are strong and that countries don't need to lose their national identity. In India, there are more
40 than four hundred languages and several different religions—and McDonald's serves mutton instead of beef and offers a vegetarian menu. In Shanghai, the television show *Sesame Street* teaches Chinese values and traditions. As one Chinese teacher said,
45 "We've got an American box with Chinese content in it."

But there is one thing that is certain—globalization **4** is here to stay. And if that means we'll understand each other better, that's a good thing.

1d First impressions

Real life opening and closing conversations

> "You never get a second chance to make a good first impression."

- Dress appropriately. A dark blue suit is great for a business meeting; a red tie or scarf suggests power and energy.
- Be punctual, courteous, and positive.
- Make sure you know the other person's name. Use it!
- Make the other person the focus of your attention. Sound interested! Ask questions!
- Know what you want to say and say it effectively!
- Don't forget to follow up on your meeting with a phone call or an email.

1 Read the information above. Then work in groups and discuss the advice. Which advice is appropriate in your country? Which is not appropriate?

2 ▶ 6 Listen to two conversations at a business skills seminar in the US. Four participants are role-playing "first meetings." Which advice in the information above do they follow? Discuss with a partner.

3 ▶ 6 Look at the expressions below for opening and closing conversations. Listen again and circle the expressions the speakers use.

4 Work in pairs. Look again at the expressions for opening and closing conversations. Which expressions are the most formal?

▶ OPENING AND CLOSING CONVERSATIONS

Opening a conversation
Let me introduce myself.
Allow me to introduce myself.
Nice to meet you. My name's …
Hello. How are you. I'm …
It's a pleasure to meet you.
I'm very pleased to meet you.

Closing a conversation and moving on
Thanks for your time.
It's been good talking to you.
Let me give you my card.
Let's stay in touch.
Why don't I give you my card?
Would you like to meet again?

5 Pronunciation short questions

a ▶ 7 Listen to these conversations. Notice how the speakers use short questions to show interest.

1   C: I mostly work on online ads.
    K: Do you?

2   K: I'm in sales.
    C: Oh, are you?

3   L: Oh, yes. My brother goes to Get Fit.
    Y: Does he?

4   Y: It's almost ready to open, in fact.
    L: Is it?

b Work in pairs. Practice the exchanges.

6 Practice the conversations from Exercise 2 with your partner. Look at the Track 6 audioscript on page 180.

7 Work in groups. Imagine you are a participant in the business skills seminar. Do the task below. Use the expressions for opening and closing conversations to help you:

> **First Impressions**
> Task: You are at a networking event. Introduce yourself to as many people as you can and arrange to follow up with useful contacts. You only have two minutes with each person.

> **networking (n)** /ˈnetwɜːrkɪŋ/ making useful business contacts

8 Work in pairs. Compare the information you found out about different people in Exercise 7.

1e About us

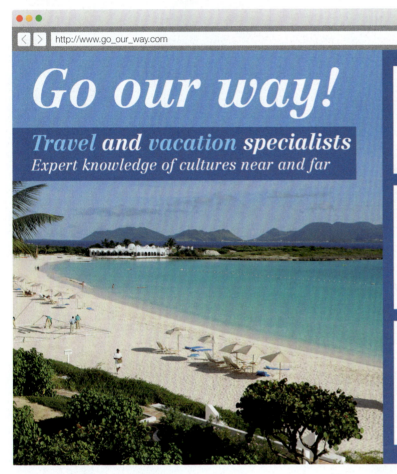

http://www.go_our_way.com

Go our way!

Travel and vacation specialists
Expert knowledge of cultures near and far

About us
We are a professional travel agency with fifteen years' experience. We offer advice for all kinds of travel. We help you find the perfect vacation destination. We lead the field in designing personalized trips.

What we do
Our team of experts can recommend the best accommodations for your needs. We work closely with small hotels and guides in twelve countries. We arrange everything from the first to the last day of your trip.

Testimonials
"*Go our way!* booked everything for us for our family trip to Vietnam. Everything went perfectly." *Sandra Lowe, Boston, MA*
"We used *Go our way!* to plan the vacation of a lifetime last year. Their ideas were just what we wanted." *Bim Okri, Miami, FL*

Writing a business profile

1 Work in pairs. Read the information about *Go our way!* What kind of traveler do you think would be interested in their services?

2 Writing skill **criteria for writing**

Work in pairs. Read the information again. Circle the correct options to describe the information. Which features of the text helped you decide your answers?

1 **text type**: website / letter
2 **style**: neutral / formal / informal
3 **reader**: current customers / possible customers
4 **purpose**: to promote the company / to advertise a product
5 **structure**: separate sections of text / a sequenced text

3 Underline these things in the text.

1 travel vocabulary
2 verbs that describe what the company does

4 Complete the sentences with some of the verbs you underlined in Exercise 3.

1 Our company can _____ closely with your staff to help you.
2 Let our market researchers _____ the best strategy for your business.
3 Our personal banking advisors _____ you save money.

5 Work in groups. Imagine you run a small business. Decide on your company name, field of work, and some current projects.

6 Work on your own. Write a profile to promote your business. Use the *Go our way!* profile and the categories in Exercise 2 to help you.

7 Work in your groups again. Read your profiles and choose the one that best promotes your company. Think about the following points:

- **Accuracy** Spelling mistakes do not look professional!
- **Clarity** Does the reader understand exactly what your business does?

A shepherd in Rajasthan, India

Before you watch

1 Work in pairs. Look at the photo and the caption. Describe the man's appearance. What does his expression tell you about him?

2 Key vocabulary

a Work in pairs. Read the sentences. The words in bold are used in the video. Guess the meaning of the words.

1 The **shepherd** has two dogs to help him move the sheep.
2 I think the eyes are often a person's most interesting **feature**.
3 It takes days to get to Rajasthan as it's fairly **remote**.
4 The local people dress in a very **particular** way.
5 My friend's funny stories always **amuse** me.

b Match the words in bold in Exercise 2a (1–5) with these definitions.

a part of the face _____
b far from other places, difficult to get to _____
c special, individual, or different from others _____
d a person who looks after sheep _____
e to make someone laugh or entertain someone _____

While you watch

3 ▶ **1.1** Watch Part 1 of the video. Complete the information about Steve McCurry.

Steve McCurry is a [1] _____ . His first job was working on a [2] _____ . His ambition was to travel and see the [3] _____ . He has worked at National Geographic for about [4] _____ years.

4 ▶ **1.2** Watch Part 2 of the video. Match the beginnings of the sentences (1–3) with the endings (a–c).

1 Rajasthan is   ○   ○   a a shy person.
2 The people of   ○   ○   b gentle and
  Rajasthan are   hospitable.
3 Steve McCurry is ○   ○   c strange and
                                          wonderful.

5 ▶ **1.1, 1.2** Watch both parts of the video again and look closely at the people you see. Then work in pairs and describe the person you remember best.

6 ▶ **1.2** Work in pairs. Can you remember what Steve McCurry says about photographing faces? Do you agree? Choose the correct option or watch the last section of Part 2 again.

It's *the eyes / the strange features / the whole face* that tell(s) the story.

After you watch

7 Vocabulary in context

a ▶ **1.3** Watch the clips from the video. Choose the correct meaning of the words and phrases.

b Answer the questions in your own words. Then work in pairs and compare your answers.

1 Can you think of two places where you feel at home?
2 What do you think is a good way to make a living?
3 Have you been anywhere that felt like another planet?
4 Have you seen anything or done anything that you could describe as "kind of strange"?
5 What activities do people do that involve getting warmed up before they start?

8 Work in groups. Steve McCurry's photos in the video focus on the people and especially their faces to "tell the story" of Rajasthan. Choose a place or a group of people you know. Plan a photoshoot of ten photos to "tell the story." Use these ideas to help you.

- What are the most important features of the group?
- Is appearance or activity more important?
- Do you need to include the place or just the people?

fortune teller (n) /ˈfɔrtʃən ˌtelər/ someone who predicts a person's future
hospitable (adj) /hɒsˈpɪtəbl/ friendly to visitors
nomad (n) /ˈnəʊmæd/ someone who moves from one place to another to live
snake charmer (n) /ˈsneɪk ˌtʃɑrmər/ someone who performs with snakes

UNIT 1 REVIEW AND MEMORY BOOSTER

Grammar

1 Complete the interview with a prize-winning travel writer at the prize-giving event.

Q: What [1] _____ (this prize / mean) to you?

A: Actually, I [2] _____ (feel) very proud of myself. I never [3] _____ (expect) to win.

Q: When you sit down to write, how [4] _____ (you / decide) what to write about?

A: I [5] _____ (not / know), really. Sometimes my readers [6] _____ (send) me ideas.

Q: [7] _____ (which places / interest) you?

A: Oh, everywhere. Every culture [8] _____ (have) something special about it.

Q: [9] _____ (you / work) on anything at the moment?

A: I [10] _____ (do) some research for a new book, and I also [11] _____ (want) to finish some magazine articles.

Q: [12] _____ (you / can / tell) me what the book's about?

A: At the moment, I [13] _____ (think) about either Brazil or Vietnam. I love both places.

2 Are the sentences about the writer true (T) or false (F)?

1 She's surprised to win prizes for her books.   T   F

2 She usually writes about what her readers want.   T   F

3 She's writing some articles on Peru and Vietnam.   T   F

3 **>> MB** Work in pairs. Say which tense is used in each blank in Exercise 1 and explain why.

4 **>> MB** Work in pairs. Each person chooses one dynamic and one stative verb from Exercise 1. Ask and answer questions using each verb.

I CAN

ask and answer questions about things that are always and generally true, and routines (simple present)	☐
ask and answer questions about things happening now (present continuous)	☐
talk about possessions and states: thoughts and mental processes, etc. (stative verbs)	☐
use different question forms: direct and indirect questions	☐

Vocabulary

5 Write the noun forms of these adjectives.

| angry | brave | cheerful | happy |
| lucky | powerful | proud | sad |

6 **>> MB** Work in pairs. Look at the adjectives in Exercise 5. How often do you feel like this? What kinds of situations make you feel this way?

I CAN

| talk about feelings and personal states | ☐ |

Real life

7 Look at the expressions (1–6). Do we use them to open (O) or close (C) conversations?

1	Hello. How are you? I'm . . .	O	C
2	Would you like to meet again?	O	C
3	Nice to meet you. My name's . . .	O	C
4	Let me give you my card.	O	C
5	Let's stay in touch.	O	C
6	Let me introduce myself.	O	C

8 Work in small groups. You are at an event for the travel industry. Act out conversations with different partners using a suitable expression to begin and end the conversation.

I CAN

introduce myself in formal and informal situations	☐
open and close a conversation	☐
ask for and give personal information	☐

Unit 2 Performing

Masked folk dancers and their audience, Ollantaytambo, Peru

FEATURES

22 Music today
How we listen to music today

24 Learning to dance
Why do we dance?

26 Living statues
Entertainment on the street

30 Taiko master
A video about a Japanese art form

1 Work in pairs. Which word doesn't belong in each group? Why?

1 actor audience dance director
dance – all the others are people
2 choreographer conductor musician play
3 concert dancer musical show
4 act comedian entertainer magician
5 band choir orchestra singer
6 ballet clown drama opera

2 ▶8 Listen to three people talking about different events. Circle the words in Exercise 1 they mention.

3 ▶8 Listen again. Work in pairs. Which person is talking about the photo? What are the other two people talking about?

4 Work in pairs. Are you interested in the arts? Discuss these questions.

1 How often do you go to concerts, shows, or the theater?
2 What are your favorite types of events?
3 What traditional events in your country or region do you enjoy?
4 Do you like taking part in things or do you prefer being in the audience?

2a Music today

Vocabulary musical styles

1 Work in pairs. Discuss the questions. Do you like the same kind of music?

1 What's your favorite album?
2 Do you like all the tracks on it?
3 How do you usually listen to music?

2 ▶9 Listen to six music clips. Discuss the clips with your partner. Use some of these words.

catchy	cheerful	interesting	lively
repetitive	sad	tuneless	unusual

3 ▶9 Listen again. Which country do you think each clip is from? Write the number (1–6) next to the country.

bhangra – India _____
bossa nova – Brazil _____
Celtic – Ireland _____
flamenco – Spain _____
reggae – Jamaica _____
township jive – South Africa _____

Reading

4 Read the article from a magazine, *Music Today*. What is the article about? Choose the correct option (a–c).

a the best live bands
b becoming a musician
c changes in how people listen to music

5 Work in pairs. Read the article again. Discuss the questions.

1 Is it easy to find music stores in your town? Why or why not?
2 Why are there more music websites nowadays?
3 How do we listen to music without buying it?
4 Why is it now easier to listen to international musicians?

6 Are any of the things in the article true for you? Tell your partner.

▶10

THE ONLINE
revolution

The way we listen to and buy music has changed enormously in recent years. These days, it's hard to find a music store downtown—so where have they all gone? The answer, of course, is online. The number of music websites has grown incredibly quickly since internet connections became faster and cheaper. But it's not only the way we buy music that's different—it's also *what* we buy. New vinyl[1] records have been hard to find for years. CD sales have fallen, and MP3 sales are slowing down. In fact, thanks to musicians' websites and other streaming websites, we can now choose the music we listen to without actually buying it. These days, our choice is much wider—bands and singers release their music online direct to the listeners—so it has become much easier to discover different kinds of music from all over the world. One thing that hasn't changed so much, however, is our love of live music. Bands still go on tour and play at festivals, often giving their audiences unforgettable experiences.

[1]**vinyl** (n) /ˈvaɪnəl/ a kind of plastic used to make records

A musician plays a trumpet on a rooftop in Cyprus.

Grammar present perfect

7 Work in pairs. Look at the grammar box. How do we form the present perfect? Which verbs have irregular past participles?

8 Underline four more present perfect sentences in the article. Then circle the correct options in these sentences (a–d).

a We *know / don't know* exactly when the activities or situations started.
b The activities or situations started in the past. They *have / don't have* an effect on the present.
c The present perfect is used with *for / since* and the point of time when the activity started.
d The present perfect is used with *for / since* and a period of time.

9 Complete the text with the present perfect form of the verbs.

Digital downloads of albums ¹ _____ (become) the most popular way to buy music in recent years, but not everybody ² _____ (lose) interest in vinyl records. Sales of vinyl records ³ _____ (rise) significantly since 2007. Many buyers are younger fans who ⁴ _____ (realize) that music sounds better on vinyl. The price of a typical pop CD ⁵ _____ (not / go up) for a while, but some collectors ⁶ _____ (pay) thousands of dollars for original vinyl records.

10 Complete the sentences with the present perfect form of these verbs.

be	happen	record	sell

1 Fado singer Mariza _____ over a million records worldwide.
2 Charanga bands _____ part of Cuban culture since the 1940s.
3 What _____ to MTV since YouTube began?
4 How many albums _____ your favorite band _____ ?

11 Work in pairs. Are these expressions used with *for* or *since*? Write F or S next to each expression.

1986	____	a couple of days	____
a while	____	ages	____
I was a child	____	July	____
lunchtime	____	a few months	____
centuries	____	last Monday	____

12 Write the present perfect form of the verbs. Then complete the sentences so that they are true for you. Work in pairs and compare your sentences.

1 I _____ (not / listen) to _____ for ages.
2 I _____ (live) in this town for _____ .
3 I _____ (be) in my current job / class since _____ .
4 I _____ (know) my best friend since _____ .

13 ▶ 11 Match the comments (1–4) with the responses (a–d). Complete the sentences with *already*, *just*, and *yet*. Then listen and check.

1 Have you heard Shakira's new single? ____
2 Do you want to borrow the new James Bond DVD? ____
3 Have you seen the musical *Wicked* _____ ? ____
4 I've _____ bought tickets to see *Stomp* in Chicago! ____

a No, thanks. I've _____ seen it. I saw it at the movies.
b Yes, we have. It's even better than the movie.
c Really? Is that show still running?
d No, not _____ . Is it as good as her last one?

Speaking my Life

14 Work in pairs. Act out conversations as in Exercise 13. Use these ideas.

an album / a song / a track
a book / a magazine / a comic
a musical / a show / a play / a concert / a movie
an exhibition / a festival

*Adele's new album has **just** come out. Have you heard it **yet**?*

2b Learning to dance

Vocabulary emotions

1 What kind of things can change your mood? Circle the correct option to complete the sentences.

1 That music is so cheerful—**it** always **puts me in a** *bad / good* **mood**.
2 That song's so sad. **I feel like** *crying / smiling* every time I hear it.
3 It's a really funny movie. **I can't stop** *crying / laughing* when I think about it.
4 I love dancing because **it** *makes me feel sad / cheers me up*.

2 Work in pairs. Tell your partner what changes your moods. Use some of the expressions in bold in Exercise 1.

I don't go out dancing very often. But when I do, it puts me in a good mood.

Listening

3 Work in pairs. Discuss the questions.

1 What kind of dances are traditional in your region or country?
2 Have you ever been to a dance class or learned a dance?
3 Do you enjoy dancing?
4 Do you dance on special occasions? Which ones?
5 Is there a dance or kind of dance you'd like to be able to do?

4 ▶ **12** Listen to a dance teacher, Bruce Daley, talking about his career. Correct the factual errors in these sentences.

1 Bruce opened the studio when he started dancing professionally.
2 A lot of young kids began coming when big TV shows started.
3 Two of Bruce's older students became professionals last year.
4 Once, a very happy young man came to class.

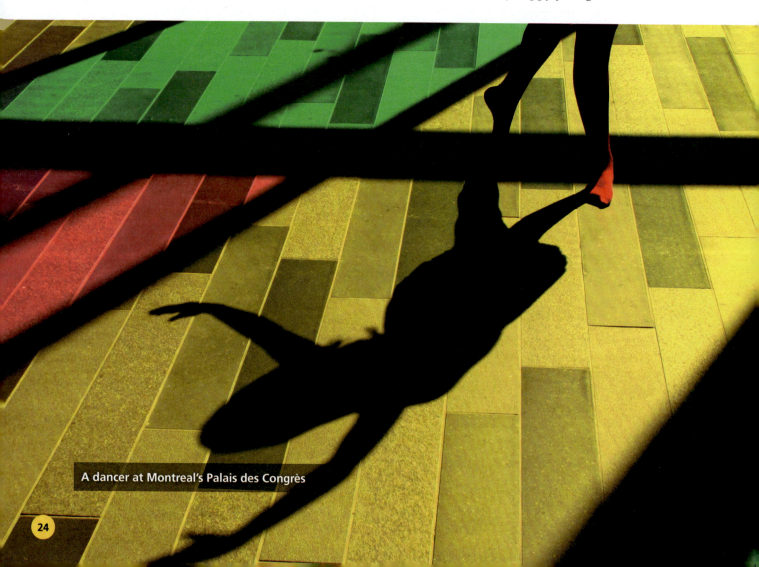

A dancer at Montreal's Palais des Congrès

5 ▶ 12 Listen again. Are the sentences true (T) or false (F)?

1　Bruce runs dance classes for professional dancers.　　T　F
2　Bruce's first students were older people.　　T　F
3　Many people have found a new social life at his studio.　　T　F
4　Bruce has seen how dancing can change people's moods.　　T　F
5　Bruce has had two careers through dance.　　T　F

6 Work in pairs. Can you think of other activities people do to:

1　make them feel young? *keeping fit*
2　meet people?
3　have a social life?
4　change their mood?

Grammar present perfect and simple past

> **PRESENT PERFECT and SIMPLE PAST**
>
> Dancing **has been** my life, really.
> And starting this school **was** the best thing **I've ever done**.
> My injuries **ended** my career as a dancer ten years ago.
> But opening the school **gave** me a new career as a teacher.
>
> For more information and practice, see page 158.

7 Look at the grammar box. Circle the simple past verbs and underline the present perfect forms. Then circle the correct option to complete the rule: We use the *present perfect / simple past* when we say—or it is clear from the situation—when something happened.

8 Underline the present perfect forms and circle the simple past verbs in the Track 12 audioscript on page 180. Which ones have different simple past and past participle forms?

9 Work in pairs. Look at the pairs of sentences. Explain why the two different verb forms are used.

1　a　Anya Paseka danced professionally for years.
　　b　Anya Paseka has danced professionally for years.
2　a　The students went to New York for a week.
　　b　The students have gone to New York for a week.
3　a　The show was at the Royal Theater all summer.
　　b　The show has been at the Royal Theater all summer.

10 ▶ 13 Circle the correct options to complete the text. Then listen and check.

Bruce ¹ *was / has been* my teacher for about two years now. ² *I started / I've started* coming here during a bad time at work. Bruce's classes are great—³ *I never had / I've never had* so much fun! ⁴ *I met / I've met* all kinds of people here. Some of them ⁵ *became / have become* really good friends. At first, I ⁶ *didn't know / haven't known* how to dance. But I soon ⁷ *realized / have realized* that you can't get embarrassed—you just have to dance! Everyone here ⁸ *felt / has felt* the same way at some point.

11 Pronunciation weak forms

a ▶ 14 Listen to four sentences from Exercise 10 again. Notice how the verb *have* is not stressed in present perfect statements.

b Work in pairs. Practice saying the four sentences.

12 Match the pairs of verbs with the sentences. Use the present perfect and the simple past form of the verbs to complete the sentences.

never try / go	not buy / not enjoy
not be / break	see / go

1　I first _____ *River Dance* in April, and I _____ three times since then!
2　I _____ zumba, but I _____ to an aerobics class a few months ago.
3　Jack _____ in the show since he _____ his ankle.
4　We _____ tickets for Enrique Iglesias this time. We _____ his last concert.

Speaking myLife

13 Work in pairs. Ask questions with *Have you ever ...?*, *Did you (ever) ... when ...?*, and *When was the last time you ...?* Ask follow-up questions using the simple past and *where, what, who, why,* or *when*.

act in a play	play an instrument
give a speech	sing in front of an audience
perform in public	tell a joke

A:　**Have you ever acted** in a play?
B:　Yes, **I acted** in Macbeth in high school.
A:　What part **did you play**?
B:　Actually, **I was** Lady Macbeth.

2c Living statues

Reading

1 Look at the photo and write three sentences to describe it.

2 Work in pairs. Compare your sentences and discuss what you think it feels like to be a living statue.

3 Read the article. Underline the parts of the article that tell you:

1. what a living statue does.
2. where you can see living statues.
3. what similar art forms in history there have been.
4. what it feels like to be a living statue.

4 Work in pairs. Read the article again and discuss these questions.

1. Who is the main audience for this kind of performance?
2. What are the main differences between living statues and *tableaux vivants*?
3. What makes a living statue successful?

5 Find these words in the article. Look at how the words are used and try to guess their meaning. Then replace the words in bold in the sentences (1–4) with these words.

illustrate (line 15)	begging (line 29)
resident (line 26)	react (line 45)

1. Sadly, we see a lot of people who are **asking people for money** in the street nowadays. _____
2. The audience was shouting at him, but he didn't **say or do anything in response**! _____
3. The pictures in the book **show** what the story is about really well. _____
4. We spoke to a **person who lives in this area** about the traffic problems. _____

6 Would you like to be a street performer? Why or why not? What kind would you be? Tell the class.

living statue	musician	magician
pavement artist	sand sculptor	

Word focus *kind*

7 Read the two examples from the article. Say if *kind* is an adjective (A) or a noun (N).

1. … you'll see a special kind of display …   A   N
2. … not everyone is so kind and generous …   A   N

8 Complete the sentences with these expressions.

a kind of	really kind of
How kind	that kind of thing

1. Flowers! _____ !
2. Grunge is _____ rock music that started in the 1980s in the USA.
3. I love going to exhibitions and _____ .
4. It's _____ you to lend me the money.

Critical thinking **balance**

9 Work in pairs. Discuss the questions.

1. What kind of reader is the article for?
2. Does the article change your opinion of living statues? How?
3. Is there anything you want to know about living statues that the article doesn't tell you?

10 According to the article, this type of street performance is not popular with everyone. Discuss the questions.

1. Who thinks negatively about living statues? What three points does the person make?
2. What does the performer from Hollywood say about one of these points?
3. Do you think the author gives equal importance to both views?

Speaking myLife

11 Work in pairs. Prepare six questions for a survey on prices and art events in your country. Use these ideas. Then ask and answer your questions in groups.

street performers / art exhibitions / museums / concerts
free of charge / tickets / admission fee / donation
too expensive / about right / not enough

Do you ever give money to street performers? How much is about right?

12 Share the results of your survey with the class. What was the majority opinion about paying for art?

Living statues

Entertainment on the street

▶ 15

Go sightseeing in many cities today and among the famous buildings, street markets, and other attractions, you'll see a special kind of display: living statues. These street performers—who are sometimes
5 dressed as famous characters from history or from popular culture—have become a common sight in tourist areas of Paris, London, Barcelona, Hollywood, and other cities. The performance involves standing completely still[1] for long periods of time.

10 This kind of performance has a long history. It has existed in various forms since the sixteenth century. The French used the term *tableaux vivants,* which means "living pictures." A group of actors stood in positions
15 to illustrate a scene, but they didn't speak or move during the display.

The subject of the displays was often religious or from mythology. In some places, they were part of royal[2]
20 occasions. In the Catalan region of Spain, *tableaux vivants* have been a popular tradition since the early eighteenth century. Nowadays, Catalonia is also famous for its modern living statues. In fact, there are so many of them on the streets of Barcelona that the city council decided
25 to control the number and give out only thirty licenses for fifteen locations. Local resident Joan Castells explained, "You can't move past the crowds on the pavement, and most of them are not really entertaining people, they're just begging." Now, each licensed artist can perform
30 either in the morning or in the afternoon.

So why do so many people want to be living statues? Joan Castells says, "It's an easy way of earning money. All you need is some makeup and a costume." But according to one of the living statues in Hollywood,
35 "Preparation takes ages—and so does getting clean at the end of the day. It's also extremely difficult to stay completely still for long periods. I can't even move my eyes or show that I'm breathing." And although it's "understood" that if you take a photo, you leave
40 some money, not everyone is so kind and generous. "Nobody gets rich doing this," said the living statue from Hollywood.

Perhaps they don't get rich, but every performer has some tricks to encourage people to give them money.
45 Every time a tourist throws them a coin, they react with a quick, small movement. Perhaps they wave or turn their head or touch the person. The statue comes to life for just a moment, entertaining the crowd and rewarding the payment. And maybe giving the tired and
50 aching performer a chance to move into a new, more comfortable position.

---

[1]**still** (adv) /stɪl/ not moving
[2]**royal** (adj) /ˈrɔɪəl/ connected to a king or queen

A living statue in São Paulo, Brazil

2d What's playing?

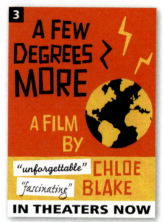

Real life choosing an event

1 Work in pairs. Look at the ads. Which event would you most like to go to? Which would you not like to go to? Tell your partner.

2 ▶ 16 Read the comments. Then listen to two people making plans to go out. Write the number of the ad (1–3) next to the comments. Which event do the speakers decide to go and see?

a It sounds really interesting. ____
b Apparently, it's absolutely amazing. ____
c It looks pretty good. ____
d Roger Whitehead is absolutely hilarious. ____
e He's not very funny. ____

3 ▶ 16 Look at the expressions for choosing an event. Listen again and circle the expressions the speakers use.

> **▶ CHOOSING AN EVENT**
>
> **Suggestions and responses**
> Do you feel like going out tonight?
> Do you want to go to the theater?
> Would you like to see a movie?
> Do you like the sound of that?
>
> Yeah, why not?
> Yes, sure.
> I like the sound of that.
> I don't really like him.
> I'm not in the mood for anything depressing.
> It doesn't really appeal to me.
> That sounds great.
>
> **Details of the event**
> What's playing?
> Who's in it?
> What else is playing / happening?
> Who's it by?
> Where / When / What time is it at / showing?
> What's it about?

Vocabulary describing performances

4 Look at the sentences in Exercise 2. Write the adverbs used before these adjectives. Which adjectives have stronger meanings?

1 _____ : amazing, hilarious
2 _____ , _____ , _____ : interesting, good, funny

5 Work in pairs. Which adverbs can you use with these groups of adjectives?

A		
fascinating	spectacular	terrible
terrific	thrilling	unforgettable

B		
boring	depressing	disappointing
dull	entertaining	

6 **Pronunciation** intonation with *really, absolutely,* etc.

a ▶ 17 Listen to the sentences from Exercise 2 again. Notice how the speaker stresses both the adverb and adjective in the affirmative statements.

b Work in pairs. Practice these exchanges. Pay attention to your intonation.

1 A: Was it a good festival?
   B: Yes, it was absolutely amazing.
2 A: How was the show?
   B: Oh, very entertaining!

7 Work in pairs. Invite your partner to see the event that you would most like to go to in Exercise 1. Include words from Exercises 4 and 5. Use the expressions for choosing an event to help you.

2e A portrait of an artist

Writing a review

1 Who is your favorite performer or artist? Tell your partner about this person and why you like him or her.

2 Read the review of Baz Luhrmann's work. What kind of information about Luhrmann is included? Circle the correct options (a–d).

a his influences
b his plans for the future
c his private life
d his work

3 Work in pairs. Read the review again. Find three facts and three opinions. Then find two direct quotes from Luhrmann.

4 Which sentence (a–c) best describes the review? Explain your choice.

a It summarizes several different opinions.
b It only talks about negative things.
c It's a personal point of view.

Baz Luhrmann is a director whose movies include *Strictly Ballroom*, *Romeo + Juliet*, *Moulin Rouge!*, and *Australia*. I have seen every one of his movies, and in my opinion, Luhrmann's work just gets better and better. He says that "putting on a show" has always come naturally to him and that Bollywood is his biggest influence. Although he is best-known as a movie director, Luhrmann has also directed opera. Consequently, his movies are usually exciting, energetic, and spectacular. They have had box office success despite being unusual: in *Romeo + Juliet*, the actors speak in verse; In *Moulin Rouge!*, they sing their lines. On the other hand, the epic *Australia* wasn't so popular with the critics. Nevertheless, as an ordinary movie fan, I thought it was absolutely fantastic. Luhrmann says the high point of his career has been "achieving so many of the dreams I had as a kid—from going to the Oscars to getting a letter from Marlon Brando." To me, his movies have the power of dreams. They take you into thrilling, unforgettable worlds.

---

5 Writing skill linking ideas

a Look at the table. Which group of words can replace each highlighted word in the review? Write the words from the review in the table.

in spite of	even though while	in contrast, but however,	because of this, for that reason, so therefore
_____	_____ _____	_____ _____	_____ _____

b Circle the correct option to complete the sentences.

1 *Although / Despite* his name is Mark, everyone calls him Baz.
2 *Although / Despite* working mainly in Australia, he has had international success with his movies.

c Rewrite the sentences using the words in parentheses. Make any changes to verbs and punctuation as necessary.

1 They have had box office success despite being unusual movies. (even though)
2 I enjoyed *Romeo + Juliet* in spite of not understanding all the dialog. (but)
3 Although they praised Luhrmann's earlier movies, the critics did not like *Australia*. (In spite of)
4 I've seen all of the movies, but I haven't seen any of the operas. (However)
5 His last movie was absolutely amazing. Because of this, I'm looking forward to seeing the next one. (so)

6 Write a review of an artist whose work you like. First, look at the headings and make notes. Then write about 150 words. Use a variety of adjectives and linking words.

> Basic biographical information
> Facts (life, work)
> Opinions (mine, others)

7 Use these questions to check your review.

- Have you used linking words correctly?
- Have you expressed clearly why you like this artist's work?

8 Read some reviews your classmates have written. Use these questions to check your classmates' reviews.

- What did you learn about the subject from reading the review?
- Do you agree with the opinions expressed in the review?

Taiko is an art form that brings together sound, body and mind.

Before you watch

1 Work in pairs. Look at the photo and the caption. Discuss the questions.

1 What is the man doing?
2 How do you think he feels?
3 What do you think the caption means?

2 Key vocabulary

a Work in pairs. Read the sentences. The words in bold are used in the video. Guess the meaning of the words.

1 After the meeting, my **mind** was full of ideas.
2 Text messages introduced a new **style** of writing.
3 When you're driving late at night, **tiredness** can be a serious problem.
4 I like music that has a fast **beat**
5 Ringo Starr was the famous **drummer** in The Beatles.
6 I'm not feeling well today. I don't have the **energy** to go to class.

b Match the words in bold in Exercise 2a with these definitions.

a a regular sound _____
b a musician who plays the drums _____
c power and force _____
d your thoughts, feelings, memories, etc. _____
e a way of doing something _____
f the feeling of being sleepy _____

While you watch

3 ◻ **2.1** Watch Part 1 of the video. Are the sentences true (T) or false (F)?

1 Japanese warriors[1] used drums 2,000 years ago.   T   F
2 The sounds of drums told people where a village boundary[2] was.   T   F
3 The sound of drums in Japan has never gone away.   T   F
4 Taiko drumming is now popular in San Francisco.   T   F

4 ◻ **2.2** Watch Part 2 of the video. Put the events (a–d) in the history of taiko drumming into the correct order (1–4).

____ a About 800 groups started in the United States and Canada.
____ b Japanese-American communities enjoyed traditional taiko drumming.
____ c People lost interest in taiko drumming.
____ d Seiichi Tanaka arrived in the United States.

5 ◻ **2.1, 2.2** Work in pairs. Circle the correct option to complete the sentences about taiko. Then watch the whole video again and check your answers.

1 Japanese warriors used drums to make their enemies *attack / fear* them.
2 The essence[3] of taiko is that it's not just people drumming. It's the unity[4] of the *audience / drummers* amongst themselves.
3 In San Francisco, *the movement of the body / the human voice* has now been added to traditional taiko drumming.
4 Taiko drummers sometimes have to play *through pain and tiredness / with 50 percent of their energy* while practicing and performing.
5 Seiichi Tanaka is giving North America the chance to enjoy the energy and excitement of *a completely new form of music / traditional taiko drumming.*

After you watch

6 Vocabulary in context

a ◻ **2.3** Watch the clips from the video. Choose the correct meaning of the words and phrases.

b Complete the sentences in your own words. Then work in pairs and compare your sentences.

1 I think I've _____ a dozen or so times.
2 In this school, there are something like _____ students.
3 I felt better when _____ went away.
4 Many people in _____ [place] in _____ [time] were just fresh off the boat.

7 Work in pairs. Discuss traditional art forms from your country. How have they changed in recent decades?

---

[1]**warrior** (n) /ˈwɔːriər/ soldier, fighter
[2]**boundary** (n) /ˈbaʊndri/ the outside limit of an area or a place
[3]**essence** (n) /ˈesəns/ the basic quality
[4]**unity** (n) /ˈjuːnɪti/ a state of being whole and complete

UNIT 2 REVIEW AND MEMORY BOOSTER

Grammar

1 Read part of a blog by a visitor to Japan. Find ten places in the blog where words are missing. Complete the blog post with these words.

didn't	for	for	has	just
since	since	for	was	yet
			went	

I've lived in Japan three months now, and I'm really enjoying it. I know any Japanese before I came, but I've learned some I got here, including the word *matsuri*, which means "festival." One of my favorite pastimes is going to matsuri. I got home from the Nango summer jazz festival—it was great to sit around in the sunshine listening to amazing music! Last week, we to Tenjin matsuri here in Osaka. It been part of Osaka summer events about a thousand years, and some performances have hardly changed then—the traditional kagura music, for example, which I loved. There also an amazing puppet show. Tomorrow there's a big procession of boats on the river. I haven't been on the river, so I'm really looking forward to that.

1 _____
2 _____
3 _____
4 _____
5 _____
6 _____
7 _____
8 _____
9 _____
10 _____

2 Answer the questions about the blog in Exercise 1.

1 When did the writer learn Japanese?
2 What time of year was it when the writer wrote the blog post?
3 What did the writer see at the Tenjin festival?
4 How many times has the writer been on the river in Osaka?

3 **>> MB** Work in pairs. Underline the present perfect verbs and circle the simple past verbs in the blog post. Explain why each is used.

4 Work in pairs. Tell your partner about a festival you have been to.

I CAN

talk about things that have happened in a time period up to or including the present (present perfect) ☐

use the correct tense when talking about things that have happened in the past (present perfect and simple past) ☐

Vocabulary

5 Work in pairs. Circle the people who are usually involved in each performance. Then choose four types of performer and tell your partner about performers you know.

1 **Movie:** actor, director, magician
2 **Concert:** clown, conductor, musician
3 **Ballet:** choreographer, comedian, dancer
4 **Musical:** living statue, singer, orchestra

6 **>> MB** Work in groups. In two minutes, write the names of as many art events as you can. Then discuss them, using the words in the box.

boring	depressing	disappointing
entertaining	fascinating	marvelous
terrible	terrific	unforgettable

7 **>> MB** Work in pairs. Describe what kind of music makes you do the following:

cry	feel happy	feel sad	laugh	smile

I CAN

talk about performers and performances ☐

describe different types of music ☐

give my opinion about art events ☐

Real life

8 Work in pairs. Circle the correct option in the questions.

1 Do you want *to go / going* out tonight?
2 Would you like *to see / seeing* a movie?
3 *Do you / Would you* like the sound of that?
4 Who's *in / on* it?
5 Who's it *by / for*?
6 What's it *about / of*?

9 Work in pairs. Act out a conversation for choosing an event. Use the questions in Exercise 8, adding more information.

I CAN

ask for and give information about arts events ☐

Unit 3 Water

A sailing crew battles a storm during a yacht race.

FEATURES

34 The story behind the photo

When things go wrong in the water

36 Return to *Titanic*

The truth about a famous underwater discovery

38 Love and death in the sea

An article by marine ecologist Enric Sala

42 Four women and a wild river

A video about a trip down a dangerous river

1 Work in pairs. Look at the photo and the caption. Answer the questions.

1 What do you think the people are thinking?
2 Have you ever tried this activity? If not, would you like to?
3 How many words can you think of to describe this experience?

2 ▶ 18 Listen to the introduction to a radio program. Look at the two groups of words. Circle the activities and places you hear.

Activities			
diving	jet skiing	kayaking	rafting
rowing	snorkeling	waterskiing	windsurfing

Places						
lake	ocean	pool	river	sea	stream	waterfall

3 Work in pairs. Where do you think is the best place to do the activities in Exercise 2?

4 Can you think of other sports and leisure activities connected with water? Do you do any of these activities? Where do you do them? Tell your partner.

I go swimming in a lake near here, but only in the summer.

3a The story behind the photo

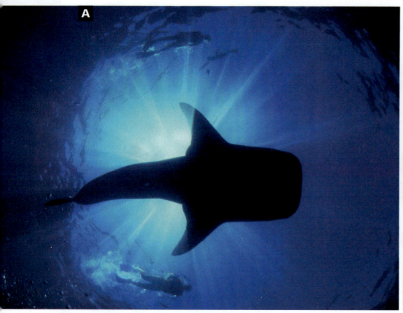

A

B

Listening

1 Look at the photos (A–C). Match the captions (1–3) with the photos.

1 diving in an underground lake in Mexico ____
2 snorkeling with a whale shark in the Indian Ocean ____
3 white-water rafting on the Zambezi River ____

2 ▶ **19** Listen to the people in two of the photos talking about their experiences. Are the sentences true (T) or false (F)?

1 The girl was rafting for the first time.   T   F
2 The raft was approaching some   T   F
  rapids.
3 She saw a hippo near the riverbank.   T   F
4 The boy learned to dive because   T   F
  he was bored.
5 He went diving in a dangerous   T   F
  cenote.
6 He wasn't concentrating on what   T   F
  he was doing.

3 ▶ **20** What do you think happened next? Choose one of the options (a–c). Then listen to the whole story and check your ideas.

1 a The hippo attacked the raft.
  b A crocodile jumped into the river.
  c The raft sank.

2 a His air ran out, and he had to go to the surface.
  b His mother saw a sea snake just behind him.
  c He almost got lost.

4 Pronunciation *d* and *t* after *-ed* endings

a ▶ **21** Listen to this sentence from the second story. Notice how the speaker links the *-ed* verb ending to the *t* at the start of the next word. Do you hear one sound or two?

I actually learned to dive while I was on vacation in Mexico.

b ▶ **22** Listen and repeat the sentences you hear.

Vocabulary describing experiences

> **WORDBUILDING adverbs with *-ly***
>
> Some adverbs are formed by adding *-ly* to adjectives. Sometimes there is a spelling change.
> add *-ly: loud* ➜ *loudly*
> drop *-e*, add *-ly: gentle* ➜ *gently*
> drop *-y*, add *-ily: lucky* ➜ *luckily*
>
> For more practice, see Workbook page 27.

5 Look at the wordbuilding box. Underline the adverb in these sentences. What is the adjective from which the adverb is formed?

1 The hippo suddenly saw us.
2 We reached the river bank safely.
3 I found the way out of the cave easily.
4 The crocodile jumped noisily into the water.
5 Fortunately, nobody was hurt in the accident.
6 I got into the pool very carefully.

C

6 Work in pairs. Think of at least two activities you can do in the manner of each adverb.

angrily	calmly	bravely
happily	politely	secretly

Grammar simple past and past continuous

▶ **SIMPLE PAST and PAST CONTINUOUS**

Simple past
It **jumped** into the water about a meter away from our boat.
My mom **realized** pretty quickly that I was missing, and she **came after** me.

Past continuous
We **were going** around a small island.
The sun **was shining** in through an opening in the roof.

For more information and practice, see page 160.

7 Work in pairs. Look at the grammar box. Which verb form do we use to talk about these things?

1 an unfinished and continuing activity or background situation
2 a short completed action or a sequence of actions

8 Underline the key event in these questions (1–2) about the rafting story in Exercise 1. Then match the questions with the answers (a–b).

1 What were they doing when they saw the hippo?
2 What did they do when they saw the hippo?

a They tried to get away. _____
b They were coming down the river. _____

9 Circle the correct option to complete the rules.

1 We often ask questions in the *simple past / past continuous* about activities at the time of the key event.
2 We often ask questions in the *simple past / past continuous* about actions after the key event.

10 Complete the text about Photo A with the simple past and past continuous forms of the verbs.

> While I ¹_____ (work) in the Maldives, I ²_____ (hear) that there were whale sharks in the area. Whale sharks are the world's biggest fish, and they aren't dangerous! I ³_____ (buy) a snorkel and ⁴_____ (set out) with some friends on a boat. Almost immediately, a whale shark ⁵_____ (swim) past the boat. It ⁶_____ (move) really quickly, but we ⁷_____ (manage) to catch up with it. We all ⁸_____ (get) into the water and ⁹_____ (spend) about two minutes with the shark. Afterwards, I ¹⁰_____ (feel) absolutely wonderful!

11 Write sentences with the simple past and past continuous forms of the verbs. Use *because, when, while,* or *so.*

1 I / have / problems / my teacher / help me.
2 We / see / bears / we / hike.
3 I / fall down / I / run / for the bus.
4 He / not look / at the road / he almost / have / an accident.

12 Work in pairs. Ask and answer questions about the sentences using the simple past and the past continuous tenses.

1 I lost my wallet.
   When did you realize you lost it?
   Were you shopping at the time?
2 I met an old friend in the street.
3 A car ran into me.
4 A friend of mine got some good news.
5 My neighbor saw a robbery.

Speaking

13 Work in pairs.

Student A: Think about an interesting thing that happened the first time you tried something new. Answer your partner's questions.

Student B: Ask ten questions and decide if your partner had a good or bad experience.

What were you trying to do?
Did you have any special equipment?

3b Return to *Titanic*

Reading

1 ▶ **23** Read the interview with the man who discovered the wreck of *Titanic*. Match three of the questions (a–e) with the paragraphs (1–3). Then listen and check your answers.

a Did you know you were looking at *Titanic* when you saw the first pieces of debris? ____
b How did you discover *Titanic*? ____
c How long did it take to locate *Titanic*? ____
d Tell me about the experience of seeing *Titanic* again in 2004. ____
e When did you find out about how *Titanic* sank? ____

2 Work in pairs. Read the interview again. Answer the questions.

1 What was the secret mission that Ballard was involved with?
2 How did Ballard and his team feel when they found *Titanic*?
3 How did Ballard feel when he returned to the wreck in 2004? Why?

3 Work in pairs. Do you think the remains of *Titanic* should be left on the ocean floor? Or should they be removed and put in a museum? Tell your partner.

RETURN *to* TITANIC

On April 15, 1912, the largest passenger steamship ever built hit an iceberg and sank in the North Atlantic Ocean. *Titanic* had left Southampton, England, five days earlier and was on her first voyage.

In 1985, the explorer Dr. Robert Ballard found the wreck of *Titanic*. He went back to *Titanic* nineteen years later to see how it had changed.

1 It was during the Cold War. I was on a secret mission when we found *Titanic*. The US Navy had agreed to pay for our new underwater video technology. In return, we had agreed to use the technology to look for two submarines that had disappeared in the 1960s.

2 Not at first, because many ships had sunk in that area. When we realized it was *Titanic*, we jumped for joy. Then we realized we were celebrating something where people had died.

3 I saw champagne bottles with the corks still in. The box holding the bottles had disappeared long ago. Suddenly, I noticed a woman's shoe. Nearby, I saw a pair of smaller shoes—perhaps they'd belonged to a child. I felt that the people who had died here in 1912 were speaking to me again. But I knew that other people had been there since my first visit. Hollywood filmmaker James Cameron had been there. A couple from New York had even got married down there. I was disappointed. It was exactly what I didn't want to happen. I'd asked people to treat *Titanic*'s remains with respect. The story of *Titanic* is not about the ship—it's about the people.

Grammar past perfect

4 Put each group of events (a–c) in the order they actually took place (1–3). Which of the verbs in the sentences are in the past perfect in the interview? Why?

1   a   Ballard jumped for joy. ____
    b   Many people died. ____
    c   Ballard realized the wreck was *Titanic*. ____

2   a   James Cameron went to the wreck. ____
    b   Ballard noticed a shoe. ____
    c   The box for champagne bottles disappeared. ____

> **► PAST PERFECT**
>
> 1 *He went back to* Titanic *nineteen years later to see how it **had changed**.*
> 2 *I saw some shoes that **had belonged** to a child.*
>
> For more information and practice, see page 160.

5 Look at the grammar box. Underline what happened first. Then circle the correct option to complete this sentence.

We use the past perfect to show that an event took place *before / after* another event in the past.

6 Circle the correct option to complete the sentences.

1   When *Titanic* hit the iceberg, it *was / had been* at sea for four days.
2   When *Titanic* hit the iceberg, it *sank / had sunk*.
3   By the time they sounded the ship's alarm, it *was / had been* too late.
4   By the time a rescue boat came, many people *died / had died*.
5   When Ballard used video technology, he *found / had found* the wreck.
6   By the time Ballard returned to the site, several people *visited / had visited* it.

7 Use the past perfect to answer the questions with your own ideas. Then work in pairs and compare your answers.

1   Why did *Titanic* collide with an iceberg?
2   Why did so many people die when the ship sank?
3   Why was Ballard upset in 2004?
4   Why do you think a couple got married at the wreck site?
5   Why do you think James Cameron visited the wreck?

8 Complete the text with the simple past and past perfect forms of the verbs.

Captain Henry Morgan [1] _____ (be) one of the most famous pirates of the seventeenth century. In 2010, archeologists [2] _____ (begin) to lift cannons from a ship they [3] _____ (discover) two years earlier, near the coast of Panama. The archeologists [4] _____ (feel) confident that the ship was Morgan's main ship, *Satisfaction*. This ship and several others [5] _____ (sink) in 1671 when they [6] _____ (hit) rocks. Three years later, after Morgan [7] _____ (become) extremely rich from pirate attacks, he [8] _____ (retire) from pirate activities to become the governor of Jamaica.

Speaking **my Life**

9 Work in two pairs within a group of four. Read these puzzles. Then follow the instructions.

Pair A: Turn to page 153. **Pair B:** Turn to page 154.

> **A** A ship came across a yacht in the middle of the ocean. There were no other ships or boats in the area. The bodies of several people were floating in the water nearby.

> **B** A man was on vacation on his yacht. He fell off the yacht into deep water. He couldn't swim, and he wasn't wearing any gear to help him float. The yacht kept moving until his friends realized he had disappeared. They found him several hours later. Why hadn't he drowned?

10 Work in pairs. Complete this sentence in as many ways as you can. Use the past perfect. Take turns beginning another sentence with *By the time*.

By the time this lesson started, ...

3c Love and death in the sea

Reading

1 Work in pairs. Discuss the questions.

1 Where is the best place to go swimming? A pool, a lake, the ocean, …?
2 What kinds of problems can swimmers have in each place?

2 Enric Sala is a marine ecologist. Read the article he wrote for World Ocean Day. Answer the questions.

1 What happened to Enric Sala?
2 Why did this happen to him?
3 How has the experience changed him?

3 Find the expressions in the article. What do they mean? Circle the correct option.

1 a couple of times (line 1)
on *a few / many* occasions
2 my heart races (line 5)
I feel *angry / afraid*
3 I decided to call it a day (line 18)
I decided to *stop / try again*
4 I was having a hard time (line 35)
it took a long time / it was difficult for me
5 I decided to let myself go (line 37)
I decided to *try again / stop swimming*
6 I have learned my lesson (line 50)
my *bad / good* experience taught me something

4 Discuss the questions with your partner.

1 Sala talks about three decisions he made. What were the decisions, and what were the consequences of each one?
2 Sala describes how he feels about the ocean. Do you think what he says is unusual? Why or why not?
3 Do you think the title of the article is a good one? Why or why not?

Critical thinking drawing conclusions

5 We can sometimes draw conclusions from a piece of writing even if the author does not state these things. Read the sentences. Which three are conclusions (C) and which one is stated in the text (S).

1 The Costa Brava is a dangerous place for swimmers. ____
2 Enric Sala has recovered from the experience now. ____
3 He was lucky to be alive after the experience. ____
4 The experience has made him wiser. ____

6 Work in pairs. Do you agree with the conclusions in Exercise 5? Give reasons for your answers.

Word focus *get*

7 Look at the verbs in bold in these sentences. Find expressions with *get* in the article that have the same meanings as the verbs. Then rewrite the sentences with *get*.

1 I **entered** the pool.
2 The weather **didn't improve**.
3 I couldn't **reach** the shore.
4 I wasn't **moving toward** the land.
5 We **receive** so much from nature.
6 We put the bird in a cage, but it **escaped**.

8 Write six more sentences with the expressions with *get* from the article. Write about your own experiences.

Speaking myLife

9 Think about an experience you had where you learned a lesson. Use these ideas to think about the details. Work in small groups. Tell each other about your experiences.

> what lesson you learned
> the place / situation
> any other people involved
> what happened
> why / how it happened
> how the experience changed your behavior afterward

A: *I almost got into an accident once when I was driving and I was really tired.*
B: *Where were you going?*

Love & death in the sea

The ocean has almost killed me a couple of times. It wasn't her fault; it was mine, for not respecting her. I still remember the last time—a stormy day off the Costa Brava of Spain, in early summer
5 2008. Every time I think about it, my heart races.

The place where I used to swim every day was hit by a storm with strong eastern winds. The clear blue waters of summer quickly changed into a dirty soup of sand and cold gray water. Waves were
10 breaking in all directions. But beyond the surf zone, the sea seemed swimmable. In a moment of Catalan bravado,[1] I put on my bathing suit, mask, and fins, and got into the water. It was crazy, but I did it. I swallowed sand and salt while I was trying
15 to swim through the surf zone. Fighting against the water, I swam—I still don't know why—for twenty minutes. The storm got worse, and I decided to call it a day. I turned to swim back. Then I realized I couldn't get to the beach.

20 Waves were breaking all around me. I tried to bodysurf one wave to the shore, but it took me down under the water. When I came up, I turned around and a second wave hit me just as hard, taking me down again. I hit the sandy bottom.

25 I pushed myself up, but once again, waves were coming and I couldn't rest or breathe. I was caught in the surf zone, with waves pushing me out and a current[2] pulling me in. I wasn't getting any closer to the beach.

30 The ocean is our mother, sister, and home, and as such I love her. We get so much from the sea. She gives us life, oxygen, and food. Without the ocean and all the life in it, our planet would be much poorer. We should thank the sea, the ocean, every
35 day. But on this day, I was having a hard time feeling grateful.

After a few more attempts, I decided to let myself go and give up the fight. I took a deep breath. The next wave took me down and forward. I hit
40 the bottom with my back. I rolled over, hit my head, and after what seemed the longest minute of my life, I found myself lying in a foot of water. I crawled[3] out of the water and onto the beach. I'd got out, but I'd lost my mask, snorkel, and one
45 fin. My whole body was sore. I sat on the beach, watching the ocean and feeling lucky to be alive. I walked back home slowly, like a beaten dog.

Some days the sea wants us and some days she doesn't. Since that day, I have not been to the ocean
50 when she does not want me. I have learned my lesson. I now thank the ocean every day the surface is calm, the waters are clear, and diving is easy.

> [1] **bravado** (n) /brəˈvɑːdəʊ/ false bravery
> [2] **current** (n) /ˈkʌrənt/ a strong movement of water in the sea or a river
> [3] **crawl** (v) /krɔːl/ to move slowly on your hands and knees

3d No way!

Real life telling stories

1 Work in groups. Which of these statements (a–d) are true about you? Tell your group.

a When I'm in a group, I listen more than I talk.
b I'm always telling funny stories about things that happen to me.
c I'm no good at telling stories, but I'm a good listener.
d People say I exaggerate, but they always laugh at my stories.

2 Look at the photo below. Which group of words (A or B) do you think are from the story of the photo? Then work in pairs. Compare your ideas and explain your reasons.

A

looking after it	food and water
empty cage	searched everywhere
taking a bath	

B

learned to fly	jump in the air
a lid on a tank	above the kitchen sink
there was some water in it	

3 ▶ 25 Listen to two stories. Which story matches the photo? What would a photo of the other story show?

4 ▶ 25 Look at the expressions for telling stories. Listen to the stories again. Circle the expressions the speakers use.

> **► TELLING STORIES**
>
> **Beginning a story**
> Did I ever tell you about …?
> I remember once …
> A couple of years ago, …
> You'll never believe what happened once …
>
> **Saying when things happened**
> after we saw …
> after a few days
> a couple of weeks later
> one day
> all of a sudden
> suddenly
> immediately
> then
> the next thing was
> while I was …
> during the night

5 Only one of the stories is true. Which one do you think is true? The answer is on page 44.

6 Pronunciation *was* and *were*

a ▶ 26 Listen to the sentences from the stories in Exercise 3. Notice the sound /ə/ in *was* and *were*.

b ▶ 26 Listen again and repeat the sentences. Pay attention to how you say *was* and *were*.

7 Work in pairs. Choose one of the stories from Exercise 3. Take a role each. Look at the Track 25 audioscript on page 181 and prepare your role. Then close your books and practice the conversation. Change roles and repeat with the other story.

8 Work in pairs.

Student A: Tell your partner about three surprising or embarrassing things that happened to you or to someone you know. One of the things should be untrue.

Student B: Try to guess which of your partner's stories is untrue.

A: Did I ever tell you about the time I found some money?
B: No, you didn't.

3e What a weekend!

Writing a blog post

1 Work in pairs. Do you read or write any blogs? What kinds of things do people write about in personal blogs? And in professional blogs?

2 Work in pairs. Read the post and answer the questions.

1 What is the topic of this post?
2 What do you think *beach gear* refers to?
3 Who do you think Ellie, Louis, and Oscar are?

3 Put the main events of the story (a–g) in the correct order.

____ a   Ellie, Louis, and Oscar **ran** to the water.
____ b   The sun **started to shine**.
____ c   There was a storm.
____ d   A ship lost a cargo of sneakers.
____ e   They **got** into the car.
____ f   They **picked up** things to take to the beach.
____ g   They **went** to the beach.

4 Writing skill interesting language

a Compare the post with the sentences in Exercise 3. Which verbs does James use instead of the verbs in bold? Why?

b Circle the verbs and adjectives that James uses instead of these words.

raining	full of people	looking
arrived	holding	

c Read the sentences. Replace the words in bold with these words.

fell down	ran	really	tired	walked

1 The kids **raced** along the street. _____
2 I felt **exhausted** after my walk. _____
3 The weather was **boiling** hot. _____
4 I **wandered** along the beach, enjoying the silence. _____
5 At the end of the game, we **collapsed** on the sand. _____

5 Think about a recent weekend when something unusual happened. Make notes of the main events. Add notes with background information.

The calm after the storm

It was pouring rain all weekend, so we spent almost the whole time indoors trying to entertain the kids. Then, unexpectedly, the sun came out late on Sunday afternoon. We grabbed our beach gear, jumped into the car, and headed down to the bay. When we got there, we realized that everyone had had the same idea! The beach was packed. But everyone was staring out over the water and picking stuff up off the sand. Ellie, Louis, and Oscar rushed down to the water's edge, full of excitement. It turned out that a ship had lost its cargo in Saturday's storm. Five containers of sneakers had washed up on the beach! Everyone was clutching odd shoes, looking for the other one to make a pair! What a strange end to the weekend!

Written by James   28 Feb., 23:17

See older posts

6 Write a first draft of a blog post about your weekend. Then look at the vocabulary you used. Use interesting language in your post.

7 Check that your post:

- uses different past verb forms correctly.
- uses interesting vocabulary to tell the story.

8 Work in pairs. Exchange posts. Can you suggest two more verbs or adjectives that your partner could use?

3f Four women and a wild river

Amber Valenti and some of her team on their trip down the Amur River

Before you watch

1 Work in pairs. Look at the photo and the caption. Then read the information. Would you like to make this kind of trip? Why or why not?

Amber Valenti was the leader of a kayak trip down the Amur River in Mongolia, Russia, and China. The river is one of few major rivers that flow from their start to the ocean without dams or reservoirs. The Amur River begins in Mongolia, and part of its 2,800 kilometers marks the border between Russia and China. The trip took two months to complete.

2 Key vocabulary

a Work in pairs. Read the sentences. The words in bold are used in the video. Guess the meaning of the words.

1 The **concept** of this new TV show is to explain how everyday objects work.
2 We found a **sponsor** to give us most of the money we need for our expedition.
3 The most **memorable** vacation I've ever had was in China.
4 I'm **passionate** about protecting animals.
5 **Conservation** is a big part of the work of the World Wildlife Fund.
6 The best **aspect** of my job is meeting people.

b Match the words in bold in Exercise 2a with these definitions.

a difficult to forget _____
b having strong feelings about something _____
c idea _____
d one part of a problem or situation _____
e someone who supports people's activities with money, equipment, etc. _____
f the protection of natural places, plants, and animals _____

While you watch

3 ▶ **3.1, 3.2** Watch the whole video. Work in pairs. Which of these words do you think describe the experience the women had? Give reasons for your answers.

| dangerous | enjoyable | frightening | relaxing |

4 ▶ **3.1** Watch Part 1 of the video again. Work in pairs. Complete the sentences with the information you hear.

1 Amber Valenti wanted to explore the Amur River and also to _____ .
2 The people she wanted to invite on the trip were _____ .
3 Having an all-woman trip was an advantage with _____ .

5 ▶ **3.2** Watch Part 2 of the video again. Work in pairs. Answer the questions.

1 Amber Valenti describes moments of the trip as "joyful and light" and "intense." What scenes in the video show this?
2 What kinds of things do you see when they reach the mouth of the river?
3 Why does Amber Valenti want people to fall in love with the "human aspect" of the river?

6 After watching the video, do you feel differently about your answer to Exercise 1?

After you watch

7 Vocabulary in context

a ▶ **3.3** Watch the clips from the video. Choose the correct meaning of the words and phrases.

b Complete the sentences in your own words. Then work in pairs and compare your sentences.

1 I think … is awesome.
2 In my experience, … is really fun.
3 I can't … all on my own.
4 People today are hungry for … .
5 I think that … take themselves very seriously.

8 Work in pairs. The trip described in the video was filmed for a documentary called *Nobody's River*. From what you have learned, why do you think the filmmakers chose that title?

---

free-flowing (adj) /ˌfriːˈfləʊɪŋ/ when a river or water moves naturally
intense (adj) /ɪnˈtens/ extremely strong or powerful
joyful (adj) /ˈdʒɔɪfəl/ very happy and cheerful
perspective (n) /pərˈspektɪv/ a point of view
showcase (v) /ˈʃəʊkeɪs/ to explain or show something in a positive way

UNIT 3 REVIEW AND MEMORY BOOSTER

Grammar

1 Choose the correct options to complete the story.

"I ¹ *learned / had learned* to surf a few years ago when I ² *was / had been* in my teens. My dad ³ *paid / was paying* for the course, because I ⁴ *just passed / had just passed* some important exams. It ⁵ *was / had been* a sunny weekend in June. Anyway, the whole first day ⁶ *went / was going* by and I ⁷ *didn't manage / hadn't managed* one successful ride. All my friends ⁸ *were watching / watched*, and of course I ⁹ *was wanting / wanted* to impress them. I eventually ¹⁰ *was paddling / paddled* out for my last attempt of the day as the sun ¹¹ *set / had set* over the bay. I ¹² *scrambled / had scrambled* onto the board, and—for the first time—I ¹³ *didn't fall off / wasn't falling off* right away. I ¹⁴ *just got up / had just got up* on my feet on the board when someone almost ¹⁵ *crashed / was crashing* right into me! But I ¹⁶ *stayed / was staying* on!"

2 >> MB Make notes about the main events from the story in Exercise 1 using single words. Then close your book and work in pairs. Exchange your notes with your partner. Retell the story using your partner's notes.

I CAN	
talk about a sequence of events in the past (simple past, past perfect)	☐
describe the background to past events (past continuous)	☐

Vocabulary

3 Circle the correct options to correct the sentences.

a He checked the exam answers very *carefully / suddenly*.
b She usually drives quite *secretly / slowly*.
c I sat *calmly / badly* in the dentist's chair.
d She *politely / suddenly* had a brilliant idea.
e He *politely / dangerously* asked a stranger for directions.

4 >> MB Work in pairs. What are these places? Can you think of two more places with water? How many examples of each place can you name?

5 >> MB Work on your own. Choose two activities you think best match each category (1–3). Then work in pairs. Explain your reasons.

diving	jet skiing	kayaking	rafting
rowing	snorkeling	waterskiing	windsurfing

1 people find this relaxing
2 people do this to get a thrill
3 it's best to do this with other people

I CAN	
use adverbs to describe experiences	☐
talk about water sports and activities	☐

Real life

6 Work in groups. Tell a story starting with this sentence. Take turns adding a sentence to the story, using one of these expressions.

"Did I ever tell you about the time my cat ate my homework?"

a few … later,	one day,
after a few …,	suddenly,
all of a sudden,	the next thing was
during the …,	then

7 >> MB Use one of these first sentences and tell another story.

"I remember once, I was waiting at the bus stop."
"A couple of years ago, I went for a job interview."

I CAN	
tell a story	☐
say when things happened in a sequence of events	☐

Page 40, Exercise 5: Story A is true.

Unit 4 Opportunities

Children playing at an entertainment center

FEATURES

46 Will a robot take your job?

The future of work

48 What's next?

We hear from people facing life-changing decisions.

50 A better life?

One reporter's view of the economic boom in China

54 Everest tourism changed Sherpa lives

A video about the people who live near Mount Everest

1 Work in pairs. Look at the photo and the caption. What do you think the children are doing?

2 Did you want to do any of these jobs when you were a child?

ballet dancer	movie star	firefighter	soccer player
pilot	police officer	rock star	scientist
train engineer	vet		

3 Work in pairs. Look at the words that can describe jobs. Are they positive or negative? Which words can describe the jobs in Exercise 2?

underpaid	boring	challenging	dangerous
dirty	enjoyable	exciting	responsible
stressful	well-paid		

4 ▶ **27** Work in pairs. Listen to three people talking about their childhood ambitions. Answer the questions for each person.

1 Which job did they want to do when they were young?
2 Which job do they do now or do they plan to do?
3 How do they describe the jobs?

5 Work in pairs. Ask and answer the questions in Exercise 4 about your own ambitions.

4a Will a robot take your job?

Word focus *job* and *work*

1 Look at the sentences. How do we use *job* and *work*?

  1 A lot of **jobs** are kind of boring, but my **job** has lots of variety.

  2 I've **worked** as a firefighter for ten years—it can be hard **work**.

2 Complete the sentences with the correct form of *job* or *work*.

  1 Where do you _____ ?
  2 Do you have an interesting _____ ?
  3 Is your company good to _____ for?
  4 My sister _____ in the same company as me.
  5 A: Is your brother around?
      B: No, he's at _____ .

3 Work in pairs. Take turns asking and answering questions 1–3 from Exercise 2. If you don't have a job, imagine you are someone you know.

Reading

4 Work in pairs. Look at the jobs. Do you think a robot could do these jobs? Why or why not?

electrician	engineer	clerical worker	nurse
taxi driver	teacher	telemarketer	

5 Read the article and check your ideas from Exercise 4.

6 Read the article again and say:

  1 which jobs are already done by robots.
  2 what the Oxford University study looked at.
  3 one job that is at risk, and one that is not.

7 Work in pairs. Find predictions in the article about these jobs. Do the predictions surprise you? Why or why not?

  1 factory work
  2 engineers
  3 taxi drivers

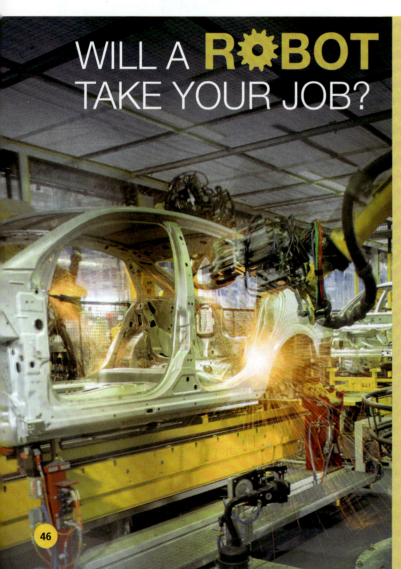

WILL A ROBOT TAKE YOUR JOB?

▶ 28 How likely is it that you'll lose your job to a robot? According to Toby Walsh, a professor of Artificial Intelligence, it's hard to think of a job that a computer won't be able to do. There are already some factories where all the work is done by robots, and there will certainly be more in the future. But what about teachers, engineers, and electricians? A team at Oxford University studied 350 different professions and suggested that 35 percent of UK jobs might go to robots in the next 20 years. In particular, work that is repetitive[1] or involves handling small objects will be at risk of automation.[2] On the other hand, jobs that involve helping other people or having original ideas will probably always need people. So journalists, nurses, engineers, and teachers won't be at risk, but clerical workers and telemarketers may not be so lucky. The Oxford study gives the probability for each of the 350 jobs. Electricians (65 percent) are more at risk than taxi drivers (57 percent). One global taxi company says driverless taxis will be on every street corner eventually. However, a spokesperson for London taxi drivers isn't convinced. "It won't happen. Driverless cars will never be able to work on roads at the same time as normal vehicles."

[1]**repetitive** (adj) /rɪˈpetətɪv/ repeating the same thing in the same way many times
[2]**automation** (n) /ɔːtɒˈmeɪʃən/ the use of machines to do tasks automatically

Grammar predictions

▶ **PREDICTIONS WITH** *WILL, MAY,* **and** *MIGHT*

Robots	will won't will certainly / definitely certainly / definitely won't may (not), might (not) will probably probably won't	do these jobs.

For more information and practice, see page 162.

8 Look at the grammar box. Underline the future forms (verb + base form) in the article.

9 Work in pairs. Look at the sentences you have underlined in the article. Which two predictions does the writer think are much less certain than the others?

10 Circle the appropriate words to complete the information about household robots.

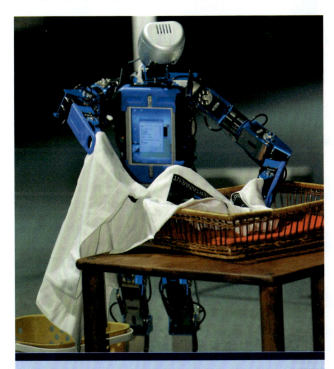

The robots are coming, according to robot manufacturers. They say that in five or ten years, we ¹ *will / won't* all have robots in our homes. Very soon, robots that can cook and fold clothes ² *might not / will* be available. In the future, there ³ *may / won't* even be robots to babysit our children. Or they ⁴ *may not / might* look after our elderly parents, and we ⁵ *will / won't* be able to watch them from a computer from wherever we are. One thing is certain: We ⁶ *might not / won't* be able to live without the help of robots in several aspects of our lives.

11 Cross out the option that is not logical to complete the sentences.

1 Hyundai is building a new factory. They *may / will / ~~won't~~* need more workers.
2 Ravi isn't very good at his job. He *might / might not / won't* get a promotion.
3 I'm bored with my job. I think I *may / might not / will* look for a new one.
4 The office changes are not important. They *might not / will / won't* affect our work.
5 Don't worry about your exam! You *may / might / won't* do better than you expect.

12 Write predictions. Use a form from the grammar box and the words below. Then compare your predictions with your partner. Do you agree?

1 My English exam results / (probably / definitely) / good / …
   My English exam results will probably be good because I've worked hard.
2 Finding a good job / (certainly / probably) / easy / …
3 People's salaries / (definitely / might) / go down / …
4 Unemployment / (definitely / probably) / get better / …
5 Environmental problems / (definitely / may) / get worse / …
6 The amount of free time we have / (certainly / might) / go up / …

Speaking my Life

13 Work in groups. How likely are you to do the following in the next two years? Give reasons. Use future forms from the grammar box in your conversations. Add ideas of your own.

1 buy a motorcycle
2 get a degree
3 get a cat
4 get married
5 look for a job
6 make new friends
7 move to a new house
8 travel to a foreign country

A: *Are you likely to buy a motorcycle in the next two years?*
B: *Actually, I **might buy** one this summer. I'd love to take a big road trip across Europe.*

4b What's next?

Vocabulary education

1 Work in pairs. Look at the expressions in the box and tell your partner what you have done or what you think you will do.

> apply to college
> become an apprentice
> take a (training) course
> get a degree
> get good / poor grades
> go to college
> graduate
> retake an exam

A: *When I left school, I applied to college. Then I …*
B: *I got good grades, so I think I'll graduate with a good degree. Then I'll …*

> ▶ **WORDBUILDING prefix** *re-*
>
> Adding *re-* to the start of a verb means "to do something again."
> *retake, reapply, redo, retrain, reread, rewrite*
>
> For more practice, see Workbook page 35.

2 Work in pairs. Ask and answer the questions. Ask follow-up questions.

1 Have you ever had to retake an exam?
2 How many times have you reread your favorite book?
3 Do you know anyone who has retrained for a different job?

Listening

3 Have you made any important decisions recently? Work in pairs. Tell your partner about one of your decisions.

I've decided to change jobs. I don't want to work in an office any more.

4 Work in pairs. Look at the women in the photos. Discuss where you think they are from and what they do.

5 ▶ 29 Listen to an excerpt from a radio program celebrating International Women's Day. Circle the correct option to complete the sentences.

1 Devi is *working / studying*.
2 Devi wants to be *a boss / a nurse*.
3 Elisabeth *has / doesn't have* a job.
4 Elisabeth intends to *leave her job / retire*.
5 Sahera has just *started / graduated from* university.
6 Sahera plans to *stay in / leave* Kabul.

6 ▶ 29 Listen to the excerpt again and correct the factual mistakes.

1 Devi isn't going to stay at home forever.
2 Devi is taking an exam tomorrow.
3 Elisabeth is going to join a new company.
4 Elisabeth is meeting her new boss on Wednesday.
5 Sahera's friend is going to work in the United States.
6 Sahera's friend is leaving Kabul next month.

7 Which of the three women is most certain about her plans? Who doesn't know yet?

Grammar future forms

8 Look at the sentences in bold in the Track 29 audioscript on page 182. Find the following.

1 something that is scheduled on a calendar
2 something Devi decides to do as she is speaking
3 something Devi has arranged to do
4 something Devi has already planned to do

9 Read what Elisabeth and Sahera say in the audioscript. Underline at least six other sentences about future plans.

> ▶ **FUTURE FORMS**
>
> 1 **present continuous:** *I'm taking the exam next month.*
> 2 *will:* *Just a minute, I'll get you some.*
> 3 *going to:* *I'm going to start my own business.*
> 4 **simple present:** *The semester starts in January.*
>
> For more information and practice, see page 162.

10 Look at the grammar box. Match the future forms (1–4) with the uses (a–d).

a a plan or intention decided before the moment of speaking ____
b a decision made at the moment of speaking ____
c an event that follows a regular schedule ____
d a fixed arrangement to do something at a specified (or understood) time in the future ____

11 Circle the correct option.

> I finished school last month. [1] *I'm going to take / I take* the summer off, but in September [2] *I'll start / I'm starting* as an apprentice in a garage. [3] *I take / I'm taking* a night class as well. That [4] *starts / is going to start* on October 9th. I'm lucky—some of my friends don't know what [5] *they're going to do / they do.* [6] *We'll meet / We're meeting* next week for the first time since our exams. Actually, I think [7] *I'll send / I'm sending* them a message about that right now.

12 Complete the responses with the most appropriate future form. Then work in pairs. Compare and discuss your answers.

1 A: Do you have any plans for when you finish college?
    B: Yes, I _____ (take) a year off.
2 A: I can't decide what to do.
    B: It's OK. I _____ (help) you.
3 A: Is it true that Samira is leaving?
    B: Yeah, she _____ (get) married next month.
4 A: Did you enroll for evening classes?
    B: Yes, _____ (go) to my first class tonight.

Speaking *my* **Life**

13 Draw a calendar for the next four weeks. Write in these things.

> plans you have made (shopping trips, etc.)
> arrangements (hair appointments, etc.)
> things you are still unsure about (weekend activities, etc.)

NOVEMBER		
2–8	**9–15**	**16–22**
6th–7th Weekend away?	10th – dentist 3 p.m.	

14 Work in pairs. You need to meet several times for a project for your English class. Find dates when you can get together.

A: *What are you up to next week? Maybe we can get together early in the week.*
B: *OK. But I'm going to the dentist on Monday, so how about Tuesday?*

4c A better life?

Reading

1 How can these things improve your opportunities in life? Make notes and then compare with your partner.

> the place you go to school
> the place you live
> the career you choose
> your family

2 Read the article quickly. Which paragraph(s) (1–4) talk(s) about these topics?

a training and education _____
b the movement of people _____
c the development of new towns _____

3 Read the first two paragraphs of the article. Put these things in the order in which they appear in a new town in China.

____ a street stalls
____ b cell phone companies
____ c clothing stores
____ d construction workers
____ e entrepreneurs
____ f stores
____ g women

4 Read the rest of the article. Are the sentences true (T) or false (F)?

1	According to the writer, the early development of new towns is always different.	T	F
2	The majority of Chinese people live in rural areas.	T	F
3	About ten million people a year move to the cities.	T	F
4	Education and training are high priorities for many workers in new factory towns.	T	F
5	It's difficult to find training courses in factory towns.	T	F

5 Work in pairs. Do you think that the people in the new towns have a better life than they did in their villages? Why or why not?

Critical thinking the author's view

6 Authors can show things in a positive, negative, or neutral way. Read these excerpts from the article and say which one expresses a positive view and which two are neutral. Which words help you decide?

1 When the town starts to grow, the cell phone companies arrive.
2 The human energy in these new towns is amazing: the brave entrepreneurs, the quick-moving builders, the young workers a long way from home.
3 Another young man I met is learning Arabic and is going to work as a translator for Middle Eastern buyers.

7 Work in pairs. Find other sentences in the article in which the author shows his view. What is his view?

8 Work as a class. How do the changes described in the article compare to a place or country you are familiar with?

Vocabulary pay and conditions

9 Work in pairs. Read the sentences. Think of one job to match each description.

1 In this job, people work **long hours**. _H_
2 Employees get four weeks' **paid vacation** a year. ____
3 Workers get regular **pay raises**. ____
4 The **salary** is excellent. ____
5 Employees can choose to work **flexible hours**. ____
6 There are lots of opportunities for **promotion**. ____
7 Staff members often have to work **overtime**. ____
8 There is a generous **pension plan**. ____

10 Put the words in bold in Exercise 9 into three groups: *money* (M), *hours* (H), and *benefits* (B). Then add these words to the groups.

> clocking in and out _H_   bonuses ____
> discounts on company   company car ____
> products ____   part-time ____
> free language classes ____   wages ____
> health insurance ____

Speaking my Life

11 Work in pairs. What four things in Exercises 9 and 10 does the perfect job have? Put them in order, 1 to 4. Then compare with another pair.

A better life?

Zhujiang New Town in Guangzhou, China

We spoke to Peter Hessler about his experience of the fast-changing life in China.

How does a new factory town begin?

1 The beginning of a new Chinese factory town is always the same: In the beginning there are many construction workers. They are men who have come from country villages, and they are quickly joined by entrepreneurs.[1] These businessmen sell meat, fruit, and vegetables from street stalls. Later, the first real stores appear. The same businessmen may start to sell construction materials.

What comes next?

2 When the town starts to grow, the cell phone companies arrive. They sell prepaid phonecards to the workers so that they can call the families they left behind. When the factories built by the men from the villages start production, you begin to see women. After the arrival of the women, clothing stores and shoe stores appear. And eventually, you see public services, like buses.

What does it feel like to be there?

3 The human energy in these new towns is amazing: the brave entrepreneurs, the quick-moving builders, the young workers a long way from home. These new opportunities have created an extremely motivated population. There are 1.3 billion people in China, and 72 per cent of them are between the ages of 16 and 64. A majority now live in towns rather than villages. Every year about ten million people move to the cities. Social scientists predict that by 2020 the urban population will be 60 per cent.

What kind of life do people want?

4 Most people in China have seen their standard of living go up in recent years. Chinese schools have been very successful, and the literacy rate[2] is over 90 percent. So the next step is to develop higher education, because many people are looking for better training or education. There's a huge number of private courses in a Chinese factory town: English classes, typing classes, technical classes. One young man I know couldn't read or write when he left his village. He now works in a factory and spends a quarter of his wages on training. Another young man I met is learning Arabic and is going to work as a translator for Middle Eastern buyers. The new factory towns of China have grown in order to make products for the rest of the world. And now, the workers want to be able to have these products for themselves.

[1] **entrepreneur** (n) /ˌɑntrəprənʊər/ someone who starts new companies
[2] **literacy rate** (n) /ˈlɪtərəsi reɪt/ the number of people who can read and write

Individual portraits in Beijing on Chinese National Day

4d Would you mind …?

Vocabulary job requirements

Assistant Researcher

NaturalHistoryNet **TV**

Full-time position. Initial 12-month contract.

You will be responsible for
- assisting the Research Coordinator on a variety of film projects.
- managing film production materials.
- dealing with queries related to current and past projects.

You will have
- a degree in a relevant subject.
- 1–2 years' experience in film production.
- excellent database and research skills.

You will be
- organized and independent.
- able to meet strict deadlines.
- good at working under pressure.

Send resume and cover letter to:
Anila.Jones@NHNTV.com
Closing date June 15th

---

1 Read the job ad and find the following:

1 duties
2 deadline for applications
3 skills and qualifications required
4 personal qualities required

2 Work in pairs. Choose three jobs you know something about. What are the most important requirements of those jobs? Compare your ideas.

Real life making and responding to requests

3 ▶31 Work in pairs. Listen to two friends, Rudi and Mark, discussing the position in the ad. Answer the questions.

1 Does Mark meet all the requirements?
2 Is his resume ready?
3 What will he need for the interview?

4 ▶31 Look at the expressions for making and responding to requests. Listen again and circle the expressions Rudi and Mark use.

▶ **REQUESTS**

Making requests
Is it all right if I list you as a reference?
Would it be OK to borrow your suit?
Is it OK to take your car?
Would it be all right if I used your phone?

Would you mind checking my application form?
Do you mind helping me with my resume?

Could you give me a ride to the interview?
Can you take a look at my cover letter?
Will you be able to do it today?

Responding to requests
Of course (not).
I'm not sure about that.
Yes, I will.
Sure, no problem.

---

5 Would you like to get a job like the one in the ad? Why or why not?

6 **Pronunciation weak and strong auxiliary verbs**

a ▶32 Listen and repeat the exchange. Notice how the auxiliary verb *will* is not stressed in the full question and is stressed in the response.

A: Will you be able to do it today?
B: Yes, I will.

b ▶33 Match the questions (1–5) with the responses (a–e). Then listen and check. Work in pairs. Practice the exchanges.

1 Are you going to apply for the job? ____
2 Will he help you with your resume? ____
3 Are they still advertising that job? ____
4 Does she meet our requirements? ____
5 Will it be an all-day interview? ____

a I don't think she does.
b I think it might.
c No, they aren't.
d Of course he will.
e Yes, I think I will.

7 Work in pairs. You are going to act out short conversations in different situations. Turn to page 155.

4e I'm enclosing my resume

Writing a cover letter

1 Work in pairs. Which do you think is the most common way to apply for a job? Tell your partner.

> a resume
> a letter
> a personal contact
> a phone call
> an application form

2 Read the cover letter in reply to the ad on page 52. Match the information (a–i) with the parts of the letter. What information (if any) can you leave out if you send the letter as an email?

a a reference to your resume
b the date
c the name and address of the person you are writing to
d the reason for your letter
e your address
f your phone number
g your qualifications
h your relevant experience
i your skills

3 Compare the letter to the style you use in your country. Answer the questions.

1 Is the layout different? How?
2 Does it include the same information?
3 Is the information in the main part of the letter sequenced in the same way?

4 Writing skill formal style

a A formal letter in English uses these features. Underline examples of each one in the letter.

1 concise sentences
2 formal phrases to begin sentences
3 no contractions
4 standard phrases to open and close the letter

b Rewrite the sentences in a more formal style.

1 I'll finish my degree soon.
2 Give me a call.
3 I saw your ad in the newspaper, and I thought it looked really interesting.
4 I've sent you my resume as well.
5 I'll be free beginning in August.
6 Thanks a lot.

9125 West 6th St., Coral Springs, Ohio 68776 ——
(227) 752-4446 ——
July 7, 2017 ——

Angela Jones, NHN TV
8334 Bruce St.
Brownsville
Rhode Island 42935   ——

Dear Ms. Jones,

I am writing in reply to your advertisement in the ——
Daily Herald for the position of Assistant Researcher.
I will graduate with a degree in Digital Media this ——
month from Cleveland University. I have experience
in film production and post-production as I have
worked part-time at my university television station ——
for the last year.

I consider myself to be hard-working and organized
in my work. As part of my job with the university
television station, I was responsible for planning   ——
schedules and program archiving.

I am available for an interview at any time and
available to start work at the beginning of August. I
am willing to relocate if necessary.

I am enclosing my resume, which gives full details of
my qualifications, work experience, and skills as well ——
as my contact information.

Thank you very much. I look forward to hearing
from you.

Yours sincerely,

Mark Nolan

5 Write a cover letter to go with an application for a job you would like. Follow the layout and style of the letter from Mark.

6 Exchange letters with your partner. Use these questions to check your partner's letter.

- Is it clear how to contact this person?
- Is the style appropriate?
- Does the person sound like a good candidate?

4f Everest tourism changed Sherpa lives

Without Sherpas, it is impossible for people to climb Mount Everest.

Before you watch

1 Look at the photo and read the caption. Where do Sherpa people live? What is the area famous for?

2 Work in pairs. Do you think Everest tourism is a good thing or a bad thing for Sherpas? Give your reasons.

3 Key vocabulary

a Read the sentences. The words in bold are used in the video. Guess the meaning of the words.

1. Some people work two jobs to increase their **income**.
2. My **lifestyle** is very different from that of my parents' generation.
3. One percent of the world's population owns more than half of the world's **wealth**.
4. There are **substantial** differences between my first job and my current job—it was a big shock at first.
5. I'm training to go on the next international **expedition** across Antarctica.
6. We live in an **agrarian** society, and mainly keep sheep and cows.

b Match the words in bold in Exercise 3a with these definitions.

a based on farming _____
b an organized exploration or journey _____
c the money that you earn from a job _____
d the way a person lives, the typical things he or she does or owns _____
e large and important (quantity) _____
f the money a person has _____

While you watch

4 🎬 **4.1, 4.2** Watch the video. Check your ideas from Exercise 2.

5 🎬 **4.1** Watch Part 1 of the video again. Circle the correct option to complete the sentences.

1. The Sherpa are one of *thirty / seventy* ethnic groups within Nepal.
2. The name "Sherpa" means *"Easterner" / "Mountain People."*
3. The Sherpa culture fundamentally changed in *1953 / 1960* when Tenzing Norgay and Sir Edmund Hillary climbed Everest.
4. Their lifestyle became much more *agrarian / modern.*

6 🎬 **4.2** Work in pairs. Look at the list of things Sherpas have gained and lost. Circle G or L. Then watch Part 2 of the video again and check your answers.

1	education	G	L
2	healthcare	G	L
3	clothing	G	L
4	wealth	G	L
5	a simple life	G	L
6	happiness	G	L

After you watch

7 What can you remember? Try to answer the questions. Then compare with the class.

1. Who gave Karma Tsering his watch?
2. What was the only thing Kancha Sherpa worried about?
3. What did Max Lowe say people are losing?

8 Vocabulary in context

a 🎬 **4.3** Watch the clips from the video. Choose the correct meaning of the words and phrases.

b Answer the questions in your own words. Then work in pairs and compare your answers.

1. Can you remember a time something happened to you just by chance?
2. Do you think some people in your country take things for granted? What kind of things?
3. If life feels rushed, what can you do to feel more relaxed?
4. Where do new people usually settle in your country?
5. Can you name any communities that have had little contact with the outside world?

9 Work in pairs. Tourism changed the Sherpa way of life. What are the effects of these things on people's ways of life?

the internet
the car
cheaper air travel

---

advancement (n) /əd'vænsmənt/ an improvement in a person's life
ethnic group (n) /eθnɪk 'gruːp/ a group of people belonging to the same culture
healthcare (n) /'helθkeər/ medical services
idyllic (adj) /ɪ'dɪlɪk/ peaceful and calm
self-gain (n) /self'ɡeɪn/ getting more money or things for yourself

Grammar

1 Complete each comment from student chefs with one or two words or a contraction.

1 "I'm sure nobody _____ be able to eat this!"
2 "I'm _____ to change jobs soon."
3 "This _____ definitely impress the customers."
4 "I'm going _____ be the best chef in the country one day."
5 "My parents _____ be so proud of me."
6 "This may _____ turn out as I expected."
7 "My friends _____ believe me when I tell them about my day."
8 "I'm _____ get take out for dinner tonight."

2 **>> MB** Work in pairs. Find two plans and two predictions in Exercise 1. Explain the use of the verbs in each comment.

3 **>> MB** Work in pairs. Ask your partner about plans he or she has for when your English course ends.

I CAN	
make predictions about future events (predictions with *will*)	☐
show different degrees of certainty about predictions (*may, might, could*)	☐
ask and answer questions about future plans and arrangements (*going to*, present continuous)	☐

Vocabulary

4 Match the verbs (1–5) with the nouns (a–e) to make expressions about education.

1 apply   ○   ○ a an apprentice
2 become   ○   ○ b an exam
3 get   ○   ○ c from university
4 graduate ○   ○ d good grades
5 retake   ○   ○ e to college

5 **>> MB** Work in pairs. For each of these jobs, discuss the qualities and qualifications you need, and the pay and conditions. Then say which job would be best for your partner and give reasons.

I CAN	
talk about stages in education and job training	☐
describe different jobs, job requirements, and conditions	☐

Real life

6 Work in pairs. Match the beginnings of the sentences (1–3) with the endings (a–c). Then act out a conversation that includes the requests and appropriate replies.

1 Could you ____
2 Is it all right if I ____
3 Would you mind ____

a borrow your phone?
b help me with this application?
c lending me some money?

7 **>> MB** With your partner, act out similar conversations for two of these situations.

> a problem at work
> an important exam ahead
> a meeting with a new boss
> your first day at college

I CAN	
make and respond to requests	☐

Unit 5 Well-being

Some fruit and vegetables are thrown away because they are "too ugly" to sell.

FEATURES

58 **Pizza with a pedigree**

Traditional dishes get special status.

60 **Imaginary eating**

Discover the power of your mind!

62 **A caffeine-fueled world**

An in-depth look at the role of caffeine in modern life

66 **Dangerous dining**

A video about an unusual Japanese delicacy

1 Find these foods in the photo. Which ones do you eat? How often do you eat them?

apple	carrot	green pepper	pear
red pepper	squash	sweet potato	

2 Work in pairs. Discuss the questions.

1 How much do you know about the different food groups you should eat each day?
2 How do you decide what is the right size of a portion of food?
3 Does everyone need to eat the same amounts?

3 ▶ 34 Work in pairs. What do you think the portion sizes of these types of food are? Listen to an excerpt from a radio program about food. Complete the table.

Type of food	Size of portion
cereal / rice / pasta / potato	_____ clenched fist
meat / poultry / fish	the palm of _____ hand
snacks: popcorn / chips	_____ handfuls
sweets: brownies / cake	_____ fingers

4 Discuss the questions with your partner.

1 Does any of the information in Exercise 3 surprise you?
2 How much attention do you pay to your diet?
3 In what ways can food and diet affect your health?

5a Pizza with a pedigree

Reading

1 Work in pairs. Discuss the questions.

1. What are the traditional dishes of your country or region?
2. How often do you eat or make these dishes?
3. How often do you eat or make dishes from other countries? Which ones?
4. What's your favorite pizza? What's on it?

2 Work in pairs. Read the article *Pizza with a pedigree*. Answer the questions.

1. What is a geographically indicated food product?
2. What are some of the other foods in the same group as Pizza Napoletana?
3. What are the rules for an "authentic" Pizza Napoletana?

Grammar modal verbs

> **MODAL VERBS**

Obligation	**No obligation**
have / has to, must	*don't / doesn't have to*
	Prohibition
	must not
Permission	**No permission**
can, is / are allowed to	*can't, is / are not allowed to*
Recommendation	
should	*should (not)*

For more information and practice, see page 164.

3 Look at the grammar box. Answer these questions.

1. Which modal verbs from the box are in the article? Underline the modal verbs in the article.
2. What verb form follows the modal verbs in the box?
3. Two of the modal verbs in the article do not express rules. Which ones?

F O O D

▶ 35

Pizza with a pedigree[1]

Pizza has a long history in Italy. The word "pizza" first appeared in an AD 997 manuscript from Gaeta, a southern Italian town. But there is pizza—and there is Pizza Napoletana. The two, experts say, have as much in common as virgin olive oil has with ordinary cooking oil. Pizza Napoletana is one of an elite[2] group of geographically indicated food and drink products—foods associated with a particular place, so much so that they are named for the place. Other well-known examples are Champagne, Kobe beef, and Parmesan cheese (from Parma, Italy).

The products usually have to meet certain requirements in order to be certified. For example, sparkling wine has to come from the Champagne region of France for it to be labeled "Champagne." Kobe beef has to be produced in Japan's Hyogo prefecture, a region around Kobe City. The cattle also have to pass strict[3] tests, and only 3–4,000 head of cattle qualify each year.

The specifications for a "real" Pizza Napoletana are very complicated— it takes almost as long to read them as it does to make the pizza. The pizza can't be over 35 centimeters (13.8 inches) in diameter, and the crust can't be more than 2 centimeters (0.8 inches) thick. The ingredients must include a special type of flour and up to 100 grams of San Marzano tomatoes. And the cheese has to be fresh "Mozzarella di Bufala." Of course, you don't have to know anything about how to make it to enjoy eating it. Everyone should try an authentic Pizza Napoletana at least once—see if you can taste the difference!

[1]**pedigree** (n) (adj) /ˈpedɪgriː/ a documented history
[2]**elite** (adj, n) /ɪˈliːt/ a small group of the best
[3]**strict** (adj) /strɪkt/ precise and rigorous

4 Read these statements from food packaging. Write sentences using one of the modal verbs in parentheses.

1 *Not suitable for vegetarians*
(shouldn't / don't have to)
Vegetarians shouldn't eat this product.

2 **NOT SUITABLE FOR PEOPLE WITH NUT ALLERGIES**
(don't have to / can't)

3 **DO NOT EAT MORE THAN THE RECOMMENDED DAILY INTAKE OF SALT**
(can / shouldn't)

4 **MULTIPACK OF FOUR – NOT FOR SALE SEPARATELY**
(don't have to / not allowed to)

5 *Heat before serving*
(can / have to)

6 **NOT RECOMMENDED FOR DIABETICS**
(allowed to / shouldn't)

5 Work in pairs. Look at these food items. Discuss the questions.

durian	eggs	fugu	hakarl
oysters	potatoes	red beans	steak

1 Have you ever eaten any of these food items?
2 Do you know of any special treatment these things need before you can eat them?

6 ▶ 36 Listen to eight short conversations about the food items in Exercise 5. Complete the notes for each item.

1 durian: you aren't allowed to
_____

2 fugu: _____ are allowed to
_____

3 hakarl: you have to
_____

4 potatoes: you don't have to
_____

5 oysters: you can't
_____

6 eggs: you should
_____

7 red beans: you must
_____

8 steak: you can
_____

ferment (v) /fər'ment/ to leave food or drink to undergo a natural chemical reaction by yeast, bacteria, or other microorganisms
peel (v) /piːl/ to remove the skin from fruit or a vegetable

7 Pronunciation weak forms

a ▶ 37 Listen to the sentences from conversations 1–4 in Exercise 6. Notice how *to* is not stressed. Repeat the sentences.

b Work in pairs. Decide if you do or don't have to do these things. Discuss with your partner.

keep eggs in the fridge
wash rice before you cook it
eat fish on the day you buy it
cook meat until it isn't pink

Speaking *my* Life

8 Work in pairs. Write down at least two ideas for each topic.

1 rules you had to follow when you were in elementary school
2 information that should be on food labels
3 places where you're not allowed to eat hot food
4 table manners

9 Work with a new partner. Compare your ideas from Exercise 8. Do you both agree?

A: *When we were in elementary school, we* **had to line up** *outside the classroom.*
B: *Oh, yes! So did we!*

fugu (puffer fish)

durians

hakarl (shark meat)

oysters

5b Imaginary eating

Reading and listening

1 Work in pairs. Discuss the statements. Do you agree with them? Give examples to support your arguments.

1 Believe in yourself: The difference between a winner and a runner-up is in attitude, not skill.
2 Willpower: You can achieve anything if you think you can do it.
3 Train your mind: People who consider themselves to be lucky have more lucky moments.

2 Read the article *Imaginary eating*. What does the imaginary eating technique involve?

3 ▶ 39 Listen to two people discussing the news article. Are these sentences true (T) or false (F)?

1 Jack believes the claims in the article.	T	F
2 Lin is open-minded about the idea of imaginary eating.	T	F
3 Both of them agree that willpower is important.	T	F
4 Jack plans to try out the technique.	T	F
5 Lin eats too many chips and snacks.	T	F
6 Jack is going to buy some chocolate.	T	F

4 ▶ 39 Listen to the conversation again. Match the beginnings of the sentences (1–6) with the endings (a–f).

1 I'll believe it ____
2 If you don't train your mind, ____
3 I won't find out ____
4 When I want to eat a snack, ____
5 I'll never need to buy chocolate again ____
6 As soon as it starts working, ____

a if this technique works.
b I'll let you know.
c I'll try imagining that I'm eating it.
d unless I try.
e when I see it.
f you won't be able to lose weight.

5 Work in pairs. Read the comment at the end of the article again. Do you agree with the comment? With your partner, write a comment to add to this section.

Imaginary eating

▶ 38

Christine Dell'Amore
National Geographic News

Obesity rates are climbing fast, so we need to find new techniques to help people control overeating. According to new research, "imaginary eating" could be one such technique. It's based on the idea that if you are less interested in a certain food, you will eat less of it. But how do you reduce your interest? A psychologist in the United States reports that if you just imagine eating a specific food, your interest in it will drop. Often people try not to think about food when they need to lose weight. But avoiding these thoughts might not be a good strategy. With imaginary eating, if you force yourself to think about chewing and swallowing food, you'll actually reduce your desire to eat.

Comments

👤 **Rpineapple23**

This study is just more proof of how powerful our brain is. The better we are at using that power when making decisions and controlling certain behaviors, the healthier we will become.

REPLY   RECOMMEND

Grammar first conditional

6 Work in pairs. Look at the grammar box. Answer the questions.

a Which verb forms are used to make the first conditional?
b Where can *if* go in conditional sentences?
c Look at the position of *if* in the sentences. When do we use a comma (,)?
d Which of the sentences refers to future possibility and which refers to something that is generally true?
e Find three sentences with the first conditional pattern in the article. Do the sentences refer to future possibility or to something that is generally true?

7 Complete the sentences with the simple present and *will* + base form. Which sentences refer to future possibility and which refer to something that is generally true?

1 If you _____ (believe) in yourself, you _____ (be) more successful.
2 I _____ (need) a lot of willpower if I _____ (want) to give up chocolate.
3 If you _____ (not buy) snacks, you _____ (not be able) to eat them.
4 If you _____ (find) any more information, _____ (you / let) me know?
5 I _____ (give up) junk food if you _____ (do), too.
6 If I _____ (not try) it, I _____ (never know).
7 _____ we _____ (eat) less if we _____ (use) smaller plates?

8 Jack and Lin are discussing Lin's efforts to eat more healthily. Circle the correct options.

1 You won't change *as soon as* / *unless* you make an effort.
2 I'll weigh myself *before* / *unless* I start my diet.
3 I'll keep trying *before* / *until* I see a change.
4 You won't see any results *unless* / *when* you try hard.
5 *If* / *Unless* you give up easily, you won't achieve your target.
6 I'll follow the diet *unless* / *until* I lose ten kilos.

Vocabulary a healthy lifestyle

9 Work in pairs. Match each verb with one or more nouns to make strategies for a healthy lifestyle. Add ideas of your own.

Verbs	Nouns
avoid	a new sport
change	an outdoor activity
cut down on	bad habits
cut out	computer and TV time
give up	fatty food
learn	heavy meals at night
quit	junk food
reduce	relaxation techniques
take up	smoking
	snacks between meals
	stress

10 Think of a specific result for each strategy from Exercise 9. Write sentences with the first conditional.

If you avoid heavy meals at night, you'll sleep better.

Speaking my Life

11 Work in pairs. Make a list of all the possible consequences you would face in these situations.

1 giving up junk food
2 changing your job / studies
3 sharing an apartment with friends
4 taking up extreme sports

12 Work in groups of four. Student A is going to do one of the things in Exercise 11. The rest of the group asks questions. Keep answering questions as long as you can, then swap.

A: *I'm going to give up junk food.*
B: *What **will you eat when you want** a snack?*
A: *Don't worry. **If I want** a snack, **I'll eat** nuts or some fruit.*
C: *And what **if you find out** you're allergic to nuts?*

5c A caffeine-fueled world

Reading

1 Work in groups. Discuss the questions.

1 Is your lifestyle very different from that of your parents' generation? In what way(s)?
2 How much tea, coffee, or other caffeinated drinks do you have in a normal day?

2 Read the article on page 63 quickly. Circle the correct option to complete the sentence.

The article is about caffeine and *children* / *daily life* / *sugar*.

3 What are the effects of caffeine? Complete the table.

Harmful effects	Beneficial effects
changes your mood	makes you less tired
1 _____ blood pressure	relieves
	3 _____
increases the	reduces
2 _____	4 _____
of heart disease	symptoms

4 Complete these sentences with words from the article.

1 Caffeine is an _____ in tea, coffee, soft drinks, energy drinks, and chocolate.
2 Caffeine is a drug that changes your _____ .
3 Several countries put health _____ on energy drinks.
4 People today have changed to a less natural work _____ .
5 Caffeine is popular with people who need to stay _____ .

5 Work in pairs. Do you think anything the writer says is true about your own lifestyle? What?

Critical thinking writer's purpose

6 What is the writer's main purpose in this article? Give reasons for your answer.

to entertain / *to inform* / *to persuade* the reader

7 Look at the list of features that are typical of informative texts. Find examples in the article.

1 the simple present
2 the third person
3 questions and answers
4 facts
5 specific examples
6 quotes, often from experts
7 linking words to show how ideas are connected

8 Work in pairs. Discuss the questions.

1 Do you think the writer is successful in his or her purpose?
2 Did you change your ideas about caffeine after reading the article?
3 In what way has the article influenced your opinion of caffeine?

Word focus *so*

9 Look at how *so* is used in the article. In which sentence can we replace *so* with *as a result*? What can replace *so* in the other sentence?

1 Why are these drinks so popular?
2 It raises blood pressure and so increases the risk of heart disease.

10 Work in pairs. Complete the sentences. Then write two-line exchanges using some of the sentences. Act out your exchanges.

1 I've had five cups of _____ so far today.
2 Thank you so much for _____ you've done.
3 I'm so happy you _____ .
4 _____ me so I know when to expect you.
5 No, I don't _____ so.
6 Oh, that's _____ ! So did I!

Speaking myLife

11 Complete the slogans about modern life with these words. Where do you think the slogans are from?

all	close	day	night	on	today

1 We never _____ .
2 See the movies of tomorrow _____ .
3 Open _____ hours.
4 "Always _____ " broadband.
5 Late-_____ shopping every Thursday.
6 All _____ breakfast served here.

12 Work in small groups. These things are typical of a 24-hour society. Discuss the questions.

1 Are the things positive or negative?
2 Which ones affect you? In what way?
3 What are some of the consequences for you or for other people?

24-hour shopping	shift work
difficulty sleeping	smartphone addiction
eating take-out food	tiredness

A caffeine-fueled *world*

▶ 40

by T.R. Reid

Over the centuries, people have created many traditions around preparing and drinking tea and coffee. Just think of the Japanese tea ceremony or British afternoon tea. Why are these drinks so popular? The answer is their secret ingredient—caffeine. In the modern world, we also get caffeine from many canned energy drinks. And the more modern our world gets, the more we seem to need caffeine.

Caffeinated drinks make you less tired and more alert.[1] This double power is part of the reason why caffeine is the world's most popular mood-changing drug. It is the only habit-forming drug we routinely serve to our children (in soft drinks and chocolate bars). In fact, most babies in the developed world are born with tiny amounts of caffeine in their bodies.

Most people don't think about their caffeine intake being harmful. However, it raises blood pressure and so increases the risk of heart disease. That's why the use of caffeine is considered to be a problem by scientists and public health authorities. In the United States, for example, many canned energy drinks carry warnings. In most European countries, manufacturers have to label cans with warnings. In France and Denmark, you are not even allowed to sell some energy drinks.

On the other hand, there's research that suggests that caffeine may have benefits for human health. It helps relieve pain, reduces asthma symptoms, and increases reaction speed.

And it seems we need coffee—or another caffeinated drinks—to get us out of bed and back to work. Charles Czeisler, a neuroscientist at Harvard Medical School, explains that people traditionally went to sleep following sunset and woke up after sunrise. Then the way we worked changed, and people did more jobs indoors. Consequently, we had to adapt. Electric light and caffeinated food and drinks allowed people to follow a less natural work pattern. Without caffeine, the 24-hour society of the developed world simply couldn't exist.

"Caffeine helps people try to ignore the natural human rhythms," Czeisler says. He warns us that "there is a heavy, heavy price to pay" for all this extra alertness. Without enough sleep—the traditional 8 hours out of each 24 is about right—the human body will not function at its best, either physically, mentally, or emotionally.

According to Czeisler, the modern desire for caffeine is a Catch-22 situation. "The main reason that people want caffeine is to stay awake," he says. "But the main reason that people can't stay awake is they don't get enough regular sleep—because they use caffeine."

[1] **alert** (adj) /əˈlɜrt/ awake and paying attention

The Shibuya Crossing in Tokyo, Japan, is always busy.

5d Eating out

Vocabulary restaurants

1 Work in pairs. What are the most important things to consider when eating out? Does it depend on what kind of occasion it is?

> the atmosphere in the restaurant
> the food choice and/or quality
> the prices and/or value for money
> the service

2 Put these stages of eating out (a–f) into a logical order (1–6).

a make a reservation *1*
b have an appetizer ____
c have dessert ____
d have the main course ____
e look at the menu ____
f pay the check ____

3 Are these comments usually said by a customer (C) or a waiter or waitress (W)?

1	Are you ready to order?	C	W
2	What's that made from?	C	W
3	What do they taste like?	C	W
4	I think I'll try that.	C	W
5	Can I take your order now?	C	W
6	And I'll have the same.	C	W
7	And for your main course?	C	W
8	Does it come with vegetables?	C	W
9	And what about you, sir?	C	W

Real life describing dishes

4 ▶ **41** Listen to the conversation in a Jamaican restaurant. Check your answers from Exercise 3.

5 ▶ **41** Work in pairs. Look at the expressions for describing dishes. Listen to the conversation again. How are the dishes in the photos described?

> **▶ DESCRIBING DISHES**
>
> It's / They're a sort / type / kind of:
> *baked / boiled / fried dish*
> *fruit / meat / fish / vegetable*
> It's / They're made from:
> *a kind of bean / meat / vegetables*
> It tastes / They taste:
> *bland / hot / salty / spicy / sweet*
> It's / They're a bit like:
> *fresh cod / potatoes / lamb*

6 Work in pairs Which of the four dishes do the customers order? Would you order the same?

7 Pronunciation disappearing sounds

a ▶ **42** Listen to the sentences with these words. Cross out the part of the word that is not pronounced—the disappearing sound—in each word. Listen again and repeat the sentences.

1 interesting   3 traditionally
2 savory   4 vegetables

b Cross out the disappearing sounds in these words. Then work in pairs. Write sentences with the words for your partner to read aloud.

chocolate	natural	restaurant
separately	technique	

8 Write a list of six food dishes, vegetables, fruit, or other food that are either from your country or that you have eaten. Make notes to describe each item. Use the expressions for describing dishes to help you.

9 Work in groups of three. Take turns describing your mystery foods. Who can guess each one the fastest?

plantain fritters
akkra
ackee and saltfish
goat curry

5e We look forward to your reply

Writing a formal letter/email

1 A group of students has written to the manager of a local supermarket. Read the letter quickly. What is its purpose? Choose the correct option (a–c).

a   to ask about prices in the supermarket
b   to complain about the supermarket's actions
c   to invite the supermarket to stock new products

Dear Sir or Madam,

1 We are writing to express our shock at the news that your supermarket is throwing out huge amounts of fresh food that is still OK to eat every day. As a result, you are contributing to the huge food waste problem in our country.

2 As you may know, many people can't afford to buy enough food to feed their families every week. If your supermarket donates the food to the less fortunate instead of throwing it away, this will mean fewer people have to go hungry.

3 There are several local charity organizations that could use this unsold food. Will your supermarket consider working with them to pass on unwanted food to people who need it? Most food is still of good quality for some time after its sell-by date, and therefore should not be thrown out.

4 In addition, if your supermarket reduces the price of food as it approaches its sell-by date (as some of your competitors do), more people will be able to buy it. This will lead to less waste and more profit for you.

We look forward to your reply.

Yours sincerely,
11th Grade Students
Springfield High School

2 Read the letter again. Work in pairs. Answer the questions about each paragraph.

Paragraph 1   What action are the students writing about?
Paragraph 2   Who can the supermarket help?
Paragraph 3   What question do the students have?
Paragraph 4   What alternative do the students suggest?

3 Writing skill explaining consequences

a Find these words in the letter. They link causes and consequences. For each word, underline the cause and circle the consequence.

1   as a result (paragraph 1)
2   mean (paragraph 2)
3   lead to (paragraph 4)

b Complete the sentences with these words. Sometimes more than one option is possible.

as a result	consequently	lead to
mean	result in	therefore

1   We object strongly to this plan. _____ , we will not be able to support it.
2   We welcome the new community kitchen. This will _____ more people eating a hot meal.
3   The prices have gone up. _____ , fewer people will shop here.
4   New price policies _____ we'll be able to buy more.
5   We suggest lowering prices as this could _____ more customers coming in.
6   We reduced our prices and _____ increased the number of customers.

4 Prepare a letter with your reaction to one of these situations. Make notes before you start. Use the questions in Exercise 2 to guide you.

• Your college is going to close the student cafeteria.
• Your favorite TV show is being canceled.
• Your employer or school has banned junk food and vending machines.
• Your local swimming pool is being closed.

5 Write your letter. Follow the structure of the paragraphs in Exercise 2. Use these questions to check your letter.

• Is the style correct for a formal letter?
• Is the purpose of the letter clear?
• Is it clear what action the person who the letter is addressed to needs to take?

6 Exchange letters with your partner. Read your partner's letter. Take the role of the person it is addressed to. Are you going to take any action as a result of the letter? Write a short reply to the letter.

5f Dangerous dining

A fugu restaurant on a busy street in Osaka

Before you watch

1 Look at the photo and write six words connected to it. Then work in pairs. Compare your list with your partner's.

2 Key vocabulary

a Read the sentences. The words in bold are used in the video. Guess the meaning of the words.

1 Sugar is a **major** cause of people's problems with their teeth.
2 Some frogs have **poison** on their skin.
3 Check the **regulations** before you enter the competition.
4 Lots of people go on vacation **annually**.
5 If you feel nervous, **breathe** in and out slowly.

b Match the words in bold in Exercise 2a with these definitions.

a something that can kill you if you eat or drink it _____
b every year _____
c take air into your lungs _____
d official rules _____
e important, big _____

While you watch

3 📹 **5.1** Watch Part 1 of the video with the sound OFF. Discuss the questions.

1 Which country are the people in?
2 What kind of food can you see?
3 What do you think could be dangerous about this food?

4 📹 **5.1** Watch Part 1 of the video again with the sound ON. Check your ideas from Exercise 3 and find out the name of the food.

5 📹 **5.2** Watch Part 2 of the video with the sound OFF. Work in pairs. What do you think the diners (Tom and Aki) and the chef are saying to each other? Then watch with the sound ON and check your ideas.

6 📹 **5.1, 5.2** Watch the whole video. Circle the correct option to complete the sentences.

1 A lot of people died from eating fugu *after / during* World War II.
2 At this time, licenses for *catching and selling / preparing and serving* fugu were introduced.
3 There were *2,500 / 10,500* deaths from fugu from 1945 to 1975.

4 Nowadays, only about three people die every year, mostly from poisoning *at home / in restaurants*.

After you watch

7 Vocabulary in context

a 📹 **5.3** Watch the clips from the video. Choose the correct meaning of the words and phrases.

b Complete the sentences or answer the questions in your own words. Then work in pairs and compare your answers.

1 I saw an ad for a vacation with a complete … experience.
2 One thing that concerns me is …
3 The last time I got sick was …
4 Do you know anyone who has been fooled by an internet scam?
5 Do people in your country eat mainly in restaurants or at home?

8 Work in pairs. Answer the questions below.

1 Why do you think people eat fugu?
2 Do you think eating fugu should be banned?
3 Would you like to try fugu? Why or why not?

9 Work in pairs to prepare a survey on risk-taking. Look at the example below and write three similar sentences for activities that include risks. Then ask your classmates their opinions.

The best way to avoid getting sick from fugu is…

a by going to a well-known restaurant.
b not to eat it.
c to take anti-toxin medicine.

---

anti-toxin (n) /ˌæntɪˈtɒksɪn/ a substance/medicine that can treat a problem caused by a toxin
cyanide (n) /ˈsaɪənaɪd/ an extremely poisonous chemical
toxin (n) /ˈtɒksɪn/ a kind of poison

UNIT 5 REVIEW AND MEMORY BOOSTER

Grammar

1 Read the conversation between two friends who are cooking. Circle the correct options.

A: Do you know how to make risotto?
B: Oh, yes. ¹ *I show / I'll show* you if you want.
A: OK, great. ² *Can / Must* I use this pan?
B: Yes, sure. You ³ *have to / don't have to* ask.
A: When the onion ⁴ *is / will be* ready, do I add the rice?
B: Yes, then the water. But you ⁵ *will / have to* add it slowly. Don't add more until the rice ⁶ *absorbs / will absorb* it.
A: OK, that's all the water. ⁷ *Am I allowed to / Should I* stir it all the time now?
B: Yes, because you ⁸ *must / can't* let it stick to the pan. If it ⁹ *sticks / will stick*, it will burn. And the risotto ¹⁰ *can't / has to* rest for a while before ¹¹ *you eat / you'll eat* it.
A: ¹² *Am I allowed to / Do I have to* taste it?
B: Of course you are. You made it!

2 Work in pairs. Answer the questions about the conversation in Exercise 1.

1 Are the friends making a hot or a cold dish?
2 Why is it important to add the liquid slowly?
3 Why is it important to stir all the time?

3 >> MB Work with a new partner. Take turns stating an intention and starting a chain.

buy a bike	quit smoking
cut down on snacks	join a gym
give up / start eating meat	take a vacation

A: *I think I'll buy a bike.*
B: *If you buy a bike, you'll get more exercise.*
A: *Yes. And if I get more exercise, …*

I CAN
ask and answer questions about obligation, prohibition, permission, and recommendation (modal verbs)
talk about the future results of present and future actions (first conditional)

Vocabulary

4 Match the phrasal verbs with the verbs that mean the same. Then write three sentences describing a change that leads to a healthy lifestyle.

1 cut down on ○   ○ a stop

2 give up ○   ○ b reduce

3 take up ○   ○ c start

5 >> MB Find four things you can eat in Unit 5. Think of two ways to describe each one. Then work in pairs. Try and guess your partner's things.

6 >> MB Work in pairs. Tell your partner if you never, always, or sometimes do these things when you eat out. Explain your reasons.

make a reservation	leave a tip
have an appetizer	look at the menu
have dessert	order a drink
have a main course	pay the bill

I CAN	
use phrasal verbs to talk about a healthy lifestyle	☐
talk about food and dishes	☐
talk about eating in a restaurant	☐

Real life

7 Complete the description of a seafood dish with these words. There is one extra word.

| fruit | kind | made | raw | tastes |

Ceviche is a Latin American dish. It's a ¹_____ of seafood dish. It's ²_____ by using the juice of citrus ³_____ , in this case limes, to cook a mixture of ⁴_____ fish and seafood.

8 >> MB Work in groups. Prepare descriptions of as many dishes from the list as you can. Then compare your descriptions with other groups. Look at page 155 to find out more about each dish.

baklava	bibimbap	borscht	couscous
dhal	fondue	guacamole	kebab
lasagna	satay	sushi	tortilla

I CAN	
ask about and describe different dishes	☐

Unit 6 Mysteries

Sunbathing cows in Andalusia, Spain

FEATURES

70 Flexible thinking

How good are you at puzzles and solving mysteries?

72 Desert art

The mysterious Nasca lines in Peru

74 Lost and found?

Current theories about Amelia Earhart's disappearance

78 Encounters with a sea monster

A video about strange creatures in the water

1 Work in pairs. Look at the image. Discuss the questions.

1 Does it look like a painting or a photo?
2 What is happening?
3 What does it make you think about?
4 Do you think the image has a message? What?

2 ▶ 43 Listen to a conversation about the image. Check your ideas from Exercise 1.

3 ▶ 43 Listen to the conversation again. What do the words in bold refer to?

1 Do you think the photographer Photoshopped **it**?
2 I'm surprised he didn't frighten **them**.
3 I can't make **it** out.
4 **They**'re parasailing.
5 It's really popular **there**.

4 Work in pairs. Why do people sometimes make fake photos? Why do people make fake versions of the items in the box?

bags	clothes	eyelashes	money
paintings	passports	watches	

6a Flexible thinking

Listening and reading

1 Work in pairs. Do you like doing puzzles? Read the puzzle and try to find the answer.

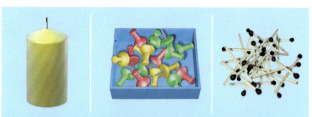

THE **CANDLE** PUZZLE

Your task is to attach the candle to the wall so that the wax doesn't drip on the floor below. You only have the candle, a box of thumbtacks, and some matches. How do you do it?

2 Compare your ideas for the candle puzzle with another pair. Then turn to page 155 to find out the answer. Was it easy or difficult to figure out?

3 ▶ 44 Work in pairs. Listen to a speaker at a conference. She asks her audience to do the puzzle in Exercise 1. What is the mystery she also talks about?

4 ▶ 44 Listen again and complete the sentences.

1. How good are you at flexible and _____ thinking?
2. Does the promise of a reward make you work _____ ?
3. Imagine I offer half of you some money to do this task more _____ .
4. I'm going to see how long it takes you so that we can find out the average _____ .
5. The people with the reward of _____ will be quicker, right?
6. The people in the first group need more time to find the _____ .

5 Read the article and find the answer to the mystery the speaker mentioned. Work in pairs. When is a reward useful? When is it not useful?

FLEXIBLE THINKING and REWARDS

▶ 45

People often think that a reward can make people work harder. However, that's not always true. Basically, it depends on the type of task or work. Rewards are great for making people concentrate, and concentration helps with tasks that have a clear set of rules, such as doing math problems or working in computer programming. But concentration doesn't help with creative and flexible thinking. When the task doesn't have a clear answer, concentration doesn't help. In fact, your brain needs to be relaxed and open so that it can look at the problem in different ways. In the workplace, the reward is usually money. So businesses need to think carefully about the relationship between work and pay—because it's true that people work harder for a reward, but only in some kinds of work.

Word focus *long*

6 Read the sentences and say if the expression with *long* refers to time (T), distance (D), or something else (S).

1	How long did it take you to do the puzzle?	T	D	S
2	Is it a long way from here to your house?	T	D	S
3	How long does the essay need to be?	T	D	S
4	I'm just going to get a coffee. I won't be long.	T	D	S
5	I love sunbathing. I could do it all day long.	T	D	S
6	I can't finish this book. It's just too long.	T	D	S
7	You can stay at my house as long as you don't mind sleeping on the sofa.	T	D	S

7 Work in pairs. Tell your partner about these things. Add follow-up comments.

1 something it took you a long time to do
2 a place a long way from here that you have visited
3 something you could do all day long
4 something you thought was too long

A: When I first started learning English, it took me forever to learn how to pronounce "daughter."
B: Oh, I had the same problem with "vegetable"!

Grammar purpose: *to, for,* and *so that*

▶ **PURPOSE: *TO, FOR,* and *SO THAT***

*Imagine I offer half of you some money **to do this** more quickly.*
*We all work **for money**, don't we?*
*Thumbtacks are **for attaching** things to other things.*
*I'm going to see how long it takes you **so that we can find out** the average time.*

For more information and practice, see page 166.

8 Work in pairs. Look at the grammar box. Answer the questions.

1 Which verb form follows *to*?
2 What can follow *for*?
3 What follows *so that*?
4 Do the sentences answer the question *how* or *why / what for*?

9 Look at the article *Flexible thinking and rewards*. Underline the patterns like those in the grammar box.

10 Circle the correct option to complete the sentences.

1 We worked together *for / to* solve the problem faster.
2 The box was useful *for / to* holding the candle.
3 We looked at the key *for / so that* the answers.
4 I went to the conference *so that / to* find out more about the brain.
5 I sit near the front *so that / to* I can hear better.
6 The speaker used pictures *for / to* make the explanation clearer.
7 Lots of people do sudoku *so that / to* keep their brain active.
8 I'm learning Chinese *for / so that* I can work in China.

11 Match the beginnings of the sentences (1–8) with the endings (a–h). Then complete the sentences with *to, for,* or *so that*.

1 I want to learn another language ____*so that*____ __*d*__
2 My friend called me _____ ____
3 I write everything down _____ ____
4 We download the homework to our phones _____ ____
5 Are you going to Colombia _____ ____
6 This notebook is _____ ____
7 Would you like to meet _____ ____
8 Did you get many chances _____ ____

a coffee after class?
b ask my advice about his course.
c help me remember it.
d I can enjoy traveling more.
e keep my passwords in.
f speak Italian on your trip?
g we can study on the bus.
h work or on vacation?

Speaking [myLife]

12 Work in small groups. Choose one of the items from the list and say why we need it. The other students in your group have to try to guess the item and add another reason why we need it.

*A: We need this **to find our way around a strange place**.*
*B: We need it **so that we don't get lost**? A map?*
A: Yes!

boots	a calculator
a credit card	a dictionary
glasses	good exam results
a guard dog	hot food
a map	a passport
a picture frame	a professional qualification
a suitcase	a window

6b Desert art

Vocabulary art

1 Complete the sentences with these words.

diagram	drawing	figure
line	pattern	shape

1 This looks like a child's _____ of a horse.
2 That cloud is in the _____ of a heart.
3 Can you draw a ten-centimeter straight _____ without a ruler?
4 I can see a _____ at the door, but I don't know who it is.
5 I prefer shirts with a striped _____ .
6 This _____ explains how to solve the puzzle.

Listening

2 Look at the photo and read the caption. Match the questions (1–3) with the exchanges (a–c).

1 What are they? ___
2 Where are they? ___
3 How big are they? ___

a A: They must be in a desert because there aren't any plants or anything there.
  B: Yes, it looks really dry.
b A: They might be roads.
  B: No, they can't all be roads. That's clearly a spider.
c A: There's a plane above it.
  B: Yeah, so they must be pretty big.

3 ▶ 46 Work in pairs. What do you think the answers to the questions in Exercise 2 are? Listen and check your ideas.

4 ▶ 47 What do you think the purpose of the lines was? Listen to another excerpt. Complete the sentences.

1 The Nasca people couldn't have seen the _____ from the air.
2 Maria Reiche was convinced that the lines must have been a type of _____ .
3 Other people thought the lines may have been ancient Inca _____ .
4 The strangest idea was the lines could have guided creatures from _____ .
5 The Nasca people can't have known the lines would still be visible _____ later.

The mysterious Nasca lines in Peru

5 Which theory do you think is most likely? Discuss your ideas with your class.

Grammar certainty and possibility

► CERTAINTY AND POSSIBILITY	
In the present	
must (not)	+ base form
might (not) / may (not) / could	+ *be* + *-ing*
can't	
In the past	
must (not)	
may (not) / might (not) / could +*have* + past participle	
can't / couldn't	

For more information and practice, see page 166.

6 Look at the grammar box. Underline the patterns in the sentences in Exercises 2 and 4.

7 Look at the grammar box again. Circle the correct option to complete the rules.

1 We use *must* to say if something is or was *possible / probable*.
2 We use *might*, *may*, and *could* to say if something is or was *possible / probable*.
3 We use *can't* and *couldn't* to say if something is or was *impossible / improbable*.

10 Complete the conversations using the correct option and the verb in parentheses. Use a present or past modal form.

1   A: Why hasn't my sister returned my phone call?
    B: Well, she *can't* / *may* _have forgotten_ (forget). She never forgets things.
2   A: Is Sandra here? I haven't seen her today.
    B: Yes, she's here. She *can't* / *might* _____ (get) coffee.
3   A: Who's Tom talking to?
    B: It *may* / *must* _____ (be) his father. He said, "Hi, Dad."
4   A: Why did the plane arrive late?
    B: I don't know. It *could* / *might not* _____ (take off) late.
5   A: Is Joe around? We have a meeting.
    B: Well, his computer is still on, so he *can't* / *must* _____ (go out).
6   A: Why is Phil wearing odd socks?
    B: He *can't* / *might* _____ (get dressed) in a hurry this morning.

11 Pronunciation weak form of *have*

a ▶ **48** Listen to the conversations from Exercise 10 and check your answers. Is *have* in past modals pronounced /hæv/ or /həv/? Is the *h* pronounced?

b Work in pairs. Read the conversations aloud. Pay attention to your pronunciation of *have*.

Speaking *my*Life

12 Work in pairs. Look at the comments and think of situations when you might say these things.

1   You must have forgotten to plug it in.
2   They may have lost your application.
3   They must be at home.
4   You might have dropped it on the way here.
5   He must have forgotten to pick it up.
6   She can't have finished so quickly.
7   They might be stuck in traffic.
8   You must have spent it on something.

13 Imagine you are in the situations in Exercise 12. Have conversations that include the comments. Take turns starting your conversations.

A: Oh, no! The battery of my phone is dead.
*B: You **must have forgotten** to charge it. Do you want to use mine?*
A: Thanks a lot.

8 Complete the sentences with present modal forms. More than one answer is possible.

1   This drawing has eight legs. Insects have six legs. So it _____ an insect.
2   "What are the straight lines?" "I'm not sure. They _____ paths."
3   "What's the plane doing?" "It _____ photographing the lines, but I can't see a camera."
4   It's summer in Europe now, so it _____ winter in Peru.
5   I'd like to walk along the lines, but they _____ let people do that.
6   The figures are so big that a plane _____ the only way to see them properly.

9 Complete the sentences about the Nasca lines with the past modal form.

1   The lines _____ something very special to the Nasca people. (must / mean)
2   We know water _____ easy to find. (can't / be)
3   The water in the area _____ . (might / disappear)
4   People _____ the drawings for fun. (might / make)
5   The animal drawings _____ roads. (couldn't / be)
6   The animals _____ in the region. (must / live)

6c Lost and found?

Reading

1 Work in pairs. Look at the photo and the title *Where is Amelia Earhart?* Discuss these statements. Which of them do you think could be true?

1 Amelia Earhart was a famous pilot.
2 She flew across the Atlantic Ocean.
3 In the photo, she's just landed her plane.
4 She lived until she was one hundred years old.

2 Read the first article quickly. Check your ideas from Exercise 1.

3 Work in pairs. Read the second article. Answer the questions.

1 What is the theory talked about in the article?
2 Which modern scientific technique might give an answer to the Earhart mystery?
3 If the new project is successful, what will it prove?
4 What is the biggest problem for the researchers on the new project?

4 Find these words in the articles. Look at how the words are used and try to guess their meaning. Then replace the words in bold in the sentences (1–4) with these words.

attempting (line 2)	financing (line 30)
samples (line 24)	distinguish (line 59)

1 My grandparents are **paying for** my studies.
2 It's easy to **see the difference** between a leg bone and an arm bone.
3 The doctor took **small amounts** of my blood to do tests.
4 The cyclist is **trying** to break the world record.

5 Work in groups. Discuss the questions.

1 The piece of bone "might have been from one of Earhart's fingers." Are there any other possibilities?
2 Is it certain that any saliva on the envelopes is Earhart's? How do you know?
3 Do you think the project will be successful?

6 Work in pairs. Complete the summary.

The new project aims to provide a way of testing [1]_____ . The success of the project depends on several things. Firstly, that the bone is from a [2]_____ , not a turtle. Secondly, that Earhart's saliva still exists on [3]_____ . And thirdly, that there is enough saliva to [4]_____ .

Wordbuilding nouns and verbs

> ▶ **WORDBUILDING nouns and verbs**
>
> Some nouns and verbs have the same form. They can have similar or unconnected meanings.
> *land* – similar; *book* – unconnected
>
> For more practice, see Workbook page 51.

7 Look at the wordbuilding box. Find these words in the two articles. Are they used as nouns (N) or verbs (V)?

1 fly (line 1) ___
2 land (line 3) ___
3 books (line 8) ___
4 records (line 11) ___
5 contact (line 13) ___
6 plan (line 23) ___
7 test (line 26) ___
8 remains (line 34) ___

8 Work in pairs. Look at the same words in these sentences. Is the meaning similar to the meaning of the word in Exercise 7?

1 Do you have any plans for the weekend?
2 We always book our hotel rooms in advance.
3 I tried to contact them yesterday without success.
4 Everyone did badly on yesterday's English test.

Critical thinking speculation or fact?

9 Read the definitions. Then decide if the sentences from the articles report speculation (S) or fact (F).

Speculation is having a theory or guessing about something.
Facts are items of information that we know to be true.

1 Amelia Earhart [...] was attempting a round-the-world flight in 1937.　　S　F
2 Earhart could have landed on a different island.　　S　F
3 About 99 percent of the genome is identical among all humans.　　S　F

10 Find one more fact and one more speculation in the articles. Then work in pairs. Do you agree with your partner's choices?

Speaking　*my* **Life**

11 Work in groups. Think of at least three news stories you have heard about recently. Suggest as many reasons as you can for what has happened.

Where Is Amelia Earhart?

Three Theories

▶ 49   *by John Roach*

Amelia Earhart, the first woman to fly solo across the Atlantic Ocean, was attempting a round-the-world flight in 1937. She planned to land on the tiny Pacific Ocean island of Howland, just north of the equator.
5 She never arrived. Exactly what happened to her and her navigator,[1] Fred Noonan, is still one of aviation's greatest mysteries. Researchers have spent millions of dollars investigating the case, and several books have been published that look at the different theories.

10 The official US opinion is that Earhart ran out of fuel and crashed in the Pacific Ocean. The radio records from a US Coast Guard ship suggest that she must have been near Howland when contact was lost.

Another theory says that Earhart could have
15 landed and later died on a different island, called Nikumaroro. Nobody lived there.

And another theory says she was captured while on a secret mission to the Japanese-controlled Marshall Islands in the North Pacific, then eventually returned
20 to the USA with a new identity.

Lost and found?
The missing pilot

▶ 50

by Ker Than

Amelia Earhart's dried saliva[2] could help solve the mystery of the aviator's 1937 disappearance. Scientists plan to create a genetic profile by taking samples of her
25 DNA from letters she wrote. This could then be used to test recent suggestions that a bone found on the South Pacific island of Nikumaroro is Earhart's.

Justin Long is a Canadian whose family
30 is financing part of the DNA project. He makes the point that at the moment, anyone who finds pieces of bones can say that they are Amelia Earhart's remains. According to Long, Earhart's
35 letters are the only existing items that are definitely hers and that might contain her DNA. The remains of Earhart, her navigator Noonan, and their twin-engine plane were never found. But in 2009,
40 researchers discovered a piece of bone on Nikumaroro, which they believed might have been from one of Earhart's fingers. However, some scientists have suggested that the Nikumaroro bone isn't human at
45 all but may be from a turtle.

The new Earhart DNA project will be organized by Dongya Yang, a genetic archeologist at Simon Fraser University in Canada. Yang will work on four
50 letters Earhart wrote to her family. It is believed that Earhart must have sealed[3] the envelopes herself.

However, geneticist Brenna Henn of Stanford University, USA, said she knows
55 of no other case where DNA has been collected from old letters. The problem is that the envelopes probably don't contain much DNA. The project needs a big sample to distinguish between
60 Earhart's DNA and that of other living people, because about 99 percent of the genome[4] is identical among all humans. To make sure that the DNA from the letters belonged to Earhart, the team
65 will compare it to DNA from Earhart's relatives who are still alive and also DNA extracted from another letter, written by Earhart's sister.

[1]**navigator** (n) /ˈnævɪˌɡeɪtər/ the person who plans the direction of a plane or ship
[2]**saliva** (n) /səˈlaɪvə/ the liquid in your mouth
[3]**sealed** (adj) /siːld/ closed safely so that it's hard to open
[4]**genome** (n) /ˈdʒiːnəʊm/ the genetic information of each living thing

6d You must be joking!

Real life reacting to surprising news

1 ▶ 51 Listen to three conversations about news articles. Choose the correct headline (a or b) in each case.

1   a   **ESCAPED SHEEP TAKE OVER LONDON PARK**

   b   **SHEEP IN GLOBAL WARMING SHOCK**

2   a   **FALSE BANK NOTES ALERT**

   b   **USA TO JOIN THE EURO ZONE**

3   a   **FUEL PRICES TO DOUBLE NEXT WEEK**

   b   **GAS PRICES FALL 50 PERCENT**

2 Can you remember? Answer the questions for each story.

1   What is the problem?
2   Does the second speaker believe the first speaker?
3   What is the date?

3 ▶ 51 Look at the expressions for reacting to surprising news. Listen to the conversations again. Put the expressions in order (1–9).

> ▶ **REACTING TO SURPRISING NEWS**
>
> ___ Are you serious?   ___ That can't be right!
> ___ Are you sure?   ___ They must have made
> ___ Come off it!   a mistake.
> ___ Oh, yeah?   ___ You must be joking!
> ___ Really?   ___ You're kidding me!

4 April Fools' Day (April 1st) is a day when people in many countries try to trick each other. Do you do anything similar in your country?

5 **Pronunciation** showing interest and disbelief

a ▶ 52 Listen to these expressions for reacting to surprising news. Notice how the speaker's intonation rises to show interest and falls to show disbelief.

1   Oh, yeah?

2   Come off it!

b ▶ 53 Listen to the other expressions for reacting to surprising news. Repeat the expressions.

c Work in pairs. Take turns responding to these statements.

1   I'm setting off on a round-the-world trip on Monday.
2   I found a wallet full of money in the street this morning.
3   I'm starting a new job tomorrow.

6 Work in pairs. Choose one of the other April Fools' Day headlines from Exercise 1. Decide what the hoax—the trick—is. Make notes about the main points of the story. Invent as many details as you wish. Practice telling the story with your partner.

7 Work with a new partner. Take turns listening and reacting to your stories. Use the expressions for reacting to surprising news to help you. Don't forget to show interest or disbelief with your intonation.

6e In the news

Writing a news story

1 Work in pairs. Read the news story. Do you think it is true or not? Explain your reasons to your partner.

2 Writing skill structuring a news story

a Work in pairs. Read the introductory sentence in the news story again. Answer the questions.

1 What happened?
2 Who was involved?
3 Where did it happen?

b Read the main paragraph and find:

1 how the woman cut the cable.
2 four things that happened after she cut the cable.
3 two pieces of background information.

c Read the main paragraph again. How are the events and background details organized?

3 Vocabulary -*ly* adverbs in stories

a Find these adverbs (1–5) in the story. Then match the adverbs with their meanings (a–e).

1 accidentally ○	○ a	at once
2 unfortunately ○	○ b	by mistake
3 temporarily ○	○ c	for a short time
4 immediately ○	○ d	it seems
5 apparently ○	○ e	we are sorry to say

b Cross out any options that are not possible. Both options may be possible.

1 *Apparently,* / *Quickly,* this type of incident is increasing in Georgia.
2 *Fortunately,* / *Incredibly,* nobody was hurt.
3 Internet services were *amazingly* / *gradually* restored across the region.
4 Software providers say hackers *deliberately* / *sadly* damaged the service.
5 *Hopefully,* / *Slowly,* the police will release the woman because of her age.

c Work in pairs. Decide which of the sentences in Exercise 3b fit into the story and where they fit.

4 You are going to write an April Fools' story or a news story that is not true. This can be invented or a story you have heard. First, make notes about the main events and the background details. Think about *what? who? where?* and also *why?* and *how?*

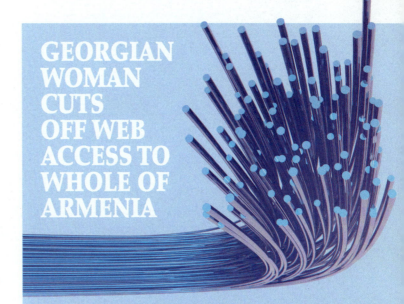

GEORGIAN WOMAN CUTS OFF WEB ACCESS TO WHOLE OF ARMENIA

An elderly Georgian woman accidentally cut through an underground cable and cut off internet services to the whole nation of Armenia.

The woman, 75, was digging for metal near the Georgian capital Tbilisi when her shovel damaged the cable. Unfortunately, Georgia provides 90 percent of Armenia's internet. Web users in the nation of 3.2 million people were left with no internet for up to five hours. Large parts of Georgia and some areas of Azerbaijan were also temporarily affected. The damage was discovered by an automatic system, and a security team immediately went to the place where the cable was cut. The cable is protected, but apparently, landslides or heavy rain may have left it exposed on the surface. The woman, called "the shovel-hacker" by local newspapers, was arrested for damaging property. She may have to spend up to three years in prison.

5 Write an introductory sentence to summarize your story. Then number your notes in the order you will write about them. Include at least three adverbs where appropriate.

6 Work on your own. Write your story in about 150–200 words. Write an interesting headline.

7 Work in pairs. Exchange your stories. Use these questions to check your partner's story.

- Did the headline make you interested in reading the story?
- Are the facts of the story clear?
- Do you think the story is true?

What could that be?

Before you watch

1 How much do you know about these monsters? Compare your ideas with the class.

Dracula	The Loch Ness monster	Godzilla
Shrek	Bigfoot	

2 Key vocabulary

a Work in pairs. Read the sentences. The words in bold are used in the video. Guess the meaning of the words.

1 Don't take the boat out past the red **buoy**.
2 Police talked to several **eyewitnesses** who saw the accident.
3 Do camels have one **hump** or two?
4 Can you turn off the boat's **motor**, please? It's very noisy.
5 It's surprising how quickly submarines can **submerge** underwater and disappear.
6 There were lots of seabirds following the **wake** of the ferry.

b Match the words in bold in Exercise 2a with these definitions.

a an engine _____
b a colored object that floats in water to indicate danger for boats _____
c people who see something happen, especially a crime, etc. _____
d something that has a round shape and that sticks out _____
e the waves behind something that moves through water _____
f to go under the surface of water _____

While you watch

3 🎥 **6.1** Work in pairs. Watch Part 1 of the video with the sound OFF. You will see Bob Iverson explaining something he was an eyewitness to. What do you think he's saying to the reporter?

4 🎥 **6.1, 6.2** Watch both parts of the video with the sound ON. You will hear a total of three eyewitness reports from Bob Iverson, Marjory Neal, and Richard Smith. Are these statements true (T) or false (F)?

All three eyewitnesses _____ .

a	saw the monster on different days.	T	F
b	saw three or more humps.	T	F
c	were in different places.	T	F
d	were alone at the time.	T	F

5 🎥 **6.1, 6.2** Work on your own. Watch the video again. Make notes to answer the questions for each speaker.

1 Where was the eyewitness?
2 What were the weather or water conditions like?
3 How far away from the eyewitness was the monster?
4 What did the monster do?

6 Work in groups of three. Compare your notes. Is there any information still missing? If you need to, watch the video again and check.

After you watch

7 Work in groups of three. Read what the reporter says at the end of the video. Discuss your ideas for possible explanations.

"… three remarkable stories, but are there more plausible explanations before we cry 'sea monster'?"

8 Vocabulary in context

a 🎥 **6.3** Watch the clips from the video. Choose the correct meaning of the words and phrases.

b Complete the sentences in your own words. Then work in pairs and compare your sentences.

1 I was on my way to class once when, all of a sudden, …
2 Sometimes when I watch TV, I wonder …
3 I spend anywhere between … hours studying English each week.
4 A news story about … caught my attention last week.

9 Would you believe a friend if he or she told you a story like the ones in the video? Why or why not?

---

plausible (adj) /ˈplɔːzəbl/ believable, likely
remarkable (adj) /rɪˈmɑːrkəbl/ unusual, extraordinary
sun deck (n) /ˈsʌndek/ a flat wooden area in a garden
tractor (n) /ˈtræktər/ a large farm vehicle

UNIT 6 REVIEW AND MEMORY BOOSTER

Grammar

1 Circle the correct options in the text about Stonehenge.

Stonehenge dates from 3–4,000 years ago. Although there [1] *are / might be* no written records from that period, some people think Stonehenge [2] *can't have / might have* been part of King Arthur's court. Others say invaders from Denmark [3] *couldn't have / could have* built it or that it [4] *can / could* be the ruins of a Roman building. The larger stones weigh 25 tons, and they come from about 30 kilometers away from the site. The smaller stones originate from Wales, 230 kilometers away.

Stonehenge [5] *is / may be* in the shape of a circle. The stones are placed [6] *so that / to* they match the sun's highest and lowest points in the sky. This has led people to suggest that it [7] *can't have / could have* been a scientific observatory or that it was designed [8] *for / to* help aliens land. On the other hand, others believe it [9] *can / may* be a kind of cemetery—a place [10] *for / so that* burying people. Every year brings new theories about the true purpose of Stonehenge.

2 Answer the questions about the text in Exercise 1.

1 What are three theories about the origins of Stonehenge?
2 What is known about the stones?
3 What are three theories about the purpose of Stonehenge?

3 ▶▶ MB Work in pairs. Which theory about Stonehenge do you think is the most likely? Why?

I CAN	
use expressions of purpose correctly	☐
talk about events in the present and past that are certain or possible (modal verbs)	☐

Vocabulary

4 Complete the sentences with an adverb ending in *-ly*. The first letter is given.

1 I'd love to come for lunch, but *u*_____ , I'm busy that day.
2 You need to reply to this letter *i*_____ . It's urgent.
3 Oh, no. I've *a*_____ deleted the email. How did that happen?
4 I'm working *t*_____ as the manager while my boss is away.
5 We checked our records, and *a*_____ the package was mailed on May 2nd.
6 I think the boys arrived late *d*_____ to miss the test.

5 ▶▶ MB Work in pairs. Answer as many questions as you can. The words in bold are in Unit 6.

1 What is **fake** money?
2 What do you understand by the expression **"flexible thinker"**?
3 When might you get a **reward**?
4 Name two activities you could do **all day long**.
5 How many **shapes** can you name?
6 Are **lines** always straight?
7 Give examples of how to use **record** as a noun and as a verb.
8 Is a **hoax** a person?

I CAN	
use adverbs ending in *-ly* in stories	☐
talk about different types of drawings	☐
talk about mysteries and puzzles	☐

Real life

6 Complete the expressions for reacting to news.

1 _____ _____ _____ joking!
2 _____ _____ me!
3 _____ _____ _____ right!
4 _____ _____ serious?
5 _____ _____ sure?

7 Work in groups. Write surprising sentences about yourself (true and false). Take turns reading your sentences aloud. Use appropriate expressions to react to the sentences about the other people and try to find out which sentences are true.

I CAN	
reacting to surprising news	☐

Unit 7 Living space

Off the Izu Peninsular, Japan, a yellow goby looks at the camera.

FEATURES

82 Before New York City

What came before the city?

84 Homes around the world

An architect talks about homes.

86 Sweet songs and strong coffee

Visit a community in Puerto Rico.

90 The town with no Wi-Fi

A video about an unusual town

1 Work in pairs. Look at the photo. Discuss the questions.

1 What can you see in the photo?
2 Do you think this is the fish's natural habitat, a temporary shelter, or a permanent home?

2 ▶ 54 Listen to three people talking about different living arrangements. Write the number of the speaker (1–3) next to the statements that summarize their comments.

____ a I can't wait to leave my parents' house and get some independence.
____ b My family's great, but I'd like to have my own home and some privacy.
____ c My roommates aren't here much, so it's just like having my own place.
____ d It's cramped and noisy, but at least you're never lonely.
____ e Sharing an apartment with friends is not as easy as I thought it would be.
____ f I love living with my mom and dad and brothers. I won't leave until I get married.

3 Work in groups. Discuss the questions.

1 Which room do you spend the most time in at home?
2 How do different family members use different rooms?
3 Do you often have friends over to your house?

7a Before New York City

Vocabulary in the city

1 Work in pairs. What kind of place is New York City? Try to describe New York in three words.

2 Complete the sentences about New York City using the words in the box.

atmosphere	blocks	built-up	financial
neighborhoods	public transportation	residents	skyscrapers

1 There's an excellent _____ system to get you around the city.
2 It has an important business and _____ district.
3 Even though most of it is really _____ , there are still a lot of open spaces.
4 The views from the _____ are spectacular, especially at night.
5 There's lots to do, for both tourists and _____ .
6 Some _____ are more dangerous than others.
7 The _____ is exciting and lively.
8 The streets divide the city into _____ .

3 Write sentences about places you know with the words from Exercise 2.

Reading

4 Work in pairs. Discuss the questions. Then read the article and check your ideas.

1 What do you think the area that is now New York City was like before the city was built?
2 What kind of people do you think lived there?

5 Read the article again. Work in pairs. Answer these questions.

1 What's the connection between Eric Sanderson and the top image below?
2 What did Sanderson aim to do with his project?
3 Why do you think the appearance of the beaver in 2007 was important for Sanderson?

Before New York

By PETER MILLER

Computer-Generated Im

▶ 55

Of all the visitors to New York City in recent years, one of the most surprising was a beaver that appeared one morning in 2007. Although beavers used to be common in the area in the seventeenth century—when people used to hunt them for their fur—there haven't been any for more than two hundred years.

For ecologist Eric Sanderson, the beaver's appearance was especially interesting. For ten years, Sanderson has been in charge of a project to show what the area used to look like before the city changed it completely. As Sanderson says, "There are views in this city where you cannot see—except for a person—another living thing. Not a tree or a plant.

¹**pristine** (adj) /prɪsˈtiːn/ pure, as new
²**wilderness** (n) /ˈwɪldərnəs/ an area in a completely natural state

How did a place become like that?"

In fact, long before the skyscrapers came to dominate the view, this place was a pristine¹ wilderness² where animals like beavers, bears, and turkeys would move freely through forests, marshes, and grassland. There used to be sandy beaches along the coasts, and ninety kilometers of fresh-water streams.

At the end of Sanderson's project, he built a 3D computer model of the area. (See the top photo on the right.) You can pick any spot in modern New York and see what used to be there. Take Fifth Avenue, for example. A family named Murray used to have a farm here. In 1782 (during the American War of Independence), the British soldiers landed nearby. "I'd like every New Yorker to know that they live in a place with amazing natural potential—even if you have to look a little harder to see it," says Sanderson.

Grammar *used to, would, and simple past*

6 Look at the grammar box. Underline the sentences in the article with *used to* and *would*. Do they refer to past habits and states or to single actions in the past?

7 Work in pairs. Look at the article again. Find three examples of single actions in the past. What is the verb form?

8 Look at the grammar box. Match the sentences with *used to* (1–4) with the uses (a or b). Then match the sentence with *would* with its use.

a past state _____
b past habit (repeated action) _____

9 Work in pairs. Rewrite the sentences using *used to* + base form.

1 New York was a lot greener than it is now.
2 The early residents didn't live in a large city.
3 People farmed the land.
4 Farmers hunted wild animals for food.
5 What was in the area where Fifth Avenue is now?

10 Complete the text with the simple past, *used to*, or *would* form of the verbs. In some cases, you can use more than one form.

> I remember when I first ¹_____ (move) to New York from California with my parents. Every day for the first month, I ²_____ (stand) in the street and stare up at the skyscrapers. They ³_____ (be) taller than anything I'd ever seen. The streets ⁴_____ (be) much busier than in California, and I ⁵_____ (run) from one side to the other holding my mother's hand. For the first few months, we ⁶_____ (not / go) farther than four blocks from home. My parents ⁷_____ (not / own) a car, so on Sunday mornings we ⁸_____ (take) the subway to Central Park. We ⁹_____ (have) breakfast at a great deli, and then we ¹⁰_____ (go) skating.

11 Complete the sentences with the simple past, *used to*, or *would* so that they are true for you. Then work in pairs. Compare your sentences and ask follow-up questions.

1 Before I worked/studied here, I …
2 When I was in elementary school, I …
3 I remember my first vacation. I …
4 Whenever I had exams at school, I …
5 The first time I went to school alone, …
6 As a child, I …

Speaking `my Life`

12 Choose two places from the list. How have the places changed? Make notes for then and now.

- my street
- my home
- my classroom
- my school
- my city / my town

my street: then – lots of cars; now – only residents

13 Work in pairs. Tell each other about the places you chose in Exercise 12. Use *used to* and *would*. Decide which places have changed the most and whether they are better now than they were in the past.

*A: There **used to be** a lot of cars on my street, but now only residents can park on it.*
B: What do visitors do? Can they drive up to your house?

7b Homes around the world

A

Homes carved into rock in Cappadocia, Turkey

B

A ger belonging to Tuvan nomads in western Mongolia

C

A wooden house on stilts in southern Cambodia

D

Modern terraced houses in Sabah, Borneo

Listening

1 Look at the photos of four homes. What are they made of?

bricks ____   cloth ____   rock ____   wood ____

2 Think of a question you'd like to ask each homeowner. Then work in pairs. Tell your partner.

3 ▶ 56 Marta Ferreira presents the TV series *Home Planet*. Read the questions (a–e) that viewers have sent in to the program's website. Then listen and match Marta's podcast replies (1–5) with the questions.

a Why are you so interested in traditional house design? _1_
b We live in a new house that my dad calls a "box." What do you think of the design of modern houses? ____
c Why are some types of house more common in some areas of the world than in others? ____
d You mentioned shelters in your last program. What's the difference between a shelter and a home? ____
e I'd like to stay in a ger, but they look kind of basic. What are they really like? ____

4 ▶ 56 Listen again and complete the sentences.

1 Traditional houses usually survive bad _____ conditions better than modern ones.
2 Rock homes heat up less quickly than _____ .
3 You can put up a ger much faster than a _____ .
4 You can live much more safely above the _____ .
5 Modern houses are getting smaller and _____ .
6 Unfortunately, sometimes _____ are also built badly.
7 Modern houses don't work as efficiently as _____ .

5 Work in pairs. Which of the homes in the photos would you like to spend time in? Why?

Grammar comparative adverbs

6 Look at the grammar box. Underline the comparative adverbs in the sentences in Exercise 4.

7 Work in pairs. Read the three sentences. Do they mean the same thing? Do you agree with the sentences?

1 A brick house heats up more quickly than a rock house.
2 A rock house heats up less quickly than a brick house.
3 A rock house doesn't heat up as quickly as a brick house.

8 Complete the text about house sales and rentals with the comparative form of the adverbs.

Last year, townhouses sold [1] _more quickly_ (quickly) than apartments, but one-bedroom apartments did [2] _____ (well) with young buyers. The number of large houses for rent rose [3] _____ (fast) than other types of home. Sales of large apartments did [4] _____ (badly) than in previous years. So what does this mean for you? You can now rent a large house [5] _____ (cheaply) than ever before, but if you're trying to sell yours, you probably won't find a buyer [6] _____ (easily) as in previous years. Renting it out is a good alternative, so come and talk to us today.

9 Write sentences comparing the pairs of things. Then look at your partner's sentences. Do you agree?

1 young people / older people (drive carefully)
   Older people drive more carefully than young people.
2 girls / boys (do well on exams)
3 children / adults (learn quickly)
4 women / men (work hard)

Grammar comparative patterns

10 Work in pairs. Look at the grammar box. Which sentences describe change? Which sentence describes two related things?

11 Read what two people say about where they live. Underline comparative patterns similar to the ones in the grammar box.

Josef: As this building gets older, things go wrong more and more often. But living in an apartment building is really good because I don't have to worry about repairs and things. Everyone pays an amount each month, so the greater the number of residents, the lower the monthly payment is.

Sandra: We're all students. So for us, the cheaper the place, the better. We don't have as much money as people who are working. Rents are getting higher and higher, but you can still rent more cheaply than buy.

12 Complete what this person says. Use comparative patterns from the grammar box above.

Frances: I love having a garden, but it's a lot of work—so the [1] _____ (small / good), I think. With a big garden, I find that as the plants get [2] _____ (big), the garden gets [3] _____ (more) overgrown.

Speaking my Life

13 Work in groups of four. Discuss ways of doing these things. What advice would you give someone who wanted to do each one?

1 learn English more quickly
2 do better on exams
3 live more cheaply
4 eat more healthily

*A: I think you can **learn English more quickly** if you go to live in an English-speaking country.*
*B: I agree. You won't learn **as quickly** if you stay at home. You won't meet native English speakers **as easily**, for example.*

7c Sweet songs and strong coffee

Reading

1 Think of one word to describe your hometown. Tell the class.

2 Read the article about a town in Puerto Rico. What is the article mainly about? Circle the correct option (a–c).

a daily life and work
b festivals and holidays
c people and traditions

3 Which paragraph gives information about:

a what life used to be like in Adjuntas? ____
b a traditional activity that people still do? ____
c a new activity that people have learned to do? ____
d what the town looks like? ____

4 Work in pairs. What do you think of Adjuntas as a place to live? Or a place to go on vacation?

Wordbuilding noun → adjective

> **WORDBUILDING noun → adjective**
>
> We can make adjectives from nouns by adding a suffix such as -al or -ic. Spelling changes are sometimes needed.
> nature → natural, person → personal, artist → artistic
>
> For more practice, see Workbook page 59.

5 Look at the wordbuilding box. Underline the adjectives in the article that are formed from these nouns.

1 romance (line 12)   2 nation (line 18)

6 Complete the sentences with adjectives formed by adding -al or -ic to the nouns.

benefit	center	coast	economy	energy
fact	history	nature	origin	person

1 The farmer never stops working. He's _____ and enthusiastic.
2 The _____ part of the island is quite flat, and the _____ part is mountainous.
3 Opening the forest park was _____ for the villagers and the wildlife.
4 We saw lots of birds in their _____ habitat.

5 The _____ crisis has greatly affected business.
6 The _____ area of the city around the old market is worth visiting.

Critical thinking descriptions

7 The writer aims to paint a picture of Adjuntas in the reader's mind. Which descriptions in the article helped you to build a mental picture of Adjuntas? Underline words and phrases in the article.

8 Work in pairs. Compare the words you have underlined with your partner. Do you think the writer has been successful in her aims?

9 Add descriptions to each sentence to help the reader build a mental image. Then exchange sentences with your partner.

1 The village is in the forest.
The tiny village is in the heart of the dense forest.
2 The houses are small.
_____
3 You can walk through the streets.
_____
4 The village center is full of people.
_____
5 People are working everywhere you look.
_____
6 From one building, you can hear music.
_____

Speaking my Life

10 Work in pairs. Choose a place that you both know well and that is attractive to tourists. Plan and practice a short presentation to persuade people to visit the destination. Use descriptions that help people to imagine the place. Talk about:

- the best things to see.
- the best things to do.
- the best places to eat.

11 Work in small groups. Give your presentations. Ask and answer follow-up questions.

A: … and finally, don't leave the area without trying the food at the Golden Lion. It's delicious and not expensive.
B: Can you tell me what kind of restaurant the Golden Lion is?

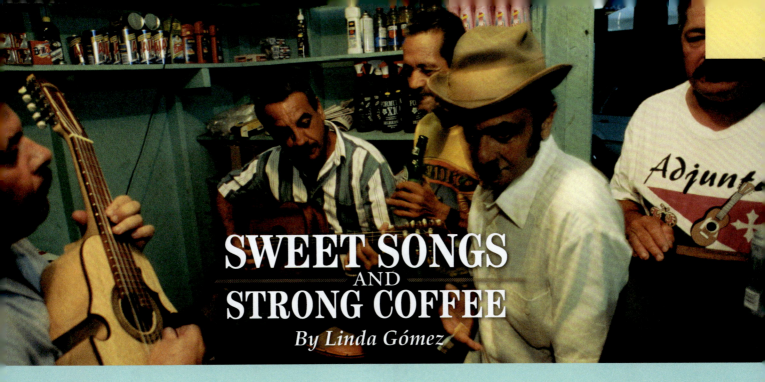

SWEET SONGS AND STRONG COFFEE

By Linda Gómez

▶ 57

1 There's a dreamy atmosphere to Adjuntas, a coffee town in the Valley of the Sleeping Giant, high in the mountains of Puerto Rico. And there's love—the love of the people for their land and its customs. People say their families have lived here "since forever." You feel this love in the streets, with the smell of food cooked at roadside barbecues. You see it in the beautiful horses that parade through town on holidays. And you feel it as you sit in the large, elegant square, with its romantic fountains and stone benches.

2 Several decades ago, this love of the land also led the local people to prevent a mining development in the surrounding mountains. They used money from the area's successful coffee production for a national park—El Bosque del Pueblo. The park opened in 1998 and runs a reforestation program allowing young and old to plant trees. "Learning to manage the forest has been a kind of new life for us," said Tinti Deya, a local resident. "It's another world where we're like children doing everything for the first time, except in our case we're grandmothers."

3 Grandmothers are everywhere in Adjuntas, and they're all respectfully addressed as Dofia. Lala Echevarria, an 85-year-old great-great-grandmother, was born on the oldest street in town, where she still lives in a small, tidy home. Dofia Lala grew up before electricity and running water, and remembers when the first car arrived in Adjuntas. "As a child, I used to spend all my time carrying water, finding firewood,[1] looking after the chickens and the cows," she said. "There were sixteen of us. We would wash our clothes in the river, and we used to cook on an open fire. At meal times, we kids would sit on the floor to eat." Dofia Lala was working as a maid when she met and married the love of her life, Mariano the mechanic. They had thirteen children and shared 44 years before he died in 1983. She shows me the dozens of photographs of four generations of her family that now fill her tiny home.

4 People in Adjuntas play old traditional songs in little shops like Lauro Yepez's place, where men meet to swap stories and have a drink. When I was there, Tato Ramos, a local singer, appeared. He began to sing in a flamenco style that hasn't changed for centuries. The shop quickly filled with working-class men clapping, tapping, and nodding to the music. Ramos improvised songs on topics requested by shop customers. "This is a forgotten art," said Yepez. "People give him a topic and he composes a song, in proper rhyme."

5 Later, I played the recording I'd made for my 88-year-old Spanish father, who has Alzheimer's disease. His dark brown eyes shone with recognition. He nodded his head, smiled, and said, "Oh, yes, this I remember, this I remember …"

---

[1] **firewood** (n) /ˈfaɪərˌwʊd/ wood that is used as fuel

7d To rent or to buy?

Victoria Park, Hong Kong

Real life stating preferences and giving reasons

1 Work in pairs. Write a checklist of things you should think about when you are looking for somewhere to live.

2 ▶ 58 Work in pairs. Listen to a conversation at a a real estate agency. Does the woman mention the things on your checklist? What four things does she specify?

3 ▶ 58 Look at the expressions for stating preferences. Listen to the conversation again. Complete the expressions.

> ▶ **STATING PREFERENCES**
>
> I think I'd rather _____ than _____, for now anyway.
> I'd prefer _____ _____ , but not too _____ .
> So, two bedrooms, and preferably with _____ _____ .
> Would you rather _____ _____ _____ places or _____ ones?
> To be honest, I prefer _____ to _____ .
> I don't have a car. I prefer to _____ or _____ _____ _____ .

4 Work in pairs. Can you remember the reasons for the customer's preferences? Compare your ideas. Then check in the Track 58 audioscript on page 185.

5 **Pronunciation** rising and falling intonation

a ▶ 59 Listen to this question. Notice how the intonation rises, then falls.

Would you rather live in a town or a village?

b ▶ 60 Listen and repeat the questions.

1 Do you prefer playing baseball or basketball?
2 Would you rather have tea or coffee?
3 Do you prefer summer or winter?
4 Would you rather go by car or by bike?
5 Do you prefer math or science?
6 Would you rather eat fish or meat?

c Work in pairs. Add at least six more pairs of items to the list in Exercise 5b. Take turns asking and answering about your preferences.

6 Work in groups of three. Where would you rather live? Ask and answer questions using these ideas. Explain your reasons. Do you think your preferences will change in the future?

1 In a new house or an old one?
2 In a city or in a town?
3 In a city center or in the suburbs?
4 By the coast or in the mountains?
5 In a historic area or a new development?

7e A great place

Writing a description of a place

1 Read the text. Where do you think it's from? Choose one of the options (a–c).

a   a personal blog
b   a real estate agent's website
c   a tourist information website

2 Work in pairs. How does the writer describe these things?

streets and buildings	shops	facilities
local residents	atmosphere	

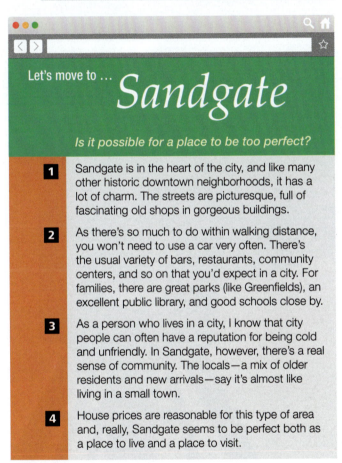

Let's move to …

Sandgate

Is it possible for a place to be too perfect?

1 Sandgate is in the heart of the city, and like many other historic downtown neighborhoods, it has a lot of charm. The streets are picturesque, full of fascinating old shops in gorgeous buildings.

2 As there's so much to do within walking distance, you won't need to use a car very often. There's the usual variety of bars, restaurants, community centers, and so on that you'd expect in a city. For families, there are great parks (like Greenfields), an excellent public library, and good schools close by.

3 As a person who lives in a city, I know that city people can often have a reputation for being cold and unfriendly. In Sandgate, however, there's a real sense of community. The locals—a mix of older residents and new arrivals—say it's almost like living in a small town.

4 House prices are reasonable for this type of area and, really, Sandgate seems to be perfect both as a place to live and a place to visit.

3 Writing skill organizing ideas

Read the text again. Write the number of the paragraph (1–4) next to the heading. There is one extra heading.

a   What kind of place is Sandgate? ____
b   What are the bad points? ____
c   Overall opinion? ____
d   What kind of people live there? ____
e   What can you do there? ____

Word focus *as* and *like*

4 Work in pairs. Look at these two excerpts from the text. Circle the correct option. Then find two more examples of *as* and *like* with the same meanings.

1   … and, like many other historic downtown neighborhoods, it has …
     It is similar to / It has many historic downtown neighborhoods.

2   As a person who lives in a city, I know …
     I am similar to / I am a person who lives in a city.

5 Work in pairs. Find two other examples of *as* and *like* in the text. Match the examples with these meanings.

1   because _____
2   for example _____

6 Complete the sentences with *as* and *like*.

1   _____ a lifelong resident of my town, I take pride in our community.
2   I love modern shopping malls _____ this.
3   It's ideal _____ a vacation destination.
4   Our public library is _____ a palace.
5   _____ all good cafés, the one in my neighborhood has a great atmosphere.
6   The old buildings, _____ the town hall, are beautiful.

7 You are going to write a description of your own neighborhood. Make notes using the headings in Exercise 3. Use these words or your own ideas.

a good range of …	close to …	easy access to …
elegant	excellent	kind of limited
modern	unfriendly	welcoming

8 Decide on the order of the paragraphs in your description. Then write about 150–200 words.

9 Use these questions to check your description.

• Are your ideas clearly organized into paragraphs?
• If you've included *as* or *like*, have you used them correctly?
• Does your description give the reader a clear picture of your neighborhood?

10 Read a description a classmate has written about his or her neighborhood. Would you like to move there or not? Give your reasons.

7f The town with no Wi-Fi

Two satellite dishes in the USA

Before you watch

1 You're going to watch a video about a town in the USA that has no Wi-Fi or cell phones. What would be the main change in your life if you didn't have Wi-Fi or a cell phone? Would it be good or bad?

2 Key vocabulary

a Work in pairs. Read the sentences. The words in bold are used in the video. Guess the meaning of the words.

1 Jack built his house to his own design— it's certainly **unique**!
2 I'd love to have a **telescope** to see the stars at night.
3 I can't call you from the beach because there's no **signal**.
4 Earth is the only planet in the Solar System with a breathable **atmosphere**.
5 I remember before **cordless** phones—you had to stand next to the phone on the wall.

b Match the words in bold in Exercise 2a with these definitions.

a a piece of equipment that makes distant things seem closer _____
b radio waves that are sent or received _____
c one of a kind, unlike any others _____
d the air in a certain place or area _____
e without a cable or wire attached to it _____

While you watch

3 ▭◀ **7.1, 7.2** Watch the whole video. Match the people you see to their descriptions.

1 Artie Barkley ○　○ a Site Director of NRAO
2 Joyce Nelson ○　○ b Business Manager of NRAO
3 Michael Holstine ○　○ c resident of the Quiet Zone
4 Karen O'Neil ○

4 Work in pairs. Discuss the questions.

1 What does *quiet zone* mean exactly?
2 What does the NRAO do in Green Bank?

5 ▭◀ **7.1** Watch Part 1 of the video again. Check your ideas from Exercise 4. What do the people say?

1 Artie Barkley says he just listens to _____ .
2 Karen O'Neil says if you have a radio _____ in an area of lots of radio noise, the signal you're looking for is destroyed.
3 Michael Holstine says that to _____ the radio atmosphere, Congress created the National Radio Quiet Zone.

6 ▭◀ **7.2** Watch Part 2 of the video again. Answer the questions.

1 Which ONE of these modern conveniences is OK to use in Green Bank? Circle it.

gasoline engines	cell phones
diesel engines	automatic door
Wi-Fi modems	openers
cordless phones	digital cameras

2 Why would it be difficult to create a new radio quiet zone?

After you watch

7 Vocabulary in context

a ▭◀ **7.3** Watch the clips from the video. Choose the correct meaning of the words and phrases.

b Answer the questions in your own words. Then work in pairs and compare your answers.

1 How many world-class athletes can you name?
2 Do any of your friends look just like someone famous?
3 What's life like in your community?

8 Work in pairs. Discuss the questions.

1 Do the residents of Green Bank seem happy to live there? Give your reasons.
2 How would you feel about living in a quiet zone like Green Bank?

Grammar

1 Look at the photo of rooftop golf. Then complete the text. Use comparative forms and patterns of adjectives and adverbs. Use the simple past and *used to* form of the verbs.

I'd never heard of rooftop golf before. I suppose that as cities get [1] _____
(big / big), people live a long way from golf courses. When I was a kid, I [2] _____
(live) in an apartment building with a basement parking garage. During the day, the garage
[3] _____ (be) almost empty, so we [4] _____ (play) soccer there.
Obviously, we played [5] _____
(well) on a real field and we couldn't kick the ball
[6] _____ (as / hard / as) when we played outside, but we [7] _____
(not mind). Having the garage meant we could play [8] _____ (often). These
days, gyms seem to be [9] _____
(more / more / popular) in cities. I suppose people spend a lot of time sitting at desks or in cars. And
[10] _____ (less / active) they are,
[11] _____ (less healthy) they feel.
Gyms have taken the place of open spaces in a lot of cities.

2 Answer the questions about the text in Exercise 1.

1 What are the advantages and disadvantages of playing soccer in a parking garage?
2 Why are gyms popular in cities?

I CAN	
talk about past states and past habits (*used to*, *would*)	☐
compare things and describe a process of change (comparative adverbs, comparative patterns with adverbs and adjectives)	☐

Vocabulary

3 Work in pairs. Which word doesn't belong in each group? Cross it out, and explain why it doesn't belong.

1	bricks	igloo	wood
2	run-down	skyscrapers	traffic
3	apartment	house	neighborhood
4	built-up	polluted	residents
5	garden	town	city

4 ▶▶ MB You are a real estate agent with an important house to sell—your own. Make notes on your home and the area that it's in. Decide on a price. Then try to sell your home to one of your classmates.

I CAN	
talk about cities	☐
talk about places to live	☐

Real life

5 Match the questions and answers (a–f). Circle the correct option in each answer.

1 A: What's wrong with this apartment? ____
2 A: Are you looking for a roommate? ____
3 A: I can show you a fantastic beach house. ____
4 A: This apartment is nice. Are you going to take it? ____
5 A: I'm not interested in looking around the downtown area. ____
6 A: Are you going to live near your job? ____

a B: *I'd rather / I prefer* to live on my own.
b B: Where would you rather *go / to go*?
c B: *I'd rather / I prefer* the country to the coast.
d B: I prefer *living / live* near my family.
e B: *I'd rather / I prefer* visit a few more places first.
f B: *I'd rather / I'd prefer* a bigger kitchen.

6 ▶▶ MB Work in groups. Ask and answer questions about your preferences. Give reasons for your answers.

fruit or cake	rice or pasta
jazz or pop	snow or sun
mornings or evenings	spring or fall

I CAN	
ask about preferences	☐
state preferences and give reasons	☐

Tourists take photos of an emperor penguin on the frozen Amundsen Sea in Antarctica.

FEATURES

94 Vacations and memories

Writers return to their roots.

96 Walking for wildlife

Mike Fay: a personal approach to saving wild places

98 All aboard!

A report on global tourism

102 Questions and answers

A video about National Geographic Explorers' lives

1 Work in pairs. Look at the photo. Discuss the questions.

1 What kind of vacation do you think this is?
2 Do you think the people take this kind of trip often? Why or why not?
3 Would you like to take a trip like this?

2 ▶ 61 Listen to three people talking about travel. Write the number of the speaker (1–3) next to the things they talk about.

being on planes ____	planning ____
business trips ____	an around-the-world trip ____
day trips ____	taking local buses and trains ____
delays ____	traveling for work ____
luggage ____	weekend trips ____

3 ▶ 61 Listen again. Each speaker shares a travel tip. What are their tips? Discuss the tips with your partner.

4 Which countries or cities have you been to? Find people in your class who have had similar experiences to you.

A: Have you been to Vietnam?
B: Yes, we visited Vietnam last year.
A: Me too! Where did you go?

8a Vacations and memories

Vocabulary vacation activities

1 Work in pairs. Why did you choose the destination of your most recent vacation?

> saw the place on TV
> followed a friend's recommendation
> wanted to visit somewhere new
> wanted to return to a place I know
> went to visit family/friends
> my parents chose the destination

2 Work in pairs. Match the activities (1–6) with the examples (a–f). What do you enjoy doing when you go on vacation? Give your own examples.

1 taking it easy
2 going sightseeing
3 having new experiences
4 being active
5 learning new things
6 spending time with friends or family

a hiking in the mountains ____
b lying on the beach ____
c playing board games ____
d riding on a camel ____
e taking a painting class ____
f visiting famous monuments ____

Reading

3 Look at the photo with the article. Which of these things (a–c) do you think it shows?

a a coastline
b a market
c a village

4 Work in pairs. Read the article. Where does each person live? Where are they traveling to?

5 Work in pairs. Circle the correct writer for each statement below—Lucy Chan (C), Liz Mullan (M), or Frank Rosselini (R). Which writer:

1	hasn't been to this places before?	C	M	R
2	has problems with the language?	C	M	R
3	is traveling with his or her parents?	C	M	R
4	has to change his or her plans? Why?	C	M	R

Vacations *and* memories

Three writers return to the lands their families came from.

▶ 62

1 *Lucy Chan*

I step off the train in Hong Kong and follow the crowd to Mong Kok, an area that has some of the city's most famous night markets. Brightly lit red, white, and yellow signs are swinging above the market stalls. I'm not very good at reading Chinese characters, in spite of being born in Hong Kong. Stall holders call out to me. I'm too embarrassed to speak. Back home in Sydney, I learned to say a few words, but right now my mind is blank. I should have brought my phrasebook with me.

2 *Liz Mullan*

Arriving at Belfast International Airport is always emotional. It feels like home. We head north to some of Europe's highest ocean cliffs. After a couple of hours, we're standing on the Giant's Causeway. The wind almost blows us off the rocks into the North Atlantic Ocean. I look west toward home and imagine sailing across this wild ocean to Canada, like my great-grandfather did in 1890. We had planned to walk along the coast like last time, but it's raining hard, so we decide to find a restaurant and hot food. Maybe tomorrow will bring the sun.

3 *Frank Rossellini*

When I was a child, my parents always promised to take me to Sicily one day. Finally, now that they are both in their eighties, we have managed to get here. In this tiny village, we sit down to a dinner with lots of aunts, uncles, and cousins. Eating together is still the most important part of the day here. After enormous plates of sausage, pasta, salads, and homemade bread, everyone enjoys telling us stories of the friends and family members who left for New York decades earlier. It feels great to be here, and I think about coming back again in the future.

Grammar verb patterns: *-ing* form and infinitive

> **VERB PATTERNS: *-ING* FORM and INFINITIVE**
>
> **-ing form**
> I *imagine sailing* across this wild ocean to Canada.
> *Eating* together is important.
> I'm not very *good at reading* Chinese characters.
>
> **infinitive**
> My parents always *promised to take* me to Sicily.
> I'm too *embarrassed to speak*.
>
> For more information and practice, see page 170.

6 Look at the grammar box. Circle the correct option to complete these sentences. Then find an example of each use in the article.

1 We use the *-ing* form of the verb after certain verbs, as the subject of a sentence, and after *adjectives / prepositions*.
2 We use the infinitive form of the verb after certain verbs and after *adjectives / prepositions*.

7 Each option in these sentences is grammatically possible, but one option isn't true, according to the article. Which one?

1 Lucy Chan *described / finished / mentioned* going to the market.
2 Liz Mullan *adores / avoids / loves* going to Ireland.
3 Liz Mullan *expected / intended / threatened* to walk along the coast.
4 Frank Rossellini's parents *planned / refused / wanted* to travel to Sicily.
5 Frank Rossellini *fails / hopes / intends* to return to the village.

8 Circle the correct option to complete the sentences. Then work in pairs. Tell your partner which sentences you agree with.

1 *Traveling / To travel* by train is usually pleasant.
2 Good hotels are easy *finding / to find*.
3 *Walking / To walk* can be a good way of seeing a new city.
4 *Sleeping / To sleep* on a plane can be difficult.
5 Some hotels are too expensive *staying / to stay* in.
6 I'm interested in *trying / to try* new things on vacation.
7 *Going / To go* on a trip with friends is always fun.
8 I get fed up with *spending / to spend* every day on the beach.

9 ▶ 63 Complete the conversation with the *-ing* form and infinitive form of the verbs. Then listen and check.

Rose: Hi there. I'm Rose.
Matt: Hi. I'm Matt.
Rose: Is this your first time in Mexico?
Matt: No, actually. We come every year. We love ¹_____ (stay) here.
Rose: So do we. We keep ²_____ (come) back year after year. It's hard ³_____ (find) somewhere with everything you need for a vacation—great beaches, fantastic weather, and something for everyone to do.
Matt: I know. Actually, there's a paragliding class later—I'd like ⁴_____ (try) that.
Rose: My friends want ⁵_____ (do) that, too! To be honest, ⁶_____ (lie) by the pool is my idea of a vacation.
Matt: Oh, I get kind of bored with ⁷_____ (do) that after the first day or two. I need ⁸_____ (move) around and do things.
Rose: Well, why not? It's a different way of ⁹_____ (relax), I suppose.
Matt: Yes, that's right. Well, if you decide ¹⁰_____ (go) paragliding with your friends, we'll see you there!

Listening and speaking

10 ▶ 64 Listen to people talking about vacations and complete the sentences. Work in pairs. Do you think they would be good travel companions for you? Which person would you prefer to go on vacation with?

1 I kind of like _____
2 I don't mind _____
3 I'd like _____
4 I can't afford _____
5 I'm really into _____
6 I don't like _____
7 I'm interested in _____
8 I can't stand _____

11 Think about how you would complete the sentences in Exercise 10. Then talk to people in your class and find someone who would make a good travel companion.

12 Work with your travel companion and decide what kind of vacation to take. Tell the class:

- where and when you would go.
- how you would get there.
- where you would stay.
- what you would do there and why.

8b Walking for wildlife

Mike Fay, *a conservationist whose work makes a difference*

 trekked[1] 10,000 kilometers in Africa and North America

 counted giant redwood trees in North America, elephant populations in central Africa

 created 13 national parks in Gabon

 protected thousands of elephants from poachers[2]

 survived a malaria attack, an elephant attack, a plane crash

 flew over the African continent for an aerial survey[3]

 uploaded thousands of photos to Google Earth

 helped create a marine park off the Gabon coast

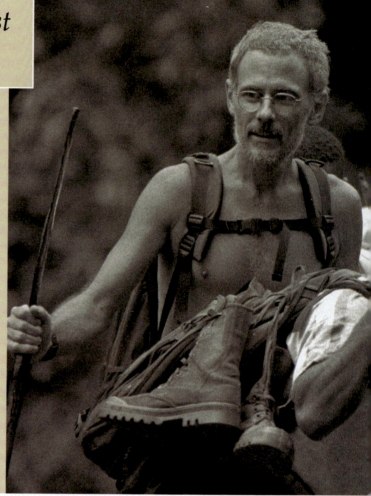

Listening

1 What kind of work do a conservationists do? What is their main goal?

2 Look at the information about Mike Fay. Do you think he's a typical conservationist? Why or why not?

Probably not, because he's trekked 10,000 kilometers, and has had some dangerous and exciting experiences.

3 ▶ 65 Listen to an excerpt from a radio program about Mike Fay. Complete the sentences.

1 Mike Fay's work is about saving the last _____ on Earth.
2 He has spent a total of more than _____ years of his life on treks.
3 He's walked in Africa, the United States, and _____ .
4 He is worried about how _____ people will affect the planet.

4 ▶ 65 Listen to the excerpt again and circle the correct options to complete the sentences.

1 Recently, Fay has been *flying / walking* across Canada.
2 Mining companies in western Canada have been *looking for / processing* gold and oil.
3 Mining companies have been *replanting / destroying* vast areas.
4 In Gabon, people have been *asking / trying* to set up mines near parks.

5 Work in pairs. Would you like to spend a year working with Mike Fay? Why or why not?

---

[1]**trek** (v) /trek/ to make a long and difficult journey
[2]**poacher** (n) /'pəʊtʃər/ someone who catches and kills animals illegally
[3]**survey** (n) /'sɜːrveɪ/ the measuring and recording of the details of an area of land

Grammar present perfect and present perfect continuous

6 Work in pairs. Look at the grammar box. Answer the questions.

1 How do we form the present perfect? How do we form the present perfect continuous?

2 Which verb form emphasizes the duration or repetition of an activity? Which verb form emphasizes an action or an activity that is complete?

7 Complete the text with the present perfect or present perfect continuous form of the verbs.

> This year, Mike Fay [1] *has been working* (work) in Gabon. He [2] _____ (check) the situation in the national parks, and he [3] _____ (discover) some problems. For example, poachers [4] _____ (kill) elephants again. Fay [5] _____ (talk) about ways of controlling poaching with the Gabonese government. As a result, the Gabonese president [6] _____ (send) soldiers to several of the parks. So far, the poachers [7] _____ (not / return). Meanwhile, for the past few years, foreign ships [8] _____ (fish) in the marine park. The Gabonese government [9] _____ (try) to find ways of dealing with this problem.

8 Write questions for Mike Fay with the present perfect and present perfect continuous forms of the verbs.

1 What / you / do / recently?
2 you / prepare for / any new trips?
3 How / you / feel / since the plane crash?
4 How many photos / you / take / in your career?
5 How long / you / travel / alone?
6 you / be / anywhere dangerous lately?

9 Match the travel preparation activities (1–6) with the results (a–f). Then write two sentences.

I've been buying vacation clothes. I've spent a fortune.

1 buy vacation clothes ___b___
2 look for cheap flights ____
3 talk to travel agents ____
4 download tourist information ____
5 pack my suitcase ____
6 practice useful phrases in Thai ____

a be on the phone all morning
b spend a fortune
c run out of space
d not learn many
e print a couple of pages
f not find any

Grammar *How long?*

10 Look at the grammar box. Which verb form is used in each question? Why?

11 Match the questions (1–5) with the answers (a–e). Then work in pairs and continue the conversations.

1 How long have you been coming to this resort? ____
2 How long did the flight from Quito take? ____
3 How long have you known each other? ____
4 How long did you spend in Canada? ____
5 How long have you been waiting for the bus? ____

a About ten hours non-stop.
b For the last four or five years.
c I was there for a couple of months.
d Not long—we met on vacation this spring.
e Only a few minutes. But I think we just missed one.

Speaking my Life

12 What kinds of activities are you interested in? How long have you been doing them? Work in pairs and tell your partner. Ask follow-up questions. Use some of these ideas.

I've been ... since/for ...
I've always/never ...

8c All aboard!

Reading

1 Work in pairs. Discuss the questions.

1 Do many tourists come to your country or region? From which countries?
2 What do these tourists do? Adventure tourism, backpacking, cultural sightseeing, ecotourism, or other vacation activities?
3 What are the advantages of this tourism? Are there any disadvantages?

2 Read the article quickly. What is it about? Choose the best option (a–c).

a It describes extreme activities tourists can do.
b It compares the positive and negative effects of tourism.
c It talks about the impact of tourists on their destinations.

3 Read the article again and complete the table.

Destination	Number of tourists	Impact
1 _____ Himalayas:	2 _____ on a single cruise ship	Falling numbers of 3 _____ _____
4 _____	5 _____ in the climbing season	6 _____ left on the mountain Negative effects on
7 _____	8 _____	9 _____

4 Work in pairs. Answer the questions with information from the article.

1 When did the tourism industry start to be successful?
2 Why are cruises bad for the environment?
3 What have groups been doing to improve the environment on Everest?
4 What action has the government of the Balearic Islands taken, and why?

5 Find these words in the article. Look at how the words are used and try to guess their meanings. Then complete the sentences (1–4).

pollution (line 12)   charge (line 41)
equipment (line 24)   ecotourism (line 50)

1 Airlines usually _____ you a lot of money if your luggage is over the weight limit.
2 You don't need much _____ for surfing—just a surfboard and a wetsuit.
3 _____ is a way of enjoying a vacation without damaging the environment.
4 Plastic is a major cause of _____ in the oceans.

Critical thinking reading closely

6 According to the article, are these statements true (T) or false (F)? Or is there not enough information in the article (N)?

1 The tourism industry has been declining in recent years.   T F N
2 There are fewer Magellanic penguins since cruises started visiting Patagonia.   T F N
3 Climbers on Everest cause problems for the local wildlife.   T F N
4 The Balearic Islands government is trying an eco tax for the first time.   T F N
5 The writer believes that tourists need to consider their impact on the environment.   T F N

7 Work in pairs. Underline the sections of the article that helped you decide about the sentences in Exercise 6. Do you agree with each other?

8 Work as a class. Discuss the questions.

1 Do you think an eco tax on tourists is a good idea?
2 What is your answer to the final question in the article?

Speaking my Life

9 Work in pairs. Look at these activities. Decide if they have a good or bad impact on the environment. Which ones does your family do?

1 flying to distant vacation destinations
2 recycling household waste
3 traveling by car
4 turning off lights and electrical appliances
5 saving water
6 using eco-friendly cleaning products

10 Work in groups. How easy is it for you and your family to live a green lifestyle?

All
ABOARD!

A plane comes in to land on the Caribbean island of Saint Martin.

▶ 66

The tourism industry started to grow rapidly in the middle of the last century, and it's been growing ever since. In the last twenty years in particular, more and more people have been traveling to distant places around the world. It's a wonderful thing, to be able to travel to destinations we had previously only read about or seen on television. But what kind of impact do large numbers of
5 people have on these places?

A voyage to the end of the Earth?

A large cruise ship can carry as many as six thousand passengers at a time, with about twenty-four million people going on cruises every year. Cruise ships drop
10 about ninety thousand tons of waste into the oceans every year, and each ship produces as much air pollution as five million cars. The effects of this are made even worse by the fact that cruises visit the same places over and over again, so the damage is repeated.
15 In Patagonia, this has been having an effect on wildlife. For example, the number of Magellanic penguins has been falling for some years now.

Climbing to the top of the world

Far fewer people go climbing or trekking in the
20 Himalayas than take a cruise, but in the short climbing season each May, about a thousand people try to climb Mount Everest. At times, there are actually lines of climbers on the route to the top. The difficult conditions mean that everyone needs to take a lot of equipment with
25 them. Unfortunately, for the last few decades, climbers have been leaving their equipment on Everest. In recent years, clean-up teams have been organizing expeditions just to pick up this trash. The teams are made up of local and international climbers. One group has brought over
30 eight tons of trash down from the mountain!

Let's all go to the beach

What happens when a region of about a million people is visited by thirteen million tourists every year? The Balearic Islands in the Mediterranean Sea
35 have been dealing with this situation for decades. Where have the fresh water, the food, the gas, and the electricity for thirteen million tourists come from? And how have the islands maintained the quality of the beaches, the roads, and the countryside?
40 Recently, the government of the Balearic Islands decided to charge tourists an eco tax of two euros a day. This has been tried once before, but it wasn't a success. However, the challenges have been getting greater every year. The money from the tax is used
45 to reduce the negative effects of tourism on the local environment.

Difficult choices

So should we travel or simply stay at home? Many destinations offer low-impact tourism—such as
50 ecotourism. It's time to ask ourselves some difficult questions. Can we really visit the world's beautiful places without destroying them?

8d Is something wrong?

Vocabulary travel problems

1 Work in pairs. Have you ever had any travel problems involving these things? Tell your partner. Which of these problems can a tour guide help you with?

baggage allowances	hotel rooms
boarding passes	passport control
car rentals	train schedules
customs checks	travel documents
flight delays	travel sickness
food poisoning	

> ▶ **WORDBUILDING compound nouns (noun + noun)**
>
> We can use two nouns together to mean one thing.
> *baggage allowance, hotel rooms*
>
> For more practice, see Workbook page 67.

Real life dealing with problems

2 ▶ **67** Listen to two conversations between a tour guide and tourists. Write the number of the conversation (1 or 2) next to the problem they talk about (a–f).

a The person has missed his/her flight home. ____
b Someone has had an accident. ____
c The luggage hasn't arrived. ____
d The flight has been delayed. ____
e The person has lost his/her plane tickets. ____
f Someone is sick. ____

3 ▶ **67** Look at the expressions for dealing with problems. Can you remember who said what? Write G (guide) or T (tourist) next to the expressions. Then listen to the conversations again and check.

> ▶ **DEALING WITH PROBLEMS**
>
> I wonder if you could help us. ____
> Is something wrong? ____
> Can I help? ____
>
> Our luggage hasn't arrived. ____
> Which flight were you on? ____
> How did that happen? ____
> Do you know where our bags have gone to? ____
> When's the next flight? ____
> It's about my wife. ____
> How long has she been feeling like this? ____
> Is there anything you can do? ____
>
> I'm afraid the luggage has gone to Los Angeles. ____
> Don't worry. We'll arrange everything. ____
> I'll ask the hotel to call a doctor. ____

4 Work as a class. Are the problems solved? How?

5 Pronunciation strong and weak forms

a ▶ **68** Work in pairs. Look at the position of *to* in these sentences. Listen to the sentences. In which sentence is *to* strong /tuː/? In which one is it weak /tə/?

1 Do you know which airport our bags have gone to?
2 Yes, I'm afraid the luggage has gone to Los Angeles.

b ▶ **69** Listen and repeat these questions. Use strong or weak forms of *at*, *from*, and *for*. Then work in pairs. Ask the questions and give your own answers.

1 Which hotel are you staying at?
2 Are you staying at the Ocean Hotel?
3 Where have you traveled from?
4 Why haven't we heard from the airline?
5 What have we been waiting for?
6 Are you waiting for the manager?

6 Work in pairs. Take the roles of a tourist and a tour guide. Choose from the problems in Exercise 2 and act out two conversations. Use the expressions for dealing with problems to help you.

8e Hello from Mexico City!

Writing a text message

1 Read the message from Lynne. Answer the questions.

1 Where has Lynne come from and where is she now?
2 Who do you think the message is for? Friends, family, or both?
3 What does Lynne say about the people and the city?
4 What has she been doing?

> Hi everyone!
> Finally made it to Mexico City after 18-hour delay in Dallas!!! 😰 Weather been rainy but people awesome. Mexico much less crowded than Seoul! So far have: been shopping in Roma Norte, visited the pyramids at Teotihuacán (wow!), taken a tour of the Frida Kahlo Museum (awesome!), had a boat trip along the canals of Xochimilco. Then slept all day & night cos jetlagged. 😣

2 Writing skill informal style

a Read the message again. Which of these features of informal style does Lynne use?

abbreviations	informal expressions
comments in parentheses	listing items
contractions	leaving out words
exclamation marks	symbols

b Look at this excerpt from the message. The words *I* and *an* are missing. Mark their positions in the complete sentence.

> Finally made it to Mexico City after 18-hour delay in Dallas!!!

c Mark the places in the message where Lynne has left out words. What are the words?

d Rewrite these as complete sentences.

1 city huge & lively
2 not been inside Leon Trotsky Museum cos closed
3 visited Museo del Palacio de Bellas Artes - stunning!
4 took selfies (lots) in the Zócalo
5 can't understand Mexican accent (trying!)
6 text from Jung - arriving Sunday

e Rewrite the sentences. Leave out words where possible.

1 The weather is sunny, and it has been very hot sometimes.
2 I've been touring all the typical places—it's exhausting!
3 The people here are very kind, and they have helped me a lot.
4 I tried some street food—it's delicious
5 I haven't heard anything from Anton yet.
6 I'm taking a bus to Oaxaca because flying is too expensive.

3 Choose a place you have visited or would like to visit. Make notes. Use the questions in Exercise 1 as a guide.

4 Decide who to write to. Write a message describing your trip. Use some of the features of informal style from Exercise 2a and leave out words that are not necessary.

5 Send your message to someone in your class. Then read the message you have received. Use these questions to check your classmate's message.

- Is everything clearly expressed?
- Are there any sections you do not understand?

6 Work in pairs. Tell your partner about the message you have received.

A: I got a message from Daisuke the other day.
B: Oh! How's he doing?

Cory Richards on the Cordillera Blanca in Peru

Before you watch

1 Work in pairs. You're going to watch two videos of National Geographic Explorers giving their personal answers to questions. Before you watch, discuss these questions.

1 What kind of work do explorers do? Where do they work?
2 What items might they need to take with them when they're exploring?
3 Why do you think people become explorers?

2 Key vocabulary

a Work in pairs. Read the sentences. The words in bold are used in the video. Guess the meaning of the words.

1 If you want to watch animals in the wild, a pair of **binoculars** is very useful.
2 I'd get really burned if I didn't use **sunblock**.
3 I'm not very good with a **paintbrush**—I prefer doing pencil drawings.
4 Children are **curious** about the world.
5 I've been making good **progress** in Italian since I started classes.

b Match the words in bold in Exercise 2a with these definitions.

a a tool to paint with _____
b cream that protects your skin from the sun _____
c equipment with lenses for looking at things far away _____
d improvement and development _____
e interested in something and wanting to learn about it _____

While you watch

Video 1: What item would you not leave home without?

3 Read what four of the explorers say about why they choose the items they take with them. What do you think they are talking about?

1 John Francis, ecologist
"...if I don't have a _____ or my binoculars then I feel nude."
2 Carlton Ward, photographer
"without a _____ , we would be still paddling in circles somewhere"
3 Amy Dickman , zoologist
"_____ , just to have a break at the end of the day"
4 Chris Thornton, archeologist
"_____ . I'm very, very white."

4 ▶ 8.1 Watch the first video. Check your ideas from Exercise 3.

5 ▶ 8.1 Watch the video again. Circle the items the explorers mention.

binoculars	camera	DVDs
family photographs	GPS	hat
headlamp	knife	local person
paintbrush	pencil	sunblock
sunglasses		

6 Work in pairs. Which of the items in Exercise 5 surprised you?

Video 2: Why is it important to explore?

7 ▶ 8.2 Read what the explorers in the video say. What do you think the missing word is? Then watch the video and check your ideas.

1 John Francis, ecologist
"If you have _____ and you don't pursue them, then to me it's a life unlived."
2 Laly Lichtenfeld, big cat conservationist
"It keeps _____ exciting, I mean that's what exploring is about."
3 Enric Sala, marine ecologist
"Without exploration, there would be no _____ ."
4 Lee Berger, paleoanthropologist
"We think we _____ how things work, but we don't."

8 ▶ 8.2 Watch the second video again. In your opinion, who gave the most interesting answer?

After you watch

9 Vocabulary in context

a ▶ 8.3 Watch the clips from the videos. Choose the correct meaning of the words and phrases.

b Answer the questions in your own words. Then work in pairs and compare your answers.

1 Does the power ever go out where you live? What do you do when that happens?
2 Do you think it's human nature to be curious? What else is human nature?
3 What kind of thing do you think drives artists? What about business people?

10 Work in pairs. Discuss the questions.

1 What would you not leave home without if you were traveling?
2 Why is it a good idea to travel?

UNIT 8 REVIEW AND MEMORY BOOSTER

Grammar

1 Complete the article about Thomas Cook with the correct verb tense or form. Use simple past, present perfect, present perfect continuous, *-ing* form or infinitive.

Before 1872, people [1] _____ (not / travel) for pleasure very much. Then a man named Thomas Cook [2] _____ (change) everything when he [3] _____ (form) a travel agency, Thomas Cook & Son. Cook aimed [4] _____ (provide) educational and cultural tours. His son was successful in [5] _____ (expand) the business around the world. At first, foreign travel was expensive, but incomes [6] _____ (rise) since those days. Nowadays, many millions of ordinary people expect [7] _____ (go) on vacation at least once a year. In the twentieth century, travelers preferred [8] _____ (book) trips with travel agencies. For the last few years, travel agencies [9] _____ (struggle) because most people [10] _____ (make) their own plans online. Thomas Cook, however, is still one of the biggest travel companies in the world.

2 Work in pairs. Answer the questions about the article in Exercise 1.

1 How has travel changed since the time of Thomas Cook?
2 Why do you think the travel agency Thomas Cook & Son was successful?

3 **≫ MB** Write four true or false sentences about yourself with these verbs. Then work in pairs and say if your partner's sentences are true or false.

have been learning	have seen
am interested in trying	want to go

I CAN	
use verb patterns correctly (*-ing* form and infinitive)	☐
talk about recent activities and experiences (present perfect simple and present perfect continuous)	☐

Vocabulary

4 Match nouns from A and B to make travel vocabulary. Then write questions with the expressions.

A		B	
baggage	flight	control	sickness
boarding	passport	allowance	checks
customs	travel	delays	pass

5 **≫ MB** Work in pairs. Which of these activities would you do in a coastal resort, a big city, a nature reserve, and a campground? Give your reasons.

be active	learn new things
go sightseeing	spend time with friends
have new	or family
experiences	take it easy

I CAN	
use travel vocabulary appropriately	☐
talk about vacation activities	☐

Real life

6 Read these sentences from a conversation at an airport. Put the sentences (a–h) in order (1–8).

a A: What? How did that happen? ____
b A: Well, let's look again. Calm down. ____
c A: Well, did you look through all your bags? ____
d A: Is something wrong? ____
e B: Yes, I have. I've even checked the suitcase. ____
f B: I've been worrying so much about everything, and now this! ____
g B: I think I've lost the boarding passes. ____
h B: I don't know. I thought they were in my pocket, but they aren't there now. ____

7 **≫ MB** Work in pairs. Act out conversations.

Conversation 1: Student A is a tourist and Student B is a tour guide. Student A has lost his/her passport.

Conversation 2: Student A is an airline employee and Student B is a customer. The flight is canceled.

I CAN	
talk about travel problems	☐
ask for and give explanations	☐

Unit 9 Shopping

Galleria Vittorio Emanuele, Milan, Italy

FEATURES

106 Shopping trends

How do you do your shopping?

108 Spend or save?

Do you buy on impulse?

110 The art of the deal

How to negotiate a price

114 Making a deal

A video about shopping in the oldest market in Morocco

1 Work in pairs. Look at the photo and the caption. Compare this place with places you usually go shopping.

2 ▶ 70 Listen to a market researcher interviewing some people who are shopping. Complete the table.

Interview	What?	Who for?
1	the latest _____	_____
2	a couple of _____	himself
3	some _____	each other

3 Work in pairs. Discuss the questions.

1 What's the best (or worst) present anyone has ever given you?
2 What kind of things do you and your family or friends buy for each other?
3 What kind of things do you prefer to buy for yourself?

4 Work in pairs. Prepare a survey on shopping habits. Ask at least three other people your questions. Then compare the results.

9a Shopping trends

Reading

1 Work in pairs. How do you prefer to shop? Tell your partner and give reasons.

> at markets (indoor or outdoor)
> in department stores
> in malls
> in small local shops
> online

2 Read what a farmer and a store manager say about selling their products. Answer the questions.

1 What kind of products do they talk about?
2 What kind of shopping do they talk about?
3 Where do they sell their products?

3 Read the article again. Find one advantage to customers and one to sellers for each kind of shopping.

4 Work in pairs. Can you think of any disadvantages to each kind of shopping?

Shopping trends

 71

Nate McGregor
Californian farmer

"Farmers' markets are becoming more and more popular these days; some are even tourist attractions. People enjoy buying fruit, vegetables, meat, and dairy directly from the growers. I have a stall in the downtown marketplace three times a week. When I sell directly to consumers, they pay less, and I still get a good price. That's because the vegetables don't have to be packaged and I don't have to pay a wholesaler[1] to distribute and sell my products. The customers are happy because the vegetables are fresher and better quality than in the supermarket, so they keep for longer. A lot of supermarket stuff has to be eaten within a couple of days."

Mark Noble,
manager at Costco store

"These days, lots of people have busy lives, and online shopping is a growing area for us. It's especially popular with people who buy the same things in the same amounts every week. At first, online shopping was used mainly by our regular customers, but since we introduced our mobile phone app, more new accounts have been set up.

Customers can browse the entire Costco selection, which offers thousands of items not found at their local store. With the app, you can save time and money. Food and household items are delivered to the customers' homes for a small charge, or people can pick them up in the store. A new free delivery service is being launched nationwide at the moment, and with that we'll be able to improve our service to customers even more."

[1]**wholesaler** (n) /ˈhoʊlseɪlər/ a company that buys products in large quantities from the maker and sells them to different stores

Grammar passives

▶ **PASSIVES**

At first, online shopping **was used** *mainly* **by our regular customers.**
A new free delivery service **is being launched** *nationwide*
A lot of supermarket stuff **has to be eaten** *within a couple of days.*

For more information and practice, see page 172.

5 Work in pairs. Look at the grammar box. Find a simple passive, a modal passive, and a continuous passive. Then answer the questions.

1 How do we form the passive? Think about the auxiliary verb and the form of the main verb.
2 What kind of information follows the word *by*?

6 Work in pairs. Underline three more passive forms in the article *Shopping trends*. Does the use of the passive emphasize the action or the person who does the action?

7 Circle the correct options to complete the text about a company that sells coffee.

We started direct trade about four years ago. This means that more of the final price [1] *pays / is paid* to the growers. We have a simple system. First, the coffee beans [2] *take / are taken* to a central collection point by each grower. When the loads [3] *have weighed / have been weighed*, the growers [4] *get / are got* the correct payment. At the moment, we [5] *are using / are being used* a standard shipping company to transport the coffee to Europe. But we [6] *are reviewing / are being reviewed* our arrangements and next year, probably, specialized firms [7] *will contract / will be contracted* to handle shipping. Once in Europe, the coffee [8] *can pack and sell / can be packed and sold* within a week.

8 Work in pairs. Write the passive form of the verbs.

1 Since its launch in 2003, 250 million *Nokia 1101 mobile phones / Apple iPods* _____ (sell).
2 With 400 shops around the world, clothing brand *Ralph Lauren / Mango* _____ (wear) by more people than any other.
3 The work of *J.K. Rowling / Agatha Christie* _____ (translate) into more languages than any other author.
4 *Solitaire / Tetris* _____ (adapt) for 65 different systems, making it the most successful computer game ever.
5 The first music video by *Justin Bieber / Lady Gaga* _____ (view) on YouTube over 500 million times.
6 A painting by *Picasso / van Gogh* _____ (buy) at auction for $106 million in 2010.

9 ▶ **72** Circle the options you think are correct in Exercise 8. Then listen and check. How many answers did you get right?

Speaking myLife

10 Work in pairs. Find out about shopping now and in the future.

Student A: Turn to page 153 and follow the instructions.

Student B: Turn to page 154 and follow the instructions.

11 Work in groups of four. You are the makers of a new bag for people of your own age group. Decide on the following details for your bag. Find images online or make your own.

- what it will be/look like
- where/how it will be made
- where/how it will be sold
- who it will be aimed at
- how much it will cost
- why people should buy it

12 Present your product to the class. Vote on the one you'd most like to buy.

9b Spend or save?

Vocabulary shopping (1)

1 Work in pairs. Have you ever bought anything on impulse? Tell your partner about it.

2 Match the beginnings of the sentences (1–8) with the endings (a–h). Check the meaning of any words in bold you are not sure about.

1 The **checkout** is where you go ___
2 When things have a **special offer**, ___
3 At most supermarkets, they help you ___
4 Fridges, washing machines, and TVs ___
5 You can often get good **deals** ___
6 Cheap and expensive items ___
7 It isn't a good idea to ___
8 A **budget** is a way of figuring out ___

a are electronics.
b buy things that you can't **afford**.
c can both be good **value for money**.
d how much money you can spend.
e on products **by buying online**.
f the price is lower.
g to bag your **purchases**.
h to pay for your shopping.

3 Work in pairs. Ask and answer questions with the words in bold in Exercise 2.

*How do you choose which **checkout** line to get in at the supermarket?*

Listening

4 ▶ 73 Listen to an excerpt from a radio program that discusses what's in the news. Check (✓) the examples of impulse buying that are mentioned.

☐ Buying lots of things when you only need bread or milk.
☐ Buying things you can't afford to buy.
☐ Buying things online.
☐ Spending too much when you're hungry.

5 ▶ 73 Listen to the excerpt again. Correct factual errors in four of the sentences.

1 Samira has written articles on impulse buying.
2 Most of us have spent more than $500 on a purchase that wasn't necessary!
3 You should always have a budget when you need to buy expensive things.
4 The researchers found that males under twenty-one are more likely to buy on impulse.
5 Many people use shopping as a way of managing their money.
6 If you make a list, you can avoid impulse buying.

6 Work in pairs. Think of three ways people can control their impulse buying.

Grammar articles and quantifiers

7 Work in pairs. Look at the words in bold in the grammar box. Which article (*a/an*, *the*, or zero article) is used when:

  a we mention something for the first time?
  b we mention something that is known (because it has already been mentioned, for example)?
  c there is only one of something?
  d we are talking about something in general?

8 Read the ideas for saving money. Complete the sentences with the correct article (*a/an*, *the*, or zero article (-)).

TOP *Saving Tips*

1 Save your small change in ____ jar.

2 Unplug ____ electrical appliances when you're not using them.

3 Buy ____ products that are close to their sell-by date.

4 Don't get ____ credit card. If you have one, cut it up.

5 Compare ____ prices before you buy ____ expensive item.

6 Keep ____ receipts and add up ____ amount of money you spend every day.

7 Take ____ lunch from home instead of buying ____ sandwiches or ____ snacks.

8 Don't buy ____ books—borrow them from ____ library.

9 Work in pairs. Look at the grammar box. Answer the questions.

  1 Look at sentences 1 and 2. Which quantifier is used with:
      a a countable noun?
      b an uncountable noun?
  2 Look at sentences 3 and 4. When do we use the quantifier *lots of*?

10 Circle the correct quantifier. Then suggest another possible quantifier for each sentence.

  1 I don't think I need to go shopping. We have *plenty of / many* food for the week.
  2 I bought *a couple of / a little* magazines. I can read them on the train.
  3 If I have *a little / one or two* money at the end of the month, I buy something nice.
  4 You can save *several / lots of* money if you buy items on sale.

11 Pronunciation linking

a ▶ 74 Listen to these sentences from Exercise 10. Notice how the speaker links the words that start with a vowel to the final consonant of the previous word.

  1 I don't think‿I need to go shopping.
  2 I can read them‿on the train.

b ▶ 75 Underline the words that start with vowels in the other sentences in Exercise 10. Then listen and repeat the sentences.

Speaking my Life

12 Work in pairs. Make true (or false) sentences with these quantifiers about things you own, have bought, or have been given. Tell your partner and ask follow-up questions.

a little	a couple of	a few	lots of
one or two	plenty of	several	some

*A: I have **some** wood I found on the beach.*
B: Do you? Why did you decide to keep it?

9c The art of the deal

Reading

1 Work in pairs. Do you like bringing souvenirs back from vacation? Discuss why you think people bring back items like the ones in the box.

> brochures from galleries, museums, etc.
> decorative objects: pictures, ceramics, etc.
> duty-free goods
> locally made products
> postcards
> T-shirts with slogans
> used tickets

2 Read the article quickly. Decide what kind of shopping experience (a–c) the article describes.

 a buying crafts direct from the maker
 b choosing souvenirs for friends and family
 c looking for bargains in local markets

3 Work in pairs. Read the article again. Answer the questions.

 1 Who are the three main people in the article and why do they go to Morocco?
 2 What two things does Sam buy and how much does he pay for them?
 3 Which is Sam's best purchase?

4 Look at the words (1–8). Find the things that are described with these words in the article. Complete the phrases. Then think of more things that can be described using these words.

 1 beautiful old ⎯⎯⎯⎯⎯⎯⎯⎯⎯⎯
 2 world-famous ⎯⎯⎯⎯⎯⎯⎯⎯⎯
 3 freshly squeezed ⎯⎯⎯⎯⎯⎯⎯
 4 deadly looking ⎯⎯⎯⎯⎯⎯⎯⎯
 5 hand-dyed ⎯⎯⎯⎯⎯⎯⎯⎯⎯⎯
 6 massive copper ⎯⎯⎯⎯⎯⎯⎯⎯
 7 tall blue ⎯⎯⎯⎯⎯⎯⎯⎯⎯⎯⎯
 8 bright yellow Moroccan ⎯⎯⎯⎯⎯

Wordbuilding compound adjectives

> ▶ **WORDBUILDING compound adjectives**
>
> Compound adjectives are adjectives made of more than one word. The hyphen shows that the words form one adjective.
> *duty-free goods, two-day lemon festival*
>
> For more practice, see Workbook page 75.

5 Look at the wordbuilding box. Then work in pairs. Answer the questions.

 1 The *world-famous marketplace* is famous around the world. What do the other compound adjectives in Exercise 4 mean?
 2 Can you name examples of:
  a a well-known athlete?
  b a best-selling book?
  c old-fashioned clothes?

Critical thinking testing a conclusion

6 The writer concludes: "Mohamed will be proud." Look at the article again and underline the pieces of advice Mohamed gives to Sam.

7 Circle the pieces of advice that Sam follows. How effective was the advice? How do you know?

Speaking myLife

8 Work in pairs. Describe typical souvenirs that people take home from your country.

9 You are a market trader. Choose four of these objects. Find or draw a picture of each object and think how you will describe it. Think about its origin, age, and material, and any interesting facts about it. Decide on a price for each object.

boomerang	bottle	box	clock
coin	figure	hat	lamp
rug	stamp	sword	watch

10 Work in groups. Choose objects from Exercise 9 that you want to buy. Visit different traders and find out about the objects you want. Then choose which trader you will buy from.

This rug is beautiful. How much is it?

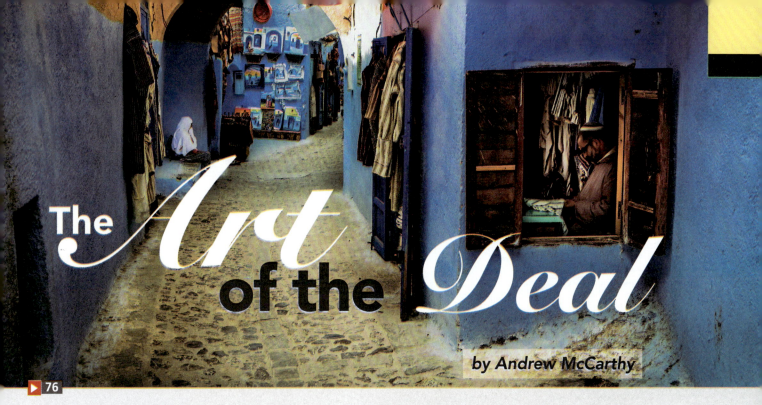

The Art of the Deal

by Andrew McCarthy

▶ 76

I'M IN MARRAKECH, the bustling[1] heart of Morocco, with my son, Sam. He's eight. We've come here with Mohamed, a friend who owns a shop in our neighborhood in New York. Sam can often be found in Mohamed's shop,
5 looking for a bargain.[2] They argue about prices and chat about swords, camels, or the desert. "You need to come to Morocco, to Marrakech," Mohamed told me. "I'll show you around and teach Sam how to really get a bargain!" So here we are.
We meet up with Mohamed over a cup of mint tea in the
10 beautiful old city of Marrakech. We're sitting in an area next to the exotic stalls of the souk[3]—Marrakech's world-famous marketplace. Market sellers with carts offer freshly squeezed juice—others sell dates or figs. Later, as we wander around, Mohamed introduces us to olive sellers,
15 tile makers, and rug merchants. He also begins the first of his lessons in bargaining for Sam.
"The price of everything in Morocco is open to discussion, Sam. When you hear a price, the first thing you say is 'Too much—*bezaf,*' and then walk away."
20 "But what if I like it?"
"When you see something you like, maybe a lamp, you ask about something else instead. Then, as you walk out, you ask, 'And how much is that lamp?' as though you'd just noticed it and aren't really that interested in it."
25 We turn a corner into another narrow street in the souk. "Don't always give an offer. Make them continue to lower the price. Oh, and wear something Moroccan," Mohamed continues as we enter a fairly large shop. Most of the stalls in Marrakech sell mainly one type of thing, but not this
30 one. Decorative and deadly looking swords hang beside soft hand-dyed fabrics; large camel bones covered in writing sit beside massive copper lamps. It is here that Sam spots a beautiful box. "Look, a treasure chest!" It's made of wood, and painted red and gold. He opens the lid, then
35 closes it. "Cool." Then he spots a tall blue bottle—an old

perfume bottle. "Four hundred dirham," the shopkeeper says. Fifty dollars. Sam says nothing. I can't tell whether he's too shy or is practicing what Mohamed has taught him. He eventually agrees to pay 200 dirham—about $24. I'd
40 say the bottle is worth $10, at most. Clearly, he needs more practice at this. "Just to get started, Dad," Sam tells me as he pays for the bottle.
We spend a few days sightseeing around Marrakech, but Sam is really interested in only one thing. Late one afternoon,
45 it's just the two of us. We return to the shop where Sam saw the treasure chest. "You have returned. Very good." The shopkeeper opens his arms. He places the chest on the floor. Sam opens the lid. He runs his fingers over it.
The shopkeeper speaks. "Give me 2,500."
50 Sam shakes his eight-year-old head. "Eight hundred."
"I like your babouches," says the man. Sam's wearing a pair of bright yellow Moroccan slippers. He ignores the comment.
"You're very good. I'll take 1,800 dirham," the shopkeeper announces.
55 "One thousand."
Both are silent. Neither blinks.[4] What happens next happens fast.
"Fifteen hundred, and it's yours."
"Twelve hundred."
60 "Thirteen hundred."
"Yes!"
The man holds out his hand. Sam grabs it. The deal is done. Mohamed will be proud.

---

[1] **bustling** (adj) /ˈbʌslɪŋ/ energetic and busy
[2] **bargain** (n) /ˈbɑːrgɪn/ something that has a lower price than usual
[3] **souk** (n) /suːk/ the name in some countries for a market
[4] **blink** (v) /blɪŋk/ to open and close your eyes very quickly

9d It's on sale

Real life buying things

1 ▶ **77** Work in pairs. Listen to two conversations. Answer the questions for each conversation.

1 What kind of store is it?
2 What does the customer want?
3 Does the customer buy the item?

2 ▶ **77** Look at the expressions for buying things. Listen to the conversations again. Circle the option the speaker uses. Identify the speakers. Write C (customer) or S (salesperson) next to the expressions.

> ▶ **BUYING THINGS**
>
> Can I look at / Could I see this silver chain? _____
> It's on sale / It's reduced, actually. It's 20 percent off. _____
> I wanted / I was looking for something lighter. _____
> Can she bring it back / return it if she doesn't like it? _____
> Excuse me, do you work in this department? _____
> What's / Do you have the reference number or the model name?
> _____
> Let me see if it's in stock / we have any on order. _____
> How much do you charge / does it cost for delivery? _____
> We accept payment / You can pay by credit card or in cash. _____

Vocabulary shopping (2)

3 Work in pairs. Can you remember the question and response for each word? Check your answers in the Track 77 audioscript on page 187.

return	exchange	receipt	gift-wrapping
reference number	model name	in stock	available
delivery	checkout		

4 Pronunciation silent letters

a ▶ **78** Listen to these words. Notice how the crossed-out letters are silent. Repeat the words.

gift-wrapping	receipt
right	though

b ▶ **79** Say these words and cross out the silent letters. Then listen and check.

answer	bought	design	friendly
hour	listen	weigh	

5 Work in pairs. Take the roles of a customer and a salesperson. Choose two of these items and act out two conversations. Use the expressions for buying things to help you.

> an item of furniture for your new home
> clothes for your father for his birthday
> toiletries for your sister
> a book for a friend
> a kitchen appliance for your brother
> sportswear for yourself

9e For sale

Writing customer reviews

1 Work in pairs. Do you read customer reviews when you buy things online? Have you ever changed your mind about a purchase after reading reviews?

2 Work in pairs. Read the customer reviews from two online shopping sites. Answer the questions.

1 Which review is about a product and which is about a seller?
2 What problems do the customers mention?
3 Are the reviews positive or negative?

★★★★★

I have no hesitation in recommending PetTown. I ordered two ID tags, but after two weeks, **they** hadn't arrived. When I emailed the company, **they** immediately sent replacement tags via express mail at no extra charge. **They** were courteous and efficient, and I would buy from **them** again.

★★★★☆

Bought this nice shirt at an even nicer 20% off. I wasn't disappointed. Great quality material and **it's** a perfect fit. Good for work and for social occasions. Slightly surprised when I washed my white shirts with it—**they** came out pale blue! This is the first time it's happened with your products, however, and is the only reason I'm not giving **it** five stars. I do recommend the product, but care must be taken when washing.

3 Writing skill clarity: pronouns

a Work in pairs. You can avoid repetition of nouns in your writing by using pronouns—as long as it is clear which noun each pronoun refers to. Look at the pronouns in bold in the customer reviews. What do they refer to?

b Work in pairs. Read the sentences. Replace the nouns with pronouns to avoid repetition.

1 I felt that the colors of the rug in the online photo weren't accurate. The colors of the rug were much darker than I expected.
2 Two of the glasses were broken on arrival, and we had to send all the glasses back.
3 My daughter received this game as a gift. My daughter loves the game.
4 This seller has always provided excellent service, and I'm happy to recommend the seller.

c Work in pairs. Read the sentences. What do the pronouns refer to? If the sentence is not clear, replace the pronoun with a noun.

1 I bought a gray jacket online. When it came, I wasn't happy with the quality.
2 I ordered the books for delivery, but they left my zip code off the address label.
3 The tracking information said the package had been sent, but it never arrived.
4 I provided my address and a phone number. The courier said he couldn't find it.

4 Prepare a customer review for something you have bought or about a seller. Use these headings and make notes where relevant. Decide how many stars to give and if you recommend the product or seller.

condition	delivery	fit/quality
item	standard of service	

5 Write your recommendation. Use these questions to check your ad.

- Did you use pronouns clearly?
- Is your feedback useful to other customers?

6 Display your review in the classroom. Read the other reviews and find out if anyone has had a similar shopping experience.

9f Making a deal

In Morocco's oldest market – a souk in Fez

Before you watch

1 Work in pairs. Look at the photo and the caption. Discuss the questions.

1 What's happening in the photo?
2 Why do you think both men are smiling?
3 What kind of things do you think you can buy in the souk?

2 Key vocabulary

a Work in pairs. Read the sentences. The words in bold are used in the video. Guess the meaning of the words.

1 When you buy things on sale, you can often get really good **discounts**.
2 I'm just going to look at the stuff in the market. I have no **intention** of buying anything.
3 We'll need to take two taxis—there are eight of us, and the **maximum** number of passengers is five.
4 The hotel tried to **cheat** us—they charged us for four nights instead of three!
5 The price to rent the bus is **fixed**. It's the same if we have ten people or twenty.

b Match the words in bold in Exercise 2a with these definitions.

a to be dishonest _____
b reductions in price _____
c can't be changed _____
d a plan _____
e the top limit _____

3 Work in pairs. Which is bigger, a half or an eighth? Put the amounts in order of size, (1–5, 5 is smallest).

| a half _____ | a sixth _____ | an eighth _____ |
| a quarter _____ | a third _____ | |

While you watch

4 ◻ 9.1 Watch Part 1 of the video with the sound OFF. Make a note of the things that you see for sale. Make a whole-class list and compare that with your ideas from Exercise 1 question 3.

5 ◻ 9.1, 9.2 Work in pairs. Watch Parts 1 and 2 of the video with the sound ON. Answer the questions.

1 What's the name of the small red hat described in the video?
2 Complete what these people say about bargaining in the souk with words from Exercises 2 and 3.
   a Vincent (Dutch tourist): "You have to start yourself at one _____ or something."
   b Consuela (Dutch tourist): "So, then you get at _____ the price they say at first."
   c Ahmed (Tour guide): "We don't really have a _____ price."
3 What does Mohcine, the jewelry seller, say about some customers?

6 ◻ 9.3 Watch Part 3 of the video. Circle the correct option to complete the answers.

1 What happens if a customer says they don't want to buy anything?
   The seller offers *a lower price / a different item.*
2 What should all tourists make sure they don't do?
   They shouldn't *pay more than something is worth / buy too many things.*

After you watch

7 Work in pairs. How do you think the tourists felt about their experiences in the souk? Give reasons for your answers.

8 Vocabulary in context

a ◻ 9.4 Watch the clips from the video. Choose the correct meaning of the words and phrases.

b Work in pairs. Answer these questions.

1 Do you prefer to take classes online or face-to-face? Why?
2 What is something a visitor to your country should watch out for?
3 What is something you learned how to do step by step?

9 Work in pairs. Do you prefer bargaining or fixed prices? Give your reasons.

---

craftsman (n) /ˈkrɑːftsmən/ someone who makes quality items by hand
dates (n) /deɪts/ a kind of fruit that grows on palm trees
dirham (n) /ˈdɪəˈræm/ the money used in Morocco
haggling (n) /ˈhæglɪŋ/ bargaining, discussing a price to come to an agreement
vendors (n) /ˈvendərz/ sellers

Grammar

1 Complete the shopping tips with articles or quantifiers where necessary. More than one option may be possible.

THE GREEN GUIDE: TELEVISIONS

The days when [1] _____ TVs came in only a [2] _____ of types—color or black and white—are gone. Today's TVs have been developed to give [3] _____ best possible picture quality, with [4] _____ different viewing options that can be set by the user.

Many people get [5] _____ new TV because they want [6] _____ bigger screen. However, bigger TVs use a lot of [7] _____ energy. A 52-inch LCD uses twice the power of a 32-inch model. Last year, new statistics were published by the United States Department of Energy. They said the amount of [8] _____ power used by TVs in America could supply electricity to all homes in [9] _____ state of New York for a year. One major factor in TV power use is the picture setting. [10] _____ people realize what a difference the settings can make. Electricity use can be cut by up to 50 percent if you change to [11] _____ efficient setting.

2 Work in pairs. Read the information in Exercise 1 and find:

1 one positive and one negative thing about modern TVs.
2 one way of reducing the amount of energy your TV uses.

3 **>> MB** Work in pairs. Underline the passive forms in the text in Exercise 1. Why are the passive forms used in the text?

4 **>> MB** Write sentences about some products and their raw materials. Use these verbs in the passive. Then work in pairs. Take turns reading your sentences.

grow	import	make
manufacture	mine	produce

1 a bar of chocolate: cocoa beans Ghana
2 a pair of jeans: cotton Egypt
3 perfume: flowers France
4 cell phone batteries: lithium Chile

A bar of chocolate is made from cocoa beans. Cocoa beans are grown in Ghana.

I CAN	
use the passive	☐
use articles and quantifiers	☐

Vocabulary

5 Work in pairs. What could a salesperson or customer say using each of these words?

delivery	exchange	gift-wrapping
in stock	receipt	return

6 **>> MB** Work in pairs. Take turns giving a definition or example of one of these things for your partner to identify.

budget	checkout	purchases
special offer	on sale	value for money

It's a way you can figure out how much you can afford to spend.

7 **>> MB** Work in pairs. Choose one of the stores in the photos and name six things you can buy there.

I CAN	
talk about shopping	☐
ask for and give product and sales information in a store	☐
talk about things we buy for ourselves and others	☐

Real life

8 Complete the questions and statements. Then write customer (C) or salesperson (S).

1 We accept _____ by card or in cash. ____
2 Can I bring it _____ if I don't like it when I get home? ____
3 Let me see if this model is in _____ . ____
4 How much do you _____ for delivery? ____
5 Do you have the reference _____ ? ____
6 Can I _____ at this watch? ____
7 It's reduced—it's 20 percent _____ . ____
8 Excuse me, do you _____ in this department? ____

9 **>> MB** Work in pairs. Take turns being the customer and the salesperson in a store. Act out conversations in which you buy a tablet, a computer, a motorcycle, and some perfume.

I CAN	
buy and sell items in a store	☐

Unit 10 No limits

In the annual *Marathon des Sables* in southern Morocco, keeping the sand out of your face can be a problem.

FEATURES

118 Leaving Earth

Could we live on another planet?

120 The superhumans

Find out about the latest advances in medicine.

122 Two journeys, two lives

Read about two people who have endured tough experiences.

126 What does an astronaut dream about?

A video about the first British woman in space

1 Work in pairs. Look at the photo and the caption. What other problems do you think runners like this face?

2 ▶ 80 Listen to an excerpt from a podcast about the *Marathon des Sables*. How many of your ideas from Exercise 1 are mentioned?

3 ▶ 80 Listen to the excerpt again and make notes about these things. Does ultrarunning appeal to you? Why or why not?

1 the age of the runners
2 the distances
3 anything else that interested you

4 Work in groups. Discuss the questions.

1 Other extreme sports include bungee jumping, BASE jumping, cave diving, and free climbing. Have you tried any of them?
2 Why do you think people push their bodies to the limit?
3 Can you think of any dangers in pushing your body to extremes?

10a Leaving Earth

Reading

1 Work in pairs. Discuss the questions.

1 Do you think the human race will ever live on another planet?
2 What kinds of things might make life on another planet difficult for humans?

2 Work in pairs. Read the article. Answer the questions.

1 Which planets does the article mention?
2 Where are the planets?
3 Which planet do scientists already know something about?
4 Why is the color blue important when looking at planets?

LEAVING EARTH

▶ 81

Professor Stephen Hawking has said that the human race has no future if it doesn't go into space. The planet we currently know most about is Mars. Two crewless[1] spacecraft have already landed on the surface and have sent a lot of information to scientists on Earth.

But if we sent astronauts to Mars, would they be able to survive? How easy would it be to set up a base? We already know there would be some difficult challenges. Communication with Earth would have a 20-minute delay, food and water would only be provided every few months, and astronauts couldn't go outside the base if they didn't wear a spacesuit. It all sounds more like science fiction than something that might actually happen.

Meanwhile, astronomers are searching for Earth-like planets outside our solar system. They hope to take images of planets in Alpha Centauri, the closest star system to Earth. According to Chris Lintott, an astrophysicist at Oxford University, it would be hugely exciting if we could get images from Alpha Centauri. From only a tiny image, astronomers could figure out the planet's orbit and its size and color. If a planet is blue, this might mean it has water and an atmosphere—and where there's water, there's life.

Of course, getting to such a distant planet is a different question—it makes a trip to Mars sound easy by comparison.

[1]crewless (adj) /'kruːləs/ without any people working on board

3 Work in groups. Do you agree with these online comments about space exploration? Give your reasons.

1 "We can't take care of Earth, so we'll never be successful on another planet."
2 "I don't understand why we need to go into space. We should spend the money on improving life on Earth."

Grammar second conditional

> **SECOND CONDITIONAL**

But **if we sent** astronauts to Mars, **would they be able to** survive?
Astronauts **couldn't go** outside the base **if they didn't wear** a spacesuit.
It **would be** hugely exciting **if we could get** images from Alpha Centauri.

For more information and practice, see page 174.

4 Work in pairs. Look at the grammar box. Answer the questions.

1 Which verb form follows *if* in the second conditional?
2 When is a comma used in a second conditional sentence?
3 Which verbs can be used before the base verb in the main clause?

5 Work in pairs. Look at how the second conditional patterns are used in the article. Answer the questions.

1 Does the second conditional refer to situations in the past or in the present and the future?
2 Does the second conditional refer to real or to hypothetical situations?

6 Complete the comments about space exploration with the second conditional.

1 I _____ (consider) training as an astronaut if I _____ (have) the right qualifications.
2 I _____ (pay) be a space tourist if it _____ (not / be) so expensive.
3 Being in space _____ (be) OK if you _____ (be able to) have Skype chats with people on Earth.
4 Even if we _____ (find) Earth-like planets, we _____ (not / be able to) travel there.
5 If I _____ (be) on a long space journey, I _____ (miss) my family.
6 What _____ (happen) if you _____ (not / get along) well with the rest of the crew on a spacecraft?

7 If you _____ (be) in charge of NASA, what _____ you _____ (spend) money on?
8 If there _____ (be) life on another planet, _____ they _____ (contact) us first?

7 Work in pairs. Look again at the comments in Exercise 6. Say which statements (1–5) you agree with and answer the questions (6–8).

8 Complete the sentences with endings that are true for you. Then work in pairs and compare your sentences.

1 If I were a tourist on a space trip,
   a I'd …
   b I wouldn't …
   c I could …
   d I might …
2 If I lived on a base on Mars,
   a I'd …
   b I wouldn't …
   c I could …
   d I might …

9 Work in two pairs within a group of four. Play a guessing game.

Pair A: Turn to page 153 and follow the instructions.

Pair B: Turn to page 154 and follow the instructions.

Speaking my Life

10 Work on your own. Think of a place you'd like to live. Write down five reasons why you'd like to live there. Then work in groups. Take turns telling your group the reasons, but don't say the place. Can they guess before you give all the reasons?

A: *I'd love to live in _____ . I'd go to all the local soccer games.*
B: *And if I lived in _____ , I'd never be cold again.*

11 Think about your answers to these questions. Then tell the class.

1 If you could start a new life, what things would you change and how?
2 What would you miss about your old life?

10b The superhumans

Listening

1 Work in pairs. Look at the photo. What do you think it shows?

2 ▶ 82 Listen to a preview of a TV program. Check (✓) the topics you hear mentioned.

- ☐ blades and wheelchairs
- ☐ Olympic medals
- ☐ Paralympic athletes
- ☐ progress in medical science
- ☐ a robotic exo-skeleton

3 ▶ 82 Match the beginnings of the sentences (1–6) with the endings (a–f). Then listen again and check.

1 The Paralympics is a sports event for people ____
2 The TV program features some athletes ____
3 A bionic device is one ____
4 Amanda Boxtel uses a robotic structure ____
5 Amanda Boxtel works with an organization ____
6 There's no limit to the things ____

a whose devices are bionic.
b that supports her body.
c bionic devices will be able to do.
d that promotes bionic technology.
e that uses electronics.
f who have a disability.

4 Work in pairs. How do you think life might be different for someone with a bionic device?

Grammar defining relative clauses

> **DEFINING RELATIVE CLAUSES**
>
> **With relative pronouns**
> 1 Tonight, there's **a documentary that features** some famous Paralympians.
>
> **With optional who/that**
> 2 **The Paralympians (who / that) you mentioned** use blades and wheelchairs.
> 3 **The range of devices (that) the program describes** is growing.
>
> For more information and practice, see page 174.

5 Look at the grammar box. Circle the correct option.

1 In sentence 1, *a documentary* is the *subject / object* of the verb *features*.
2 In sentence 2, *the Paralympians* is the *subject / object* of the verb *mentioned*.
3 In sentence 3, *the range of devices* is the *subject / object* of the verb *describes*.
4 When *who* or *that* refers to the *subject / object*, we can leave it out.

6 Look at the sentences in Exercise 3. Find the relative pronouns. Add a relative pronoun to the sentences that don't have them.

7 Look at the diagram of a bionic body. Complete the information for each numbered part with the words in the box. Use two words twice.

when	where	who	that	whose

1 implants in the ears _____ allow people _____ are deaf to hear
2 prosthetic arms _____ can receive signals from the brain
3 temporary artificial hearts for people _____ are waiting for transplants
4 the first replacement hips—from a time _____ bionics was an idea from science fiction
5 healthy area of bone _____ the bionic limb is attached
6 bionic limbs _____ movement mimics the body's natural steps

8 Read the comments from a hospital patient. Write *who* or *that* in the correct place.

1 The doctor I spoke to was very positive. *who*
2 I thought the treatment I got was very good.
3 The injections the nurse gave me didn't hurt much.
4 The other patients I met had similar injuries.
5 The hospital ward I was in had only one other patient.

9 ▶ 83 Cross out any optional words in these sentences. Then listen and check your answers.

1 I know someone who has a bionic arm.
2 The hospital that we go to isn't far away.
3 Cochlear implants are devices that improve hearing.
4 Wheelchairs are often used by patients whose legs are paralyzed.
5 The doctor who we saw in the film is a pioneer in bionics.

10 Pronunciation sentence stress

▶ 83 Listen to the sentences from Exercise 9 again. Notice how the relative pronouns are not stressed. Then listen again and repeat.

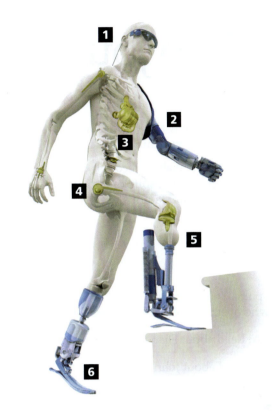

Vocabulary medicine

11 Work in pairs. Circle the correct option.

1 It's just a small cut. It will *treat / heal* naturally.
2 What time is your doctor's *appointment / date*?
3 They can't *cure / heal* this yet, but they can relieve the symptoms.
4 Where does it *hurt / pain*?
5 The *healing / treatment* has some unpleasant side effects.
6 The doctor is *controlling / monitoring* the patient's condition.
7 The injection isn't *hurtful / painful*.

12 Work in groups. Take turns choosing a word and then give a definition of the word.

*Botox is something **that** celebrities use to make themselves look younger.*

surgeon	injection	Botox
operating room	blood test	first aid
paramedic	scan	ambulance
stitches	donor	crutches
surgery	radiographer	ward
X-ray	ER (emergency room)	

Speaking *my*Life

13 Work in pairs. Choose two of the words from Exercise 12 and talk about your own experience.

I've never been in an ambulance.

10c Two journeys, two lives

Reading

1 How much do you know about these people? Circle the option (a–c) you think links them.

a   They broke "unbreakable" records.
b   They were successful in spite of difficulties.
c   They became rich and famous in their chosen careers.

J.K. Rowling	Marie Curie
Nelson Mandela	Stephen Hawking

2 Work in pairs. You are going to read about two people who overcame obstacles in their lives.

Student A: Read about Diane Van Deren.

Student B: Read about John Dau.

Make notes to answer these questions.

1 Who?	4 Distance covered?
2 Where?	5 Time taken?
3 When?	6 Food and drink?

3 Tell your partner about the story you read. Use your notes to help you. Ask your partner at least one question about his or her story.

4 Now read your partner's story. Is the story what you expected to read? Did anything surprise you?

Word focus *take*

5 Look at these excerpts from the stories. What do the expressions with *take* mean or refer to? Circle the correct option (a–c).

1   Diane Van Deren was […] **taking part** in the Yukon Arctic Ultra.
    a leaving   b participating   c winning
2   Van Deren […] had an egg-sized piece of her brain **taken out**.
    a removed   b repaired   c returned
3   […] a journey that had **taken** him **more than half of his life**.
    a distance   b speed   c time
4   Dau […] **took care of** a group of younger children.
    a controlled   b watched over   c played with

6 Work in pairs. What do the expressions with *take* mean in these sentences?

1   The Yukon Arctic Ultra **takes place** every two years.
2   Diane Van Deren **took up** running after an operation to cure her epilepsy.
3   Diane Van Deren couldn't **take off** her boots because they had frozen to her feet.
4   John Dau's plane to New York **took off** from Nairobi airport.

7 Work in pairs. Using the information in the stories and your own understanding of them, discuss the questions with your partner.

1   Why did Diane Van Deren and John Dau begin their journeys?
2   Did they make their journeys through choice or necessity?
3   What have they achieved for themselves and others as a result of their journeys?

Critical thinking reading between the lines

8 Work in pairs. Read the quotes. Who do you think said each one—Diane Van Deren or John Dau? Give your reasons.

1   "I think people refuse to try things because they fear failure."
2   "All I have to think about is my body."
3   "There have been many impossible situations in my life, but I keep trying."
4   "You can't give up."

9 Do you know of other people who have overcome obstacles to achieve something in unexpected ways?

Speaking *my* Life

10 You are nominating an inspirational person for a prize. Choose someone from one of these categories. Make short biographical notes about the person and the reasons why you find him or her inspirational. Then give your presentation.

- art or music
- business
- movies and television
- science and medicine
- sports and adventure
- technology

Diane Van Deren

▶ 84

On February 15, 2009, Diane Van Deren was one of a dozen runners taking part in the Yukon Arctic Ultra, a 700-kilometer race across the frozen Arctic in the middle of winter. Not a single woman had ever completed
5   it. With temperatures of 30 degrees below zero and only seven hours of daylight each day, it's probably the hardest race in the world. But then, there is no woman like Diane Van Deren.

Twelve years earlier, Van Deren, a former professional
10 tennis player, had an egg-sized piece of her brain taken out. It was part of a treatment for epilepsy.[1] The operation was successful, and she noticed an unexpected result: She could run without stopping for hours.

At the start of the Arctic Ultra, icy winds froze Van
15 Deren's water supplies, so she had nothing to drink for the first 160 kilometers. She kept going by sucking on frozen fruit and nut bars. On the eleventh day, the ice beneath her feet cracked open and she fell up to her shoulders into a freezing river. She managed to climb
20 out, but it was hard to continue. Her boots had frozen to her feet.

Somehow, Van Deren remained positive through it all. This was perhaps helped by another curious result of her operation. "I have a problem with short-term memory. I
25 could be out running for two weeks, but if someone told me it was day one of a race," she jokes, "I'd say, 'Great, let's get started!'"

On February 26, 2009—exactly twelve years after her surgery—Van Deren crossed the finish line of the Arctic
30 Ultra. She was one of eight people who finished—and the first and only woman.

[1] **epilepsy** (n) /ˈepɪˌlepsi/ an illness affecting the brain

John Dau

▶ 85

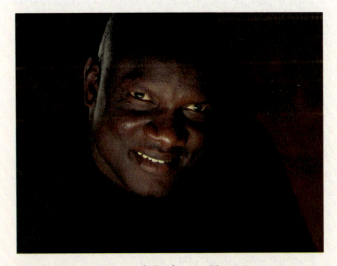

In 2001, John Dau boarded a plane to New York. It was the beginning of one trip but the end of a journey that had taken him more than half of his life. In 1987, aged thirteen, Dau had run away from his home in southern
5   Sudan, escaping from the soldiers who came to destroy his village. He met up with a small group of boys like himself, and together they walked for weeks to reach a refugee camp[2] in Ethiopia. "I had no shoes and no clothes; at night, the desert was so cold. We thought
10 about our parents all the time," remembers Dau. The boys had no food and nothing to drink. "We chewed grass and ate mud to stay alive."

The boys walked by night and slept by day. Eventually they reached the camp, where Dau spent the next four
15 years. As one of the older boys, Dau led and took care of a group of younger children that eventually numbered 1,200. But Dau was forced to run again when soldiers came to the camp. Along with 27,000 other boys, he set off to walk back to Sudan. To get there, they had to
20 cross the Gilo River. "Soldiers were shooting at us, so we had to dive into water full of crocodiles," Dau recounts. Thousands of boys were killed or caught, and only 18,000 of them arrived in Sudan. But the area was soon attacked again, so Dau and the other "Lost Boys" of
25 Sudan set off south again, this time to a camp in Kenya. By now, Dau had walked more than 1,600 kilometers.

Ten years later, Dau was one of a handful of "Lost Boys" who were sponsored to study in the USA. A new kind of journey was about to begin.

[2] **refugee camp** (n) /ˌrefjʊˈdʒiː kæmp/ a temporary home for people who have left their country of origin

10d First aid

Vocabulary injuries

1 Work in pairs. Complete the chart with the things that cause these injuries. Some things can cause more than one kind of injury. Add at least one more cause of each injury.

Cuts and bruises	Sprains and breaks	Allergic reactions

1 blades and knives	4 insect bites
2 falling off something	5 tripping
3 falling down	6 wasp and bee stings

2 With your partner, decide what is the best treatment for each injury in the chart.

Real life talking about injuries

3 ▶ 86 Work in pairs. Look at the expressions for describing injuries. Which expressions do you think refer to the injuries in Exercise 1? Then listen to three conversations and check.

> ▶ **TALKING ABOUT INJURIES**
>
> **Describing injuries**
> I feel kind of sick.   It's just a sprain.
> I got stung.   It's painful.
> It doesn't hurt.   That looks nasty!
> It hurts when I move it.   You might have broken
> It looks kind of swollen.   something.
> It might need stitches.   It's nothing.
>
> **Giving advice**
> If I were you, I'd go to the emergency room. ____
> I would keep an eye on it. ____
> I wouldn't just ignore it. ____
> You should put some antihistamine cream on it. ____
> You'd better clean it right away. ____
> Why don't you go and see Rosana? ____
> It might be worth getting it X-rayed. ____
> It's probably best to get it looked at. ____
> Have you tried putting cream on it? ____

4 ▶ 86 Listen to the three conversations again. What advice is given in each case? Write 1, 2, or 3 next to each piece of advice.

5 Pronunciation *and*

a ▶ 87 Listen to these expressions. Notice how *and* is not stressed.

cuts and bruises	bites and stuff
sprains and breaks	go and see Rosana
wasp and bee stings	

b ▶ 87 Listen to the expressions again. Notice how *and* is linked to the word before it and how the *d* isn't pronounced. Repeat the expressions.

c Match words from A with words from B. Practice saying the pairs of words.

A
day	doctors	eyes	food
fruit	hands	mind	rich

B
body	drink	ears	famous
knees	night	nurses	nuts

6 Work as a class. You will be assigned a role as a patient or a doctor.

Patients: Choose one of the injuries from the box below. Visit each doctor and describe your problem.
Who gives the best advice?

Doctors: Listen to each patient and give advice. Which is the most difficult case to treat?

> a deep cut on your thumb from a kitchen knife
> a painful ankle after jumping off a trampoline
> feeling sick after being stung by a wasp
> cuts and bruises after a biking accident
> strange skin rash after eating at a restaurant
> neck and shoulder pain after a horse-riding accident

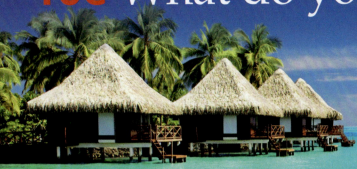

10e What do you think?

Writing a personal email

1 Who do you talk to when you need advice about these things? Work in pairs. Compare your ideas.

> car trouble   personal or relationship problems
> health worries   difficulties at work or school

2 Read the email. What is the writer's purpose? Circle the best option (a–c). What advice would you give Kate?

a   to ask for information about a job opportunity
b   to get in touch with an old friend
c   to ask for some help making a decision

> Hi there,
>
> Thanks so much for the get well card! I'm feeling a lot better now, actually. And I've been meaning to write to you for a while—I want your advice about something.
>
> I have the chance to spend a year away, on a project in the South Pacific. (I know, it sounds like paradise—I bet you wish you were me!) It's a job in a community health clinic on Vanuatu. I'd have to do some training if I took the position, of course. I can do basic first aid, but I'd need to know more than that.
>
> The thing is, I'm not sure if I should go. It would mean giving up the job I have now, obviously. But I wouldn't mind that—it's not a great job! And I've often thought about a career in nursing …
>
> So what do you think?
>
> Hope all is well with you. By the way, did you manage to sell your car?
>
> Take care,
>
> Kate

3 Is the style of the email formal, neutral, or informal? Underline the words or expressions that show this.

4 Writing skill linking ideas

a Look at the chart. Each group of words can link ideas in the same way. Use the highlighted words from the email to complete the chart.

1	clearly naturally	_____ _____
2	in fact to be honest	_____
3	Before I forget, Incidentally,	_____
4	Anyway, Well,	_____
5	All the same, Even so, However,	_____

b Complete the sentences with expressions from Exercise 4a. Remember to add a comma where necessary. More than one answer is possible.

1   Your problem sounds familiar. I had to make a similar decision once, _____ .
2   It's a long way to go. You'd miss your family at first, _____ .
3   I hope I've helped you a little! _____ how's your sister?
4   That's what I did. _____ I hope I've been of some help.
5   It could be interesting. _____ it's going to be difficult.

5 Think about a problem you need help with. Write an email to someone in your class.

6 Use these questions to check your email. Then send your email to the person you have chosen.

- Have you used a variety of linking expressions?
- Have you used linking expressions correctly?

7 Write a reply to the email you have received.

10f What does an astronaut dream about?

Helen Sharman, the first British astronaut to go into space

The Mir space station

Before you watch

1 Work in pairs. What do you think astronauts might dream about?

2 Key vocabulary

a Work in pairs. Read the sentences. The words in bold are used in the video. Guess the meaning of the words.

1 The best part of being a flight attendant is the great **crewmates** I get to work with.
2 Stones don't **float** on water, but pieces of wood usually do.
3 Since I left home, the thing I **miss** most is my dad's cooking. He makes great pizza!
4 I've visited China so many times, and have a lot of friends there. I feel really **connected** to the country.
5 We'd read amazing reviews of the movie, and when we saw it, we weren't **disappointed**. It was fantastic.

b Match the words in bold in Exercise 2a with these definitions.

a to move slowly on the surface of water or in air _____
b members of a team on a ship, plane, or spacecraft _____
c to feel sad about things or people you aren't with now _____
d feeling unhappy with something that wasn't as good as you'd hoped _____
e linked or associated with a thing, place, or person _____

While you watch

3 ◁[10.1] Work in pairs. Watch Part 1 of the video. What do you think astronaut Helen Sharman dreams about?

4 ◁[10.1] Watch Part 1 of the video again. Circle the correct option.

1 She dreams about *the liftoff from Earth / being in space*.
2 She floats toward *a door / a window*.
3 She *sees / doesn't see* the stars.
4 Sergei and her other crewmates *are / aren't* in the dream.
5 She *looks out of / wants to leave through* the window.

5 ◁[10.2] Watch Part 2 of the video. Complete the sentences with one word.

1 Everyone says the Earth looks _____ .
2 Helen Sharman felt disconnected and _____ to the Earth.
3 She knew it was her _____ .
4 She wanted to _____ .

6 ◁[10.3] Work in pairs. Watch Part 3 of the video. Answer the questions.

1 Astronauts talk about different things at the start of a space trip and after a couple of days. What do they talk about?
2 What do they think about when they go over different countries?

7 ◁[10.4] Work in pairs. How do you think Helen Sharman feels when she wakes up? Watch Part 4 of the video and check your ideas.

After you watch

8 Work in pairs. Compare your personal reactions to the video. Do you think the animation went well with Helen Sharman's words? Did anything surprise you? What was the overall message for you?

9 Vocabulary in context

a ◁[10.5] Watch the clips from the video. Choose the correct meaning of the words and phrases.

b Complete the sentences in your own words. Then work in pairs and compare your sentences.

1 I only … on the odd occasion.
2 I don't think that … has anything to do with a person's success.
3 If you asked me … , my response would be "absolutely!"
4 On a cold night, it's nice to feel the warmth of …
5 I find it hard to … and … at the same time.
6 It's best to tell someone gently if …

10 Work in small groups. Discuss the questions.

1 How often do you dream?
2 Do you usually have dreams or nightmares?
3 Do you remember your dreams?
4 Some people say dreams have meanings. Do you know of any common interpretations?
5 What do you think of the idea of interpreting dreams?

UNIT 10 REVIEW AND MEMORY BOOSTER

Grammar

1 Look at the photo of BASE jumping. Complete the comments about the activity with the second conditional.

1 You _____ absolutely terrified if it _____ the first time you did this. (feel / be)

2 If I _____ to the top of the cliff, I definitely _____ off. (get / jump)

3 If you _____ the last person left on the cliff top, _____ you _____ and go back? (be / turn around)

4 I _____ do this if you _____ me there. (not be able to / take)

5 You _____ yourself if something _____ wrong. (can kill / go)

6 If I _____ over the edge, I _____ sick. (look / feel)

2 Work in pairs. Read the comments again. Which ones do you agree with?

3 >> MB Work in pairs. For each of these things, agree on a definition and an example. Then compare with another pair.

1 an adrenaline junkie
2 bravery
3 a dangerous place
4 extreme sports
5 a life-threatening situation

I CAN
talk about improbable situations in the present or the future (second conditional)
give descriptions or definitions of things that include essential information (defining relative clauses)

4 >> MB Work in pairs. Discuss reasons for and against making BASE jumping illegal in the place in the photo. Use terms from Exercise 3. What's your conclusion?

Vocabulary

5 Complete the sentences with one word. The first letter is given.

1 This cut on my finger is taking forever to h_____ .

2 These machines m_____ the patient's condition.

3 The treatment is uncomfortable, but it's not p_____ .

4 Has she made an a_____ to see the doctor?

5 Ouch, this bright sunlight h_____ my eyes!

6 Doctors t_____ several people for burns after the fire.

6 >> MB Work in pairs. Answer the questions in your own words.

1 How might you sprain your ankle?
2 What would you do if a bee stung you?
3 What kind of things are people allergic to?
4 Have you ever broken a bone?
5 Do you know anyone who is afraid of injections?
6 How serious is food poisoning?

I CAN
talk about the body and injuries
talk about medicine and emergency medical treatments

Real life

7 Circle the correct option. Then decide what injury or illness each piece of advice could refer to.

1 You should *get / getting* an X-ray.
2 You'd better *call / calling* an ambulance.
3 It might be worth *go / going* to the doctor.
4 Have you tried *take / taking* antihistamines?
5 If I were you, I'd *put / putting* some cream on it.

8 >> MB Work in pairs. Act out two conversations using advice from Exercise 7.

I CAN
describe injuries and give first-aid advice

Unit 11 Connections

This woman speaks Koro, a language that has just been identified by linguists.

FEATURES

130 Uncontacted tribes

How a viral video revealed a controversial story

132 Sending a message

What's the best way to get your message across?

134 Spreading the news

An article about the impact of social networks

138 Can you read my lips?

A video about what it's like to have difficulty hearing

1 Work in pairs. Look at the photo and the caption. Which of these parts of a news website do you think this photo would appear in?

business section	homepage
celebrity news	national news
comment and analysis	politics and society
current affairs	sports section
entertainment	technology
features	world news

2 Work in pairs. Read the comments about the news. Think of at least two ways to complete each comment.

1 "I get the headlines direct to my phone so that …"
2 "I don't usually click on headlines unless …"
3 "I don't believe everything I read because …"
4 "I sometimes send a story to friends if …"

3 ▶ 88 Listen to four people answering questions about the news. Compare their comments with your ideas from Exercise 2.

4 Work in pairs. Look at the Track 88 audioscript on page 188. Add two more questions to the four questions in the audioscript. Then work on your own and ask at least three other people your questions. Compare your results.

11a Uncontacted tribes

Reading

1 Work in groups. Look at the title and the photo. Discuss the questions.

1 What do you think the photo shows?
2 In which parts of the world would you expect to find uncontacted tribes?

2 Work in pairs. Read the article. What kind of organization is:

1 FUNAI?
2 *Survival*?
3 *Science*?

3 Work in pairs. Find this information in the article.

1 what happened when the photos were published
2 what Survival and *Science* disagree about
3 who has had experience with contacting isolated tribes
4 who has collected information about isolated tribes for many years
5 what kind of life the Awá man had in the forest

4 Work in pairs. Read the Awá man's comments at the end of the article. Do you think he agrees with *Science* or with Survival? Give your reasons. Who do you agree with?

One of the world's last uncontacted tribes

Uncontacted TRIBES

▶ 89

Some years ago, the Brazilian department for Indian affairs (FUNAI) published photos of an uncontacted Amazonian tribe. FUNAI said that the tribe was under threat from exploitation[1] of the Amazonian forest. Around the same time, a documentary showed video of the same tribe. The photos went viral, leading to a reaction worldwide. Many online commentators asked what was being done to save the tribe. Some people also asked if contact with the outside world was actually a bad thing.

Several years after the viral video, the subject was still controversial. An article in the magazine *Science* said that it was possible to contact isolated[2] Amazonian tribes safely. However, the NGO[3] Survival disagreed. It quoted Sydney Possuelo, a former head of FUNAI who was talking about his experience with these tribes. He said that originally he had believed it would be possible to make safe contact and that he had organized one of the best prepared attempts

at contact. He said at the time that he wouldn't let a single Indian die. "But," he said, "when the contact came, the diseases arrived, the Indians died."

The authors of the article in *Science* said that isolated tribes aren't viable[4] in the long term. However, FUNAI said that the populations of the tribes they had been monitoring via satellite images had increased over a 30-year period.

Speaking to Survival, an Awá man from Brazil's north-eastern Amazon said that when he'd lived in the forest, he'd had a good life. If he met one of the uncontacted tribes, he'd tell them that "there's nothing in the outside for you."

[1]**exploitation** (n) /ˌeksplɔɪˈteɪʃn/ the unfair use of someone for another person's benefit
[2]**isolated** (adj) /ˈaɪsəˌleɪtɪd/ apart from others, alone
[3]**NGO** (n) abbreviation of nongovernmental organization
[4]**viable** (adj) /ˈvaɪəbl/ able to be successful

Grammar reported speech

5 Look at the grammar box. Circle the actual words (direct speech) the people used. What has changed in the reported speech?

1 FUNAI said, "The tribe *is / was* under threat."
2 He said, "I *won't let / wouldn't let* a single Indian die."
3 FUNAI said, "The populations *have increased / had increased* over the last 30 years."
4 Commentators asked, "What *is being done / was being done* to save the tribe?"
5 People asked, "*Is / Was* contact with the outside world a bad thing?"

6 Work in pairs. Look at this sentence from the article. Circle the correct option.

> The authors of the article in *Science* said that isolated tribes aren't viable in the long term.

When we report words that are still true at the time of reporting, we *need to / don't need to* change the verb form.

7 Write the direct speech as reported speech, changing the tenses correctly. Make changes to the pronouns and time expressions as necessary.

1 The camera operator said, "I've been filming from a plane this morning."
2 The camera operator said, "We didn't speak to the people in the video."
3 The FUNAI spokesperson said, "We'll publish the photos tomorrow."
4 The FUNAI spokesperson said, "A million people have seen these photos in only three days."
5 A viewer asked, "How long did it take to make the film?"
6 Several viewers asked, "Can I watch the video online?"
7 The spokesperson said, "The movie is being shown tonight."
8 The interviewer asked, "Will you go back again next year?"

8 Read about the first contact some tribes had with outsiders. Complete the text with the correct form of the verbs for reported speech.

In the Survival video *Stranger in the Forest*, tribal people of Brazil spoke of their experiences of first contact. One man said that his father [1] _____ (make) friends with three outsiders and then he [2] _____ (become) sick. Another man explained that they [3] _____ (never have) contact with diseases like measles or malaria before—although there [4] _____ (be) diseases in the forest, they [5] _____ (not kill) people. He said a lot of useful knowledge about forest life [6] _____ (be) lost because older tribespeople [7] _____ (die). The final speaker said that his tribe [8] _____ (be suffering) as a result of contact with outsiders and asked the filmmakers how they [9] _____ (can stop) this from happening.

Speaking and writing myLife

9 You are going to act out a news item. Work in two pairs within a group of four.

Pair A: Turn to page 153 and follow the instructions.

Pair B: Turn to page 154 and follow the instructions.

10 Work in your group again. Act out the dialog. Then write a short news story about what happened to the other pair.

11 Compare your report with the original news item.

11b Sending a message

Novice monks smile as they pose
for a New Year's photo, Bodh Gaya, India.

Vocabulary communications technology

1 Work in pairs. Which of these things do you use? Which apps or companies do you prefer for each one?

instant messaging	social media
search engines	video messaging

2 Work in pairs. Complete the questions in your own words. Then ask and answer the questions.

1 Do you follow anyone on _____ ?
2 Do you know how to upload videos to _____ ?
3 Do you prefer calling or _____ your friends?
4 Do you take many _____ ?

Listening

3 Work in pairs. Read the headlines. What do you think the stories are about? Write one sentence for each headline.

a Firm fires workers by text

b YouTube or "UFO-tube"?

c How to enjoy tomorrow's eclipse of the sun

d Email alert warns of traffic chaos

e Tweet your way around the world

4 ▶ 90 Listen to four conversations about the headlines. Write the number of the conversation next to the headline. There is one extra headline.

5 ▶ 90 Listen to the conversations again. Circle the correct option (a–c).

1 The journalist asks her followers ____ .
   a to meet her for breakfast
   b to send in photos
   c to suggest things to do
2 The website reminds readers ____ .
   a not to bookmark the eclipse page
   b not to use telescopes
   c to check the weather
3 The company told people ____ .
   a not to show up for work
   b not to use text messages
   c to come to work early on Monday
4 The politician has invited aliens ____ .
   a to come to his house
   b to come to a meeting
   c to watch his video

Grammar reporting verbs

6 Work in pairs. Look at the grammar box. Then answer the questions.

1 Underline the reporting verbs in the sentences in Exercise 5. How many verbs are there?
2 What follows the reporting verbs in the sentences in Exercise 5—a verb, a noun, or the word *that*?
3 Which verb form is used for the reported words?

7 Match the words in these sentences with the reporting verbs in the grammar box. Then write sentences reporting what the people said.

1 Dalia to Amy: "Don't forget to turn off your phone."
   Dinah reminded Amy to turn off her phone.
2 Joseph to Dalia: "Can you set up my email account?"
3 Amy to Joseph: "Come and watch the movie on our new TV."
4 Dalia to Amy: "Plug in the battery charger first."
5 Joseph to Dalia: "I can put those photos on the computer for you."
6 Amy to Joseph: "Don't worry. I'll turn it off when I'm finished."

8 Read the reported comments. Write the actual words the people used.

1 Dalia invited me to join her group online.
2 I asked Dalia to send me a link with the address.
3 I reminded Joseph to sign out of his account.
4 Dalia offered to help me set up my email accounts.
5 I told Joseph to delete the tweet.
6 Joseph promised to upload the video for me.

9 Look at the Track 90 audioscript on page 188. Underline reported thoughts with the verbs *realize, think, wonder,* and *know.*

10 Pronunciation contrastive stress

a ▶ 91 Listen to these exchanges from two of the conversations in Exercise 4. Notice how the words in bold are stressed. Repeat the exchanges.

1 A: It's a great idea to use social media for something like that.
   B: I didn't realize social media could actually be useful for **anything**!
2 C: It says here there's an eclipse tomorrow. Did you know?
   D: Tomorrow? I thought it was **today**.

b ▶ 92 Listen to four other exchanges. Repeat the exchanges.

Speaking 〔*my*Life〕

11 Think of an offer, an invitation, a promise, and a request for other people in the class. Write each one on a piece of paper. Make sure you include your name and the name of the other person.

from Francesca: I'll help Belinda upload her video.

12 Work in pairs. Exchange your pieces of paper. Then find the people and report what your partner said. Then report each person's reaction to your partner.

A: *Hi, Belinda. Francesca **has offered to help** you **upload** your video.*
B: *Oh, great!*

11c Spreading the news

Reading

1 Work in pairs. How many different things do you use your phone for?

2 Work in pairs. Are you familiar with these terms? What do you think they mean? Read the article quickly and underline the terms. Check your ideas.

internet access	community journalism
the digital divide	traditional media
media organizations	affordable technology

3 Read the article again. Find information about these things. Compare with your partner.

1 internet access in different places
2 cell phone ownership in different places
3 *HablaGuate*
4 *CGNet Swara*

4 Work in pairs. Answer the questions using information from the article.

1 What kind of technology is used by the community journalism projects described?
2 What kind of news stories don't usually appear in traditional news media?
3 What happens to the stories received by *CGNet Swara* before they are shared?
4 How successful is *CGNet Swara*?

5 Work in pairs. Find how these words are used in the article and decide if they are adjectives, nouns, or verbs. Then try to think of another word that could replace them.

1 rural (line 6)
2 enables (line 28)
3 links (line 30)
4 debate (line 31)
5 highlighting (line 54)
6 issue (line 54)

6 Look at how the words in bold are used in these sentences. Which words in Exercise 5 have a similar meaning? You may need to change the form of the word.

1 Living in a small **country** village, we are a long way from the city. _____
2 Our class is going to **discuss** the main ideas of the film we watched today. _____
3 There are some serious environmental **problems** around the factory. _____
4 The highway **connects** the two cities. _____
5 The news reports **emphasize** the fact that nobody was hurt in the accident. _____
6 There's a bus twice a day that **makes it possible for** us to get to school. _____

7 Work in pairs. How is the community journalism described in the article different from traditional local journalism?

Critical thinking opinions

8 Work in pairs. Look at the question in the title of the article again. Do you think the writer successfully answers this question?

9 Read these excerpts from the article. The writer is expressing her opinion. Which words or phrases tell you this? What is her opinion in each case?

1 It seems clear that the digital divide is also a problem for media organizations.
2 Obviously, this has great benefits for rural communities.
3 Clearly, community journalism works.

10 Underline two places in the article where the author gives the opinion or view of other people. What two phrases does she use to introduce the opinion or view?

11 Which sentence (a–c) best summarizes the writer's view of the digital divide?

a The digital divide is a problem that needs to be solved as soon as possible.
b The digital divide doesn't exist any more, since so many people have cell phones.
c The digital divide has resulted in successful alternative ways of connecting communities.

Speaking *my* Life

12 Work in two pairs within a group of four. You are going to find out about new apps for phones.

Pair A: Turn to page 153 and follow the instructions.

Pair B: Turn to page 154 and follow the instructions.

13 Tell the other students in your group about the most useful apps on your phone. Which one do you use most?

SPREADING the news

Can we overcome the digital divide?

Men in Kyrgyzstan using their cell phones

▶ 93

These days, the popular view is that we're all connected, all of the time, by the internet. But are we? On the one hand, we have people who live in cities. In many cities around the world, internet access is close to 100 percent. On the other hand, we have those who live in rural areas. Even in richer countries, the number of rural households with internet access is much less than 100 percent. And in some rural areas of India, for example, it's less than one percent. This situation is what is known as the digital divide—the gap between those who have and those who don't have the communications technology that gives them easy access to information. It seems clear that the digital divide is also a problem for media organizations.

Fortunately, lack of internet access doesn't always mean that people can't connect to the wider world. That's because there is one type of technology that over three billion people do have access to—the cell phone. And the great advantage of cell phones is that you don't need the internet to use them. Cell phones connect people to their friends and family, but they can also help to connect communities. In fact, a new type of community journalism can exist thanks to cell phone technology.

Let's look at Guatemala—a country of fifteen million people with twenty-two million registered cell phones. Guatemalan journalist Kara Andrade developed a project, *HablaGuate*, that enables people to send their stories to a community website from their cell phones. *HablaGuate* links communities, making it easier to debate and participate in the kind of local issues that don't usually make headlines in the traditional media. Obviously, this has great benefits for rural communities. Following its success in Guatemala, Andrade adapted the idea for other countries in Central America. As she says, affordable technology—like cell phones—enables people to become active in local affairs that affect their lives.

Halfway across the world, another journalist had a similar idea. Shubhranshu Choudhary used to report for the BBC in his home country, India. According to Choudhary, the best people to report on local issues are local people. He set up *CGNet Swara*, a current affairs network based around news sent on cell phones. Since 2010, more than three hundred thousand stories have been sent to the network, of which about five thousand have been fact-checked and shared. To listen to the stories, users call the number of the network and choose an option on a menu. For example, one story was from a man who reported that elephants were causing problems for his village. Another audio clip was from a woman who called in with the news that a local company had finally paid its workers the wages they were owed. This was a direct result of her previous story highlighting the issue. What's more, the national media are now featuring some of the stories from *CGNet Swara*.

Clearly, community journalism works. And although the digital divide may be a problem for more traditional media organizations, some local communities have found ways of overcoming it.

11d Can I take a message?

Real life telephone language

1 ▶ 94 Listen to two telephone calls. Note down the information.

1 Who is the call for?
2 Who is the call from?
3 What is the call about?

2 ▶ 94 Look at the expressions for telephone messages. Listen to the telephone calls again. Check (✔) the expressions the speakers use.

> ▶ **TELEPHONE LANGUAGE**
>
> **Introductions**
> This is a message for Anna Price. ____
> Could I speak to Jess Parker, please? ____
> Is Jess there? ____
> Can I take a message? ____
> I wonder whether I could leave a message. ____
>
> **Message content**
> Can you ask her to call me? ____
> It's about the apartment. ____
> I'm returning her call. ____
> I'd like to speak to her as soon as possible. ____
>
> **Caller's details**
> My number is 96235601. ____
> Can I have your name, please? ____
> Who's calling? ____
>
> **Endings**
> I'll try to call you later. ____
> I'll call back. ____
> I'll let her know that you called. ____
> She'll get back to you. ____

3 ▶ 95 Work in pairs. Listen to the conversations about the phone calls. Answer the questions.

1 Who is going to call Roger back?
2 How many messages does the secretary give Jess?

4 Pronunciation polite requests with *can* and *could*

a ▶ 96 Listen to four requests. Notice how the speaker's voice rises at the end in order to sound polite.

b Work in pairs. Practice making requests with *can* and *could* and these ideas.

1 give me your name / number / address
2 leave my name / number / address
3 ask him/her to call me back / get in touch / give me a call
4 make an appointment
5 stop by

5 Work in pairs. You are going to leave a message for someone in your class. Use the expressions for telephone messages to help you.

Student A: Choose a classmate (Student C). Decide what your message is. Call Student B and leave the message for Student C.

Student B: Take the message for Student C.

Then change roles and repeat the telephone call.

6 Work in a new pair with the classmate you took the message for. Give this person the message.

11e A point of view

Writing an opinion essay

1 Work in pairs. Look at the title of the essay. Discuss the question and make notes on at least two reasons to support your answer.

2 Work in pairs. Read the essay and answer the questions.

1 Do you agree with the writer of the essay?
2 Does the essay include the ideas you had in Exercise 1?
3 What (other) ideas does the essay include?

DOES THE INTERNET MAKE IT EASIER FOR PEOPLE TO **KEEP IN TOUCH?**

1 These days, there are many different apps that allow you to communicate with other people. I think this makes it easier to stay in touch with friends and family, and also to make new friends.

2 Firstly, many people now have constant access to the internet via smartphones as well as tablets and PCs. This means that if you send someone a message, they will see it right away. I think that you stay in touch more easily when you can communicate quickly.

3 In addition, there are lots of different apps available. For example, you can share photos, videos, and links with people as well as text messages. It's also very easy to have video chats. You can do all of these things either for a small charge or completely for free. Some people say it's not "real" conversation, but I disagree. In my opinion, it's the same as writing letters used to be.

4 To sum up, I believe that the number of apps on the internet and the low cost make it very easy to keep in touch with people.

3 Writing skill essay structure

a Match the functions (a–d) with the paragraphs (1–4).

a additional opinions / other opinions / examples _____
b concluding statement referring to the ideas in the essay _____
c general statement and short response to the title _____
d statement to support your response _____

b Write the words and expressions from the essay that are used for these functions.

Starting a paragraph	
Giving your opinion	
Contrasting opinions	
Giving examples	

4 Work in pairs. You're going to prepare an essay with four paragraphs. Choose one essay title. Write the introduction (paragraph 1) together. Make notes and decide which ideas can go in paragraphs 2 and 3.

- Do people spend too much time online these days?
- Is it a good idea to have one day a week off the internet?
- Do children under the age of ten need cell phones?

5 Work on your own. Write paragraphs 2 and 3 to follow your introduction. Then write the concluding paragraph. Use expressions from Exercise 3b.

6 Use these questions to check your essay. Then exchange your essay with a new partner.

- Have you organized your essay correctly?
- Is your opinion clearly expressed?
- Have you used expressions from Exercise 3b correctly?

7 Work in pairs. Ask your new partner about one thing he or she wrote in their essay.

11f Can you read my lips?

Learning sign language at school

Before you watch

1 Work in groups. Why do people use these three things? How much do you know about them?

1 a hearing aid
2 sign language
3 lip-reading

2 Key vocabulary

a Work in pairs. Read the sentences. The words in bold are used in the video. Guess the meaning of the words.

1 We used to play the same games every **recess** when I was a kid.
2 The art exhibition was also an **auditory** experience, because each room had different music playing.
3 This note from Jim isn't very **legible**—I can't figure out what he wrote.
4 Some children **mumble** because they are too shy to speak loudly in front of the class.
5 Some people don't accept the concept of climate change, but I don't think it's hard to **grasp**.
6 We had to **wade** across a river, but luckily nobody fell in.

b Match the words in bold in Exercise 2a with these definitions.

a describing sounds and hearing _____
b a period of play between lessons at school _____
c to walk with difficulty through something wet _____
d to understand something that seems difficult _____
e written clearly enough to be understood _____
f to speak too quietly and not clearly enough to be understood _____

While you watch

3 **■ 11.1** Work in pairs. Watch Part 1 of the video. Discuss what you think the video is demonstrating.

4 **■ 11.2** Watch Part 2 of the video. Write down the things that can make lip-reading difficult. Compare your answers with the class.

5 **■ 11.3** Watch Part 3 of the video. Answer the questions.

1 Does Rachel Kolb prefer to lip-read or to sign?
2 What does she say happens when lip-reading works well for her?

6 **■ 11.3** Watch Part 3 again. What is the girl, Rachel Kolb, saying at the end of the video?

After you watch

7 Work in pairs. What did you learn from this video?

8 Vocabulary in context

a **■ 11.4** Watch the clips from the video. Choose the correct meaning of the words and phrases.

b Answer the questions in your own words. Then work in pairs and compare your answers.

1 Can you remember a time when something clicked for you?
2 How does it feel to launch into an explanation of something, then realize you don't really understand it?
3 Being successful in life isn't a given. Do you agree with this statement?

9 **■ 11.5** Work in small groups. Watch part of the video again. What do you think the girl is signing? Take turns telling the group about something that has happened to you recently using only signs. How successful are you?

10 Look at the signs below. Practice spelling your name.

11 Work in pairs. Take turns spelling words for your partner to guess.

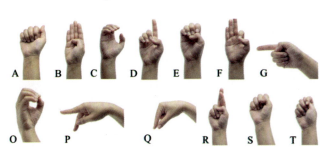

Grammar

1 Work in pairs. Underline six reporting verbs in the article below. Change the reported speech to direct speech.

Worries over lives lived online

The executive chairman of Google, Eric Schmidt, once said that there were only two states for children: "asleep or online." Recent studies claimed that vulnerable young people could become addicted to the online world and be unable to cope with the challenges of the real world. One study reported that many teenagers used social media late into the night, damaging their sleep. The study said this would increase the risk of anxiety and depression in teenagers. Teenagers who tried "unplugging" for a week told researchers that they had enjoyed the break, but they were worried about conversations they had missed. Meanwhile, some organizations asked why the government wasn't looking at ways of educating young people more on this matter.

2 Work in pairs. Read the article again. Answer the questions.

1 What are the main risks associated with being online for young people?
2 How did some teenagers feel when they didn't go online for a week?

3 >> MB Work in pairs. Tell your partner about three stories you have read or heard recently in the news. Say:

- where you read or heard the stories.
- why you remember them.
- what people involved in the stories said.

I CAN	
report people's words (reported speech)	
use appropriate verbs to report people's words (reporting verbs)	

Vocabulary

4 Work in pairs. Give an example of the kind of story you would read about in these sections of a news website.

1 business section
2 celebrity news
3 entertainment
4 home page
5 national news
6 politics and society
7 sports section
8 world news

5 Match the beginnings of the sentences (1–4) with the endings (a–d).

1 I usually text _____
2 I've never followed _____
3 It's really easy to upload _____
4 My friend takes _____

a anyone on Twitter.
b my friends because it's quicker than calling them.
c photos of all her meals with her phone!
d videos these days.

6 >> MB Work in pairs. What do you think are the most common ways of staying in touch with these groups of people? Why?

ex-work colleagues	immediate family
friends	old school friends
grandparents	people you met on vacation

I CAN	
talk about news media	
talk about communications technology	

Real life

7 Work in pairs. Put the sentences from one half of a telephone conversation (a–d) into a logical order. Then act out the conversation, adding the other person's words.

_____ a It's about the books he ordered. He asked me to call him.
_____ b OK. Well, could I leave a message?
_____ c Yes. He can reach me at 555–6481 until about five this afternoon.
_____ d Is Adam Meyer there, please?

I CAN	
leave, take, and pass on telephone messages	

Unit 12 Experts

Sheep in the Scottish Hebrides islands

FEATURES

142 The man who ate his boots

Looking back at the mistakes of some British explorers

144 Experts in the wild

Listen to two stories about unexpected trouble.

146 The legacy of the samurai

Find out about Japan's famous warriors.

150 Shark vs. octopus

A video about an encounter between a shark and an octopus

1 Work in groups. Look at the photo and the caption. What do you think the man's job is? What is he doing?

2 ▶ 97 Listen to an interview with a farmer from the Hebrides. Check your ideas from Exercise 1.

3 ▶ 97 Can you remember the answers to the interviewer's questions? Listen to the interview again and check.

1 Why do you need to move the sheep like this?
2 When do you bring them back?

4 Work in groups. Can you figure out the solution to this farmer's problem? When you're finished, check the answer on page 155.

A farmer has a fox, a chicken, and a bag of grain. He needs to cross a river. He has a boat, but he can only carry one other thing with him in the boat. Remember that foxes eat chickens, and chickens eat grain. How does he get everything across the river?

Reading

1 You are going to read a review of a book about Arctic expeditions called *The Man Who Ate His Boots*. Work in pairs. Discuss the questions.

1 What kind of environment is the Arctic region?
2 What might go wrong on an expedition to the Arctic?
3 How much do you know about the lifestyles of people who live in the Arctic?

2 Read the first paragraph of the book review. Work in pairs. Find the following information.

1 the reason for the British expeditions
2 what happened to the expeditions in the end
3 two words to describe the British explorers

3 Read the whole review. Are these sentences true (T) or false (F)?

1 The British explorers learned a lot   T   F
  from the local Inuit people they met.
2 Tents were an appropriate type of   T   F
  shelter for Arctic conditions.
3 The British wore adequate clothing   T   F
  for the weather in the Arctic.
4 The British pulled their own sleds   T   F
  rather than use dog teams.
5 The British used fresh vegetables   T   F
  to treat scurvy.

4 What do you think the title of the book refers to? Tell your partner.

▶ 98

The Man Who Ate His Boots is a fascinating account of expeditions that went wrong. The book tells the story of the nineteenth-century British search for a route to Asia via the Arctic (the Northwest Passage). Author Anthony Brandt describes many attempts by both land and sea that ended in failure and tragedy, including the 1845 expedition led by Sir John Franklin. Brandt shows how these brave, yet sometimes foolish, British explorers could have avoided starvation,[1] frostbite,[2] and even death if they had copied the survival techniques of the local Inuit. Some of the more surprising details the book reveals include:

Tents
The British had seen how the Inuit built igloos, but they still used tents. Tents freeze in sub-zero temperatures, and they don't keep the people inside them warm. If the British had built igloos, they would have been warm even in the worst Arctic weather.

Clothing
Frostbite was common among the British but rare among the Inuit. If the explorers had worn sealskin and furs like the Inuit, they wouldn't have suffered from frostbite.

Dog teams
Why didn't the British use dog teams to pull their sleds?[3] British explorers pulled their sleds themselves right into the early twentieth century. It cost Scott and his men their lives on their return from the South Pole in 1912.

Salad
The British did get something right, however, when Captain Edward Parry grew salad vegetables in boxes on board his ship. It was known that fresh vegetables and fresh meat prevented scurvy,[4] although at that time the reason for this—not enough vitamin C—hadn't been discovered. Parry's men wouldn't have stayed healthy if they hadn't eaten the salads.

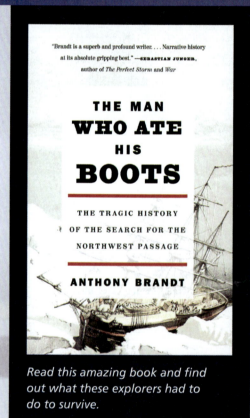

"Brandt is a superb and profound writer. . . . Narrative history at its absolute gripping best." —SEBASTIAN JUNGER, author of *The Perfect Storm* and *War*

THE MAN
WHO ATE
HIS
BOOTS

THE TRAGIC HISTORY
OF THE SEARCH FOR THE
NORTHWEST PASSAGE

ANTHONY BRANDT

Read this amazing book and find out what these explorers had to do to survive.

[1]**starvation** (n) /stɑːrˈveɪʃən/ death or loss of strength caused by not eating
[2]**frostbite** (n) /ˈfrɒs(t)baɪt/ severe damage to the body caused by freezing conditions, usually affecting toes and fingers
[3]**sled** (n) /sled/ a wooden object for transporting people and things across snow
[4]**scurvy** (n) /ˈskɜːrvi/ an illness caused by lack of vitamin C, which affects the mouth and teeth

Grammar third conditional

5 Work in pairs. Look at the grammar box. Which verb forms are used to make the third conditional?

6 Work in pairs. Look at the grammar box again. Answer the questions.

  1 a Did the British build igloos?
    b Were they warm in the worst Arctic weather?
  2 a Did Parry's men stay healthy?
    b Did they eat salads?

An Inuit man eating narwhal skin.

7 Find two more third conditional sentences in the book review.

8 Complete the sentences using the third conditional and the verbs in parentheses.

  1 If the British _____ (wear) furs, they _____ (not / get) frostbite.
  2 The men _____ (not / be) exhausted if they _____ (use) dogs to pull their sleds.
  3 If the men _____ (take) only essential items the sleds _____ (not / be) so heavy.
  4 One expedition _____ (not / get) stuck on the ice if they _____ (speak) to local people.
  5 If the expeditions _____ (follow) local customs, they _____ (be) successful.

9 Look at your completed sentences in Exercise 8. Say what actually happened.

  1 *The British didn't wear furs. They got frostbite.*

10 Work in pairs. Match the pairs of sentences. Then write a new sentence using the third conditional.

  1 We forgot to check our flight times. __c__
    If we hadn't forgotten to check our flight times, we wouldn't have missed the plane.
  2 We couldn't ask anyone for information. ____
  3 A local man gave us a map. ____
  4 We didn't plan things very well. ____
  5 We didn't get into the museum for free. ____
  6 We didn't check the weather forecast. ____

  a The trip was a disaster.
  b We found our way to the castle.
  c We missed the plane.
  d We didn't take a phrase book.
  e We didn't take appropriate clothes.
  f We didn't have our student ID with us.

Speaking [myLife]

11 Think of times in your life when you had to make a decision. Think about the answers to these questions.

  1 Was it easy or difficult to decide what to do?
  2 How did you decide?
  3 What would have happened if you had done something different?

12 Work in pairs. Tell your partner about your decisions. Ask your partner follow-up questions. Would you have done the same things?

  A: *When we were sophomores in high school, we had to choose which foreign language to study.*
  B: *Oh, so did we. What were your options?*
  A: *French or German. And **if I'd chosen** German instead of French, …*

12b Experts in the wild

Listening

1 Work in pairs. Discuss the questions.

1 Have you ever been camping? If so, what did you take with you? What was it like?
2 If you haven't been camping, would you like to? Give your reasons.

2 Work in pairs. Read about Emma Stokes and Beth Shapiro. Answer the questions.

1 What do they do?
2 What kind of places have they traveled to?
3 What kind of things could cause problems in those areas?

Emma Stokes is a wildlife researcher who has led projects to protect gorillas and tigers. She often has to cut paths through the forest and set up a camp. Her first ever expedition was to the Central African forest, where she had an unexpected experience.

Beth Shapiro is a biologist and an expert on extinct mammal species. Much of her work is done on expeditions. She often goes to Siberia, where she hopes to find mammoth bones or tusks. On her first visit there, however, living animals caused the problem.

3 Work in pairs. You are going to listen to the stories of two difficult experiences Emma (E) and Beth (B) had. Before you listen, match the words below to their definitions (1–4).

mammoth	tracker	trumpeting	tusks

1 two long teeth on the outside of the mouths of some animals _____
2 a person who shows you the way in a wild place _____
3 an extinct animal, similar to an elephant _____
4 the noise made by elephants _____

4 ▶ 99 Work in pairs. Listen to the stories. What was the difficult experience in each story?

5 ▶ 99 Work in pairs. Look at the events from the two stories. Decide if they are about Emma (E) or Beth (B).

1 She got her gear and got out of the tent.   E   B
2 She had to take her mosquito net off her face to eat.   E   B
3 She was bitten by mosquitoes.   E   B
4 The trackers woke her up by shouting.   E   B
5 They made a meal of rice and fish.   E   B
6 When she went back, three of the tents were destroyed.   E   B

6 Work in pairs. What would you have done if you were Emma or Beth?

Grammar *should have* and *could have*

7 Work in pairs. Read the comments. Who do you think said each one—Emma or Beth?

1 "We could have died."
2 "We couldn't have avoided the insects."
3 "We should have checked the area before we camped."
4 "We should have gone there at a different time of year."
5 "We shouldn't have put up our tents there."

8 Look at the sentences in Exercise 7 again. Match the sentences (1–5) with the meanings (a–d).

  a This was the right thing to do, but we didn't do it. ____
  b This was the wrong thing to do, but we did it. ____
  c This was possible, but it didn't happen. ____
  d This was impossible, and it didn't happen. ____

▶ **SHOULD HAVE** and **COULD HAVE**

should (not) could (not)	have + past participle

For more information and practice, see page 178.

9 Look at the grammar box. Circle the best option to complete the sentences.

  1 We *would / should* have brought more water—I'm really thirsty now.
  2 The elephants came so close we almost *could / couldn't* have touched them.
  3 We've run out of food. We *should / shouldn't* have known this would happen.
  4 If I'd followed you, I *should / could* have got there more quickly.
  5 I *should / would* have asked what was in the drink before I drank it.
  6 If we'd taken the other road, we *wouldn't / shouldn't* have got lost.

10 Complete the story with *should (not) have*, *could (not) have*, and past participle forms.

I'm an anthropologist, and once when I was working in a remote area of Brazil, I ate something [1] I _____ (eat). I was pretty sick. [2] I _____ (feel) any worse, actually! I suppose [3] I _____ (have) some medicine with me, but I didn't. Anyway, the *curandeira*—the local healer—brought me the strongest of their local medicine. [4] I _____ (take) it right away, but I didn't because it smelled so bad. Of course, because of this I got much worse. So, the next day, I accepted the medicine. And after a few terrible days, I got better. I really think [5] I _____ (die) without it, though.

11 Pronunciation *should have* and *could have*

  a ▶ 100 Listen to the sentences with *could have* and *should have* from Exercise 10. Notice the weak form of *have* /həv/.

  b ▶ 100 Listen again and repeat the sentences.

Wordbuilding prefixes *in-*, *un-*, *im-*

▶ **WORDBUILDING prefixes *in-*, *un-*, *im-***

We can add *in-* and *un-* to the beginning of some adjectives to mean "not." We can also use *im-* before some adjectives that begin with the letters *p* or *m*.
an inappropriate place, an unexpected experience, It was impossible.

For more practice, see Workbook page 99.

12 Look at the wordbuilding box. Replace the words in bold with an adjective beginning with *in-*, *un-*, or *im-*.

  1 We might see an elephant today, but it's **not likely**. _____
  2 The guide is great even though he's **not experienced**. _____
  3 In my country, it's **not polite** to speak while you're eating. _____
  4 I hate sleeping in a tent—it's cold and **not comfortable**. _____
  5 Don't worry about what to wear. The invitation says it's **not formal**. _____
  6 My colleague is friendly, but he's **not patient**. _____

Speaking my **Life**

13 Look at the activities below, and the problems you may have when doing them. Write one or two solutions for each one. Then talk to other students and find out what advice they would give for one of the problems.

Activity	Problem
doing homework	can't find information
packing a suitcase	don't have enough room
taking photos	come out blurry
making a meal	burning everything
going to visit a friend	getting lost

14 Work in pairs. Compare the advice you were given and decide which was the best advice.

12c The legacy of the samurai

Reading

1 Work in pairs. How much do you know about the samurai?

1 Who were the samurai?
2 Where were they from?
3 When did they live?
4 What did they do?

2 Work in pairs. Look at these words. Make connections between them.

army	enemies	generals
martial arts	opponents	soldiers
sword	warrior	weapon

An army is made up of soldiers.

3 Read the article about the samurai. Check your answers from Exercise 1. Find the words in Exercise 2.

4 Read the article. According to the article, are these statements true (T) or false (F)?

1 The early samurai were similar to European knights.   T   F
2 The samurai eventually died out following their defeat in battle.   T   F
3 Samurai soldiers had a wide range of cultural interests.   T   F
4 The military skills of the samurai have been lost.   T   F
5 The legacy of the samurai has spread outside Japan.   T   F

5 Find these words in the article. Look at how they are used and try to guess their meaning. Then replace the words in bold in the sentences (1–4) with these words.

unarmed (line 38)	lone (line 52)
appeal (line 50)	fierce (line 61)

1 I don't understand the **attraction** of war movies. _____
2 That boxer is frightening. He's so **intense and aggressive**. _____
3 We fought **without any weapons**. _____
4 The police say they're looking for a **single, unaccompanied** gunman. _____

Critical thinking relevance

6 Work in pairs. Which of these sentences could be included as additional information? Where should the sentences go in the article?

1 His words might easily have been spoken by a Bushido master from three centuries ago.
2 The samurai promised to be loyal to these men, who needed soldiers to protect and increase their power.
3 Samurai also played *go*, a board game about land conquest.
4 The classic movie *Seven Samurai* by Japanese director Akira Kurosawa has been described as one of the most influential movies ever made.

Word focus *go*

7 Look at these excerpts from the article. What do the expressions with *go* mean? Circle the correct option (a–c).

1 The original samurai were soldiers **who went into battle** riding horses.
   a fought   b sat   c traveled
2 Things **didn't go well** for the samurai.
   a didn't move   b were fine   c weren't good
3 Samurai fighting skills **went into decline**.
   a improved   b influenced others   c weakened
4 The "samurai" is asked if he would like to **go back in time.**
   a return home   b return to the past   c start again

8 Work in pairs. What do the expressions with *go* mean in these sentences?

1 The battle plan **went wrong** and ended in disaster.
2 The battle **went on** for six days non-stop.
3 The number of injured soldiers **is going up** daily.
4 Suddenly, everything **went quiet**.
5 We've decided to **go ahead** with our plan.

Speaking my Life

9 Would you like to go back in time and experience life in a different age and country? Or would you prefer to live in the future? Think about these points.

- when and where
- why that time appeals to you
- your role or position in that society
- opportunities
- possible dangers

10 Work in groups. Ask questions to find out about your classmates' time-traveling choices. What is more popular—the past or the future?

▶ 101

The Legacy of the
SAMURAI

Samurai history

The samurai (the word means "one who serves") were the elite[1] warriors of Japan for nearly seven hundred years. In the tenth century, the rulers[2] in Kyoto tried
5 and failed to organize a conscript[3] army. If they had succeeded, the rich landowners might not have decided to employ private soldiers, and the samurai might never have existed. The original samurai were warriors who went into battle riding horses and who fought their
10 opponents following ancient traditions. If they had ever met European knights, their customs would have seemed familiar. Later, as the armies became larger and the fighting more violent, most samurai trained for hand-to-hand fighting. However, during a long period
15 of peace, things didn't go well for the samurai and eventually, in the 1860s, they lost their position of power.

Samurai identity

The sword of a samurai is a symbol of authority and luxury. It was both a weapon and an art
20 object. This double identity mirrored the samurai themselves. As well as being warriors, they used to socialize with artists, writers, and philosophers. Samurai generals did flower arranging and went to the theater. But of all their cultural activities,
25 the tea ceremony was the most important. It was a slow and calm tradition. It took place in a small room where swords were forbidden, even to samurai. It must have been very inviting to battle-weary soldiers.

30 Bushido

Bushido is the warrior's code. It was first written down as a kind of self-help manual during the long period of peace when samurai fighting skills went into decline. The martial
35 arts tradition continues in Japan to this day. Millions of Japanese children still practice the classic skills of sword fighting (kendo), archery[4] (kyudo), and hand-to-hand, unarmed fighting (jujitsu) at school. But Bushido is also a code of
40 ethics: honor, loyalty, and sacrifice. As Terukuni Uki—a martial arts teacher—explains, "Here we teach the spirit of winning, but it's not so much defeating an opponent as overcoming one's own self. These days, it seems everyone
45 is looking for someone to blame rather than focusing on himself. Our message here is that if you try hard, at kendo or anything else, you will enjoy life."

Samurai today

50 The continuing appeal of the samurai is due to a simple fact: He is one of the world's greatest action figures. He's the lone swordsman who kills dozens of enemies in the name of duty and individual glory. The samurai is the cowboy, the
55 knight, the gladiator, and the Star Wars Jedi all rolled into one. The samurai have inspired hundreds of movies, video games, comic books, and TV dramas. Each spring, in Japan, men put on samurai armor and act out famous
60 samurai battles. These "weekend" samurai look fierce and realistic, but with their plastic goggles and swords, they wouldn't have been a threat to the real thing. One of the "samurai" is asked if he would like to go back in time.
65 "Hmm," he replies. "They seem like better times, but I don't think they were, really. It was live or die."

---

[1]**elite** (adj) /eɪˈliːt/ referring to the richest and most powerful people in a society
[2]**ruler** (n) /ˈruːlər/ the leader of a country
[3]**conscript** (n) /ˈkɒnskrɪpt/ a soldier who is called up to fight by the authorities
[4]**archery** (n) /ˈɑːrtʃəri/ a sport using bows and arrows

12d I'm so sorry!

Real life making and accepting apologies

1 Work in pairs. Do people apologize a lot in your culture? Would you apologize in these situations?

- arriving late for a meeting
- forgetting someone's name
- serving food a guest doesn't like
- not liking the food someone cooks for you
- taking someone's chair in a restaurant
- asking someone to repeat something you didn't hear
- losing or breaking something that belongs to someone else
- handing in some work after the deadline has passed at college

2 You are going to listen to three conversations in which people make apologies. Look at the expressions below for making and accepting apologies. What do you think the three conversations are about?

3 ▶ 102 Listen to the three conversations and check your ideas from Exercise 2.

4 ▶ 102 Listen to the conversations again. Then answer the questions.

1 What is the problem?
2 How is the situation resolved?

> ### ► MAKING AND ACCEPTING APOLOGIES
>
> **1**
> I'm really sorry you went to all this trouble.
> There's no need to apologize—it's not a problem.
> It's my fault. I'll make you something else.
>
> **2**
> I couldn't help it—I slipped.
> Don't blame me—this floor is slippery.
> Look, it was an accident! It could have happened to anyone.
> It's not your fault. Sorry I got upset.
>
> **3**
> I'm so sorry I kept you waiting.
> Don't worry about it—that bus is terrible.
> Sorry about that!
> It's just one of those things—buses are unreliable!

5 Work in pairs. Do you think all of the expressions would be appropriate in all three situations? Why or why not?

6 Pronunciation sentence stress

a ▶ 103 Look at the language box again. Listen to the expressions for making and accepting apologies. Notice which word is stressed in each statement. Repeat the expressions.

b Work in pairs. Take turns speaking and responding using an appropriate expression. Pay attention to the words you stress.

1 Excuse me. This is a no-smoking area.
2 I'm so sorry. I forgot to bring your book back.
3 Excuse me. That seat is taken.
4 You should have told me you didn't eat garlic!
5 Why is there no milk left?
6 I'm really sorry I didn't tell you I was coming!
7 Excuse me. Please wait until the waiter shows you to a table.
8 Sorry, we don't accept credit cards.

7 Work in pairs. Choose one of the problems in Exercise 1 or use your own idea. Decide what your relationship is and take a role each. Prepare a conversation that includes at least one apology.

8 Act out your conversation in front of another pair. Can they identify the situation and the relationship?

12e How to behave …

Writing a website article

1 Work in pairs. Have you ever spent time in an English-speaking country? If so, tell your partner three things (apart from the language!) you found strange or different there.

2 You are going to read an article from a website that arranges host families for foreign language students in the United States. What advice do you expect to find there? Tell your partner.

3 Read the article. Work in pairs. What do you think of the advice? Does any of it surprise you?

http://www.homestayfamily.com

How to behave with a **homestay family**

I've stayed with several families in the US, and each of them has been different. But there are some key things I can pass on about getting the best out of your stay. I hope these things are useful!

Even though you are a paying guest in their home, take a small gift for your hosts. You'd expect a gift from a guest, I'm sure.

It is not just about learning English. American people will expect you to show an interest in American culture.

Take some photos from home so that you can talk to your hosts about the photos. Taking the photos will also give you more opportunities to actually speak English, too.

You're not a tourist, so don't behave like a tourist. Your host family will be getting on with normal life. That is what you are there to experience!

And finally, remember the importance of being punctual (two o'clock means two o'clock!), polite (be careful with expressions you've picked up from pop music and movies!), and sociable (join in with things—at least the first time).

4 Writing skill checking your writing

a Look at this list of seven things that you should use to check your writing. Has the writer of the website article already checked all the things?

grammar	spelling
linking words	style
organization	vocabulary
relevance	

b The writer can improve the article by avoiding some words that are repeated. Look at the first line of the article. Who or what does *them* refer to?

c Replace the other highlighted words in the article with these words. There is one extra word.

one	She	the same	their
them	there	they	This

5 Work in groups. You are going to write an article for students coming to your country. Brainstorm ideas. Use these categories or ideas that are more relevant to your culture.

- celebrations
- dress
- food
- formality
- greetings
- house rules
- meal times
- money

6 Work on your own. Choose three to five ideas from your list in Exercise 5. Write an article of 150–200 words.

7 Use the list in Exercise 4a to check and revise your article.

8 Exchange articles with the other members of your group. Which were the most common topics?

12f Shark vs. octopus

A giant Pacific octopus interacts with a scuba diver in the North Pacific Ocean.

Before you watch

1 Work in groups. Look at the photo and the caption. Discuss the questions.

  1 What do you know about this animal?
  2 How would you feel if you were the diver? Why?
  3 Which animal would frighten you more: an octopus or a shark? Why?
  4 What do you think might happen in a meeting between an octopus and a shark?

2 Key vocabulary

a Read the sentences. The words in bold are used in the video. Guess the meaning of the words.

  1 We have a **tank** with eight different kinds of tropical fish in it.
  2 Mice can be killed by several **predators**, such as foxes and birds.
  3 A tiger's stripes help to **camouflage** it as it moves through grass and bushes.
  4 Polar bears are the same color as their **surroundings** in winter, when everything is white.
  5 Some animals **release** a strong smell when they are in danger.

b Match the words in bold in Exercise 2a with these definitions.
  a to use patterns and colors so that it's difficult to be seen _____
  b the place where you are and the things that are there _____
  c to allow a liquid or gas to escape _____
  d animals that kill and eat other animals to survive _____
  e a large container of water to keep fish and similar animals in _____

While you watch

3 [12.1, 12.2] Watch both parts of the video and check your ideas from Exercise 1 question 4. Are you surprised?

4 [12.1, 12.2] Try to complete the summary of what happened in the tank. Watch the video again to check your answers if necessary.

The spiny dogfish shark is a predator, but the octopus is not its usual prey. If it was, the aquarium staff wouldn't have put them in the same [1] _____. But then, dead [2] _____ started to appear at the bottom of the tank. The [3] _____ were worried. But then they discovered that the [4] _____ was attacking the [5] _____. Nobody had expected this to happen. The octopus was more dangerous than the sharks!

5 [12.1] Work in pairs, Student A and Student B. Watch Part 1 of the video again. Make notes about your animal. Then tell your partner.

Student A: the spiny dogfish shark
  1 usual food
    _____
  2 how it gets its name
    _____
  3 usual behavior
    _____

Student B: the giant Pacific octopus
  4 three ways it keeps itself safe from predators
    _____
    _____
    _____
  5 usual food
    _____

After you watch

6 Vocabulary in context

a [12.3] Watch the clips from the video. Choose the correct meaning of the words and phrases.

b Answer the questions in your own words. Then work in pairs and compare your answers.

  1 What other words can you use to get someone's attention when you start to speak?
  2 Think of some well-known inventions or products. Do you know how they got their names?
  3 What do you usually do when a piece of technology doesn't work?

7 Work in small groups. Brainstorm as many animals as you can in two minutes. Then discuss the connections between them—which are predators and which are prey? How many animals can you connect into a food chain?

UNIT 12 REVIEW AND MEMORY BOOSTER

Grammar

1 Complete the article about the photo with the correct form of the verbs.

This is one of the most famous photos of the rare snow leopard. What makes it so extraordinary? Firstly, patience. The photographer, Steve Winter, spent ten months on this assignment. If he [1] _____ (be) in a hurry, he [2] _____ (not get) his shots. Secondly, dedication. Steve camped out for six weeks at 30 degrees below zero, conditions in which he [3] _____ (freeze) to death! Next, cooperation. Steve credited the knowledge of local experts Tashi Tundup and Raghu Chundawat, without whom he [4] _____ (not be able) to go ahead with the project. Finally, the animal itself. Steve says the photo "was a real collaboration between the snow leopard and myself." And it's true. Imagine how differently the photo [5] _____ (turn out) if the snow leopard [6] _____ (not go) hunting, slowly and silently, on that snowy night.

2 Read the article again. Are the statements below true (T) or false (F), according to the information given?

1 Steve Winter was able to get this photo quite quickly.   T F
2 Steve Winter nearly died on this assignment.   T F
3 Winter needed help to find the leopard.   T F
4 The photo shows the leopard while it's hunting.   T F

3 **>> MB** Work in pairs. Read the sentences about Steve Winter. Discuss what would/might/could have happened if the situations had been different.

1 His first camera was a gift from his father on his seventh birthday.
2 Steve didn't get any shots until he moved higher up the mountain.

Vocabulary

4 Write adjectives with the correct prefix that mean the same as:

1 not appropriate   _____
2 not comfortable   _____
3 not experienced   _____
4 not formal   _____
5 not likely   _____
6 not patient   _____
7 not possible   _____
8 not expected   _____

5 Write sentences with four of the adjectives from Exercise 4.

6 **>> MB** Work in pairs. Tell your partner about a time when:

- something went wrong.
- something went on for longer than you expected.
- something went up in price or number very quickly.

Real life

7 Work in pairs. Complete the exchanges with these expressions. Then continue the conversations.

> a Don't worry about it.   b It's not your fault.
> c Well, don't blame me.

1 A: I'm so sorry I forgot to call you last night.
   B: ____ I wasn't home, anyway.

2 A: Oh, no. We don't have any orange juice left.
   B: ____ I don't even drink it.

3 A: I'm really sorry about getting upset yesterday.
   B: ____ I shouldn't have yelled!

UNIT 1b, Exercise 14, page 13

Pair A: The blue quiz

Ask Pair B the quiz questions without the options. Give them 5 points if they can answer the question immediately. Give them 3 points if they need to hear the options. The answer is in bold.

Pair B will then ask you the yellow questions.

1 Where does the blue-footed booby live?
   a   in South Africa
   b   in Australia and New Zealand
   c   on the west coast of Central and South America
   The color comes from the fish the birds eat.

2 Who lives in the Blue House in South Korea?
   a   the president
   b   the king
   c   the prime minister
   It's the official residence, and it has a blue-tiled roof.

3 Do you know the name of the country where the Blue Nile begins?
   a Sudan   **b Ethiopia**   c Uganda
   It originates in Lake Tana, then joins the White Nile to form the Nile River.

4 Which part of the US is famous for blues music?
   a   the West Coast
   b   the Deep South
   c   the Midwest
   Blues singers sing about their difficult life or bad luck in love. These people can be said to "have the blues."

UNIT 3b Exercise 9, page 37

Pair A

Read the solution to puzzle A. Pair B will ask you questions to discover the answer to this puzzle. Then ask Pair B questions to discover the answer to puzzle B. Then turn back to page 37.

> **Solution to puzzle A**
> The people on the yacht decided to have a diving competition. When they were all in the water, they discovered they had forgotten to put a ladder down the side of the yacht. They couldn't get back onto the yacht, so they drowned.

UNIT 9a Exercise 10, page 107

Student A

Complete the sentences with the passive form of the verb in parentheses. Then read the sentences to your partner. Student B must say whether they agree or disagree with the statement, and why. Then swap.

   1   Same-day shipping _____ by over 80 percent of online shoppers nowadays. (*demand*, simple present)

   2   By 2030, a mobile device _____ by three out of four people globally. (*own*, future)
   3   By 2030, cash _____ no longer _____ in most stores in Europe. (*accept*, future)
   4   More and more brands _____ to show that their products are ethical. (*expect*, present continuous)
   5   In the next few years, over a quarter of all purchases _____ following recommendations on social media. (*make*, future)

UNIT 10a Exercise 9, page 119

Pair A

1 Think of one example for each of these categories. Write at least four clues for two of your examples using the second conditional.

a job	an animal	a person

job – airline pilot; If we did this job, we'd spend a lot of time traveling.

2 Read the sentences to Pair B. They must guess your job, person, etc. Be prepared to give extra clues. Then swap.

UNIT 11a Exercise 9, page 131

Pair A

Read the news story. Write a short dialog between the man and a rescuer. Practice your dialog so that you are ready to act it out for Pair B. Then turn back to page 131.

> A walker who got lost in the hills was rescued this weekend after taking a photo with his phone and emailing it to the Volunteer Rescue Service. The man had fallen and was injured, but with no maps, he couldn't tell the rescuers where he was. He took the photo after advice from the rescue team, who recognized the location immediately.

UNIT 11c Exercise 12, page 134

Pair A

Read the notes. Practice describing the apps with a partner and make up names for the apps. Then tell Pair B about them.

1   audio clips of different sounds—when you need to invent a reason to end a conversation
2   food app—tells you how many calories in food
3   clean clothes app—tells you when clothes are dirty and need washing

UNIT 1b, Exercise 14, page 13

Pair B: The yellow quiz

Pair A will ask you the blue questions. You will get 5 points if you can answer the question immediately. You will get 3 points if you need to hear the options.

Then ask Pair A the yellow questions.

1 Where are yellow taxi cabs from originally?

    a **Chicago**   b New York   c Washington

Mr. Hertz started the Yellow Cab Company (in 1915) because yellow is easy to see from a distance.

2 Which yellow fruit does the California Fruit Festival celebrate?

    a the banana   b **the lemon**   c the pineapple

There are lemon festivals in California every year.

3 Which sport gives a yellow jersey to the winner?

    a golf   b horse racing   c **cycling**

More than 100 years ago, a newspaper gave money to pay for the Tour de France. The leader's jersey is the same color as the paper the newspaper was printed on.

4 Can you tell me where the house that inspired Van Gogh's "Yellow House" painting is?

    a in Holland   b in Spain   c **in France**

Van Gogh spent the summer of 1888 in Arles, in the south of France.

UNIT 3b Exercise 9, page 37

Pair B

Ask Pair A questions to discover the answer to puzzle A. Then read the solution to puzzle B. Pair A will ask you questions to discover the answer to this puzzle.

> **Solution to puzzle B**
> The man had fallen into the Dead Sea. This is actually a saltwater lake. The salt density is so high that you can easily float on the surface of the water.

UNIT 9a Exercise 10, page 107

Student B

Complete the sentences with the passive form of the verb in parentheses.

Then listen to your partner's sentences. Decide if you agree or disagree with each statement, and say why. Then swap.

    1 The amount of money that _____ by the middle class around the world will triple by 2030. (*spend*, simple present)

    2 By 2030, over $500 billion _____ via mobile payments, compared to $75 billion in 2016. (*spend*, future)

    3 Larger and larger stores _____ to meet increasing demand from shoppers. (*build*, future)

    4 Delivery in 1–3 hours _____ by over 60 percent of online shoppers nowadays. (*request*, present continuous)

    5 Personal information _____ with retailers by the majority of shoppers in the next few years. (*share*, future)

UNIT 10a Exercise 9, page 119

Pair B

1 Think of one example for each of these categories. Write at least four clues for two of your examples using the second conditional.

> a job   a famous person   an animal

job – airline pilot; If we had this job, we'd spend a lot of time traveling.

2 Listen to Pair A's sentences. Guess the job, person, etc. Then swap.

UNIT 11a Exercise 9, page 131

Pair B

Read the news story. Write a short dialog between Adam and Corey. Practice your dialog so that you are ready to act it out for Pair A. Then turn back to page 131.

> A message in a bottle that was put into the Atlantic Ocean in Florida has reached Ireland. Adam Flannery, aged 17, found the bottle, which had been sent by high school student Corey Swearingen. The message gave Corey's contact information and asked the finder to get in touch with details of where the bottle ended up.

UNIT 11c Exercise 12, page 134

Pair B

Read the notes. Practice describing the apps with a partner and make up names for the apps. Then tell Pair A about them.

1 how much sunscreen?—tells you how sunny it is
2 late homework excuses—gives you different things to say to your teacher
3 positive messages—sent to your phone each day: "I'm wonderful," etc.

UNIT 4d Exercise 7, page 52

Student A: Choose a number (1–12). You are going to make this request.

Student B: Look at your partner's number. Choose an appropriate situation (a–d) for this request. You are going to respond to the request.

Act out a conversation in this situation. Use the expressions on page 52 to help you. Take turns making requests and responding.

Request
1   You want to sit down.
2   The phone number on a letter isn't clear.
3   You don't know where the company buildings are.
4   You want an application form sent in the mail.
5   You don't have a pen.
6   You need a taxi.
7   You need to know the time.
8   You want help with an application form.
9   You need a ride somewhere.
10   You want to leave your coat somewhere.
11   You want to wash your hands.
12   You want to use the phone.
Situation
a   You're with a friend.
b   You're in the reception area of a company.
c   You're in an interview.
d   You're on the phone.

Unit 12 Exercise 4, page 141

The man can leave the fox and the grain together, so he takes the chicken across the river. He leaves the chicken on the other side of the river and goes back across.

Then he takes the fox across the river, and since he can't leave the fox and chicken together, he brings the chicken back.

Again, since he can't leave the chicken and the grain together, he leaves the chicken. This time he takes the grain across and leaves it with the fox.

The man then returns to pick up the chicken and heads across the river one last time.

UNIT 5 Review Exercise 8, page 68

Baklava
A rich, sweet pastry with chopped nuts and syrup or honey. From Turkey, the Caucasus, and Central Asia.

Bibimbap
A Korean dish of rice served in a bowl with vegetables, meat, egg, and sauce on top.

Borscht
A soup popular in many Eastern and Central European countries. Main ingredient: beetroot.

Couscous
From North Africa. A dish of semolina served with a meat or vegetable stew.

Dhal
An Indian soup dish made from spiced beans or lentils. Often eaten with rice or flat bread.

Fondue
Popular in Switzerland and France. Pieces of bread are dipped into a dish of melted cheese.

Guacamole
A Mexican dip made from mashed avocados.

Kebab
Cubes of meat (or fish) on a skewer, cooked over an open fire. Originally from Central and Western Asia.

Lasagna
An Italian dish of pasta sheets layered with cheese, meat, and tomato sauce and baked in the oven.

Satay
Originally from Southeast Asia. Small strips of meat cooked over a fire on wooden skewers. Usually served with a peanut sauce.

Sushi
From Japan. Small balls of rice served with fish, vegetables, or egg.

Tortilla
1   A type of flatbread made from corn or wheat in Mexico and Central America.
2   A potato omelet from Spain.

UNIT 6a Exercise 2, page 70

The secret to this trick is to realize that the box can be used not only for holding the thumbtacks, but also for holding the candle. First, empty the thumbtacks from the box, and place the candle in the box. Then use thumbtacks to fasten the box to the wall.

GRAMMAR SUMMARY UNIT 1

Simple present and present continuous

We use the simple present to talk about things that are permanent or generally true, such as facts, repeated behavior, habits, and routines.

> She **works** for the United Nations.
> I **don't drive** to work. I always **walk** or **ride** my bike.

We use the present continuous:

- to talk about something in progress at the time of speaking.
  *Wait a minute—I'm just **writing** an email.*

- to talk about things that are in progress around the time of speaking, but not necessarily at that exact moment.
  *He's **looking for** a new job at the moment.*

- to talk about a changing situation.
  *Smartphones **are getting** more sophisticated all the time.*

▶ Exercise 1

Dynamic and stative verbs

Most verbs have dynamic meaning—they describe actions or things that happen. We can usually use dynamic verbs in both the simple and continuous form.

> I usually **read** books about travel and culture.
> I'm **reading** a great book at the moment.

Some verbs have stative meaning—they describe states such as thoughts and mental processes, the senses, emotions, qualities, and existence. We usually use stative verbs only in the simple form.

> Do you **know** Sue? (not ~~Are you knowing Sue?~~)
> I **don't understand.** (not ~~I'm not understanding.~~)

Common stative verbs include:

Thoughts and mental processes	admire, agree, appear, believe, care, depend, expect, feel, forget, hope, imagine, know, look (like), mean, mind, realize, recognize, remember, seem, sound, suppose, think, understand
The senses	feel, hear, see, smell, taste
Emotions, likes, and desires	hate, like, love, prefer, need, want
Qualities and possession	come (from), consist of, contain, cost, deserve, fit, involve, measure, sound, suit, weigh belong, have (got), own, possess
Existence	be, be from, come from, exist

Some stative verbs can sometimes be used in the continuous form, especially in more informal contexts. We do this when we want to emphasize that the situation, feeling, or attitude is at the moment, and is not permanent.

> I'm **feeling** much better today.

Some verbs can be both stative and dynamic. The meaning changes if you use the continuous form.

> I **think** it's a good idea. (stative: *think* = believe)
> Sssh! I'm **thinking**. (dynamic: *think* = use your brain)

▶ Exercises 2 and 3

Question forms: direct questions

We normally form questions with auxiliary verb + subject + main verb.

> **Are you leaving** now? (*are* = auxiliary verb, *you* = subject, *leaving* = main verb)

Most tenses include an auxiliary verb. For the simple present and simple past, we add a form of the auxiliary verb *do*.

> Where **do** you live?
> **Did** you like the movie?

Some questions ask about a subject.

> A: **Who** wants coffee?
> B: <u>Valentina</u> wants coffee. (*Valentina* = subject)

When we ask about the subject of a sentence, we use the same word order as in a statement.

> **Who's seen** this movie? (not ~~Has who seen this movie?~~)

We don't use *do*, *does*, or *did* for the simple present or past.

> Who **speaks** Arabic? (not ~~Who does speak Arabic?~~)
> What **happened**? (not ~~What did happen?~~)

▶ Exercises 4 and 5

Question forms: indirect questions

We use indirect questions to be less direct, because we want to be more polite or formal, or when we think the person we are asking may not know the answer.

Indirect questions begin with a question phrase such as *Do you know ...* , *Can you tell me ...* , and *Could you tell me ...* .

> **Do you know** where they are from?

In *wh-* questions, we put the *wh-* word after the question phrase.

> Could you tell me **where** she lives?

In *yes/no* questions, we put *if* after the question phrase.

> Do you know **if** we can book in advance?

We use the same word order as in a statement. We don't need to add *do*, *does*, or *did*.

> Can you tell me where **the museum is**?
> (not ~~Can you tell me where is the museum?~~)
> Do you know where **she went**?
> (not ~~Do you know where did she go?~~)

▶ Exercise 6

Exercises

1 Complete the exchanges with the simple present or present continuous form of the verbs.

1   A: They _____ (have) really
    good seafood here. It's what I usually
    _____ (eat) when I _____
    (come) here.
    B: Oh, I'm vegetarian. I _____ (not /
    eat) seafood.
2   A: Oh, no! It _____ (rain) again!
    B: Yeah, I'm afraid it _____ (rain) a lot
    here at this time of year.
3   A: You _____ (work) at the university,
    right?
    B: Normally, yes. But I _____ (not /
    work) there at the moment. I _____
    (take) a year off. I _____ (write) a
    book, actually. I'm about halfway through.

2 Complete the sentences with the simple present or present continuous form of the verbs.

1   I _____ (not / remember) my first day
    of school.
2   We _____ (prefer) the blue hats to the
    red ones.
3   Kate isn't sure about going to the conference,
    but she _____ (think) about it.
4   They're in the kitchen. They _____
    (have) lunch.
5   Ben _____ (not / realize) what he
    _____ (need) to do.
6   I _____ (think) this jacket
    _____ (belong) to Lauren.

3 Choose the correct options to complete this excerpt from a book about the world's cultures.

The word "culture" [1] *comes from / is coming from*
the Latin "colere," which [2] *means / is meaning*
to cultivate and grow. Culture [3] *is / is being* the
characteristics, knowledge, and behavior of a
particular group of people. This [4] *includes /
is including* language, religion, cuisine, social
habits, music, and arts. Today, cultural diversity
across the planet [5] *increases / is increasing* faster
than ever. This is because people [6] *move / are
moving* more easily and freely around the planet.
At the same time, and as a result, more and more
people, especially the younger generation, [7] *feel /
are feeling* that they [8] *don't belong / aren't belonging* to
a particular culture.

4 Write questions for these answers.

1   Where _____
    People wear white at funerals in East Asian
    countries.
2   When _____
    _____ Hong Kong became
    independent from the UK in 1997.
3   How many _____
    About half the European countries use the euro.
4   What _____
    Ciao means both "hello" and "goodbye" in
    English.
5   Which _____
    _____ The two South American countries
    that don't have a coast are Paraguay and Bolivia.

5 Look at the interview with a travel writer. Write
the questions.

1   _____
    I became a travel writer by writing about my
    travels on a blog. A magazine saw it and liked
    what I did and asked me to write for them.
2   _____
    The qualities you need to be a travel writer
    are a love of travel, independent thinking, and
    cultural sensitivity.
3   _____
    At the moment, I'm working on an article about
    some of the smaller ethnic cultures in Southeast
    Asia.
4   _____
    I usually choose my destinations. However,
    sometimes a magazine will ask me to go to a
    particular place.
5   _____
    I prepare for a trip by reading as much as
    possible about the place I'm visiting and getting
    advice from other authors who know the place.

6 Rewrite the direct questions as indirect questions.

1   What language do they speak in Mauritius?
    Do you _____
2   Where is Robert Fisher's office?
    Could you _____
3   Which terminal does the flight leave from?
    Do you _____
4   Where did Julia go?
    Could you _____
5   Do people usually bow when they meet?
    Do you _____
    _____
6   Why do you need a new passport?
    Can you _____

GRAMMAR SUMMARY UNIT 2

Present perfect

Form

We form the present perfect with *have/has* + past participle. We normally use the contractions *'ve* and *'s* after pronouns.

> The record store **has closed.**
> I **haven't bought** any CDs recently.
> How many bands **have** you **seen?**
> I**'ve read** that book.

Many common past participles are irregular. They can be the same as an irregular simple past form (e.g., *buy – bought – bought*) or different from an irregular simple past form (e.g., *see – saw – seen*).

Use

We use the present perfect:

- when we don't know exactly when an activity or situation started.
  > Millions of people **have bought** their music.

- when an activity or situation started in the past and has an effect on the present.
  > It **has become** much easier to listen to music.
  > (= It became easier in the past and it's still easier.)
  > They**'ve released** a new album. (= They produced it in the past, but it's new and available now.)

- to talk about activities and situations that started in the past and continue in the present.
  Use *for* to talk about a period of time.
  > I **haven't been** to a concert **for** years.
  > Use *since* to talk about a point in time.
  > They**'ve lived** here **since** 1960.

- with superlatives.
  > I think that's the best song they**'ve written.**

gone and been

The past participle of *go* is *gone*. It means "go and stay away."

> William**'s gone** to his brother's house. (= He went there, and he's still there.)

But we also use *been* as a past participle of *go*. It means "go and come back."

> I**'ve been** to the store. (= I went there, and now I'm home again.)

▶ **Exercises 1 and 2**

already, just, and yet

We often use the present perfect to talk about the recent past with *already*, *just*, and *yet*.

- We use *already* in affirmative sentences and questions to say what has happened or is complete, often earlier than we expected.
  > I've **already** called Paul.
  > Julie has **already** bought the tickets! (= I didn't expect this.)

- We use *just* in affirmative sentences to say that something happened very recently.
  > He's **just** come back from work. (= He came back a few minutes ago.)

- We use *yet* in questions to ask if something is complete.
  > Have you made lunch **yet?**

We put *just* and *already* before the past participle. We put *yet* at the end of a question.

> Have you spoken to Mike **yet?**
> (not ~~Have you yet spoken to Mike?~~)

▶ **Exercise 3**

Present perfect and simple past

We use both the present perfect and the simple past to talk about situations and events in the past.

We use the present perfect when we don't say when something happened.

> They**'ve given** concerts in over sixty different countries.
> Robert**'s bought** a new car.

We also use the present perfect with *ever* and *never* to talk about experiences in our whole life.

> Have you **ever** sung in front of an audience?
> I've **never** listened to their music.

We use the simple past when we say—or it is clear from the situation—when something happened.

> I **started** a new music course last week.

With the present perfect, we use time expressions like *just, yet, already, for,* and *since*. We also use the present perfect with unfinished time periods, like *today, this week, this month,* etc.

With the simple past, we use time expressions like *yesterday, last week, last month, in 2015, two weeks ago,* etc.

▶ **Exercises 4, 5, and 6**

Exercises

1 Complete the sentences with the present perfect form of the verbs in parentheses. Use contractions where possible.

1 The concert _____ (start).
2 They _____ (make) lunch for us.
3 My sister _____ (not buy) any vinyl records.
4 _____ you _____ (finish) writing your report?
5 We _____ (know) each other since 2015.
6 _____ he _____ (see) this band play live before?
7 Our neighbors aren't here. They _____ (go) on vacation.
8 I _____ (not go) to a ballet for a long time.

2 Read the sentences (1–6). Choose the correct option (a–b) to explain each sentence.

1 I've broken my arm.
   a My arm is better.
   b My arm is still broken.
2 They've recorded three albums.
   a We know when this happened.
   b We don't know when this happened.
3 They've gone on vacation.
   a They're at home now.
   b They're on vacation now.
4 She's lived here for three years.
   a She lives here now.
   b She doesn't live here any more.
5 Sally's been to Mexico.
   a She's there now.
   b She's home now.
6 I've traveled a lot.
   a I'm talking about a general experience.
   b I'm talking about a specific time.

3 Put the word in parentheses in the correct place in the sentences.

1 Have you eaten? (already)
2 The play has started. (just)
3 The train hasn't arrived. (yet)
4 He's had coffee. (just)
5 We've seen this movie. (already)
6 Has she woken up? (yet)
7 I haven't sent the message. (yet)
8 My brother has heard the album. (just)

4 Choose the correct option to complete the sentences.

1 I've lived in this part of Melbourne *for two years / in 2005*.
2 My sister's been a music teacher *in 2000 / since 2000*.
3 I haven't seen my cousins *for 1995 / since 1995*.
4 We went to Japan *since three years / three years ago*.
5 Have you seen her *yesterday / today*?
6 I've worked in this office *since two years / for two years*.
7 We've started dance classes *last month / this month*.
8 My parents saw the show *in February / since February*.

5 Complete the sentences with the present perfect or simple past form of the verbs in parentheses.

1 Our teacher _____ never _____ (go) to France.
2 My piano lesson _____ (start) at ten o'clock.
3 _____ you ever _____ (see) a musical?
4 She _____ (not work) yesterday because she was very tired.
5 My brother _____ (get) married two weeks ago.
6 We _____ already _____ (read) this book.
7 _____ you _____ (go) to any concerts last month?

6 Complete the conversation with the present perfect or simple past form of these verbs.

do	enjoy	go	not be
have	open	hear	not see

A: What [1] _____ you _____ over the weekend?
B: I [2] _____ to a concert.
A: Lucky you! I [3] _____ a band play live for years.
B: This was a band called The Dotcoms. [4] _____ you _____ of them?
A: No. [5] _____ you _____ the concert?
B: Yes. It was amazing! I [6] _____ a great time.
A: Wow! Where was it?
B: It was at the new concert hall. It [7] _____ last month.
A: Oh, I [8] _____ there. Is it nice inside?
B: It's great!

GRAMMAR SUMMARY UNIT 3

Simple past and past continuous

We use both the simple past and the past continuous to talk about situations and events in the past.

We use the simple past for:

- a short, completed action.
  *He **opened** the car door.*

- a sequence of actions.
  *He **opened** the door, **got** out, and **walked** towards the animal.*

We use the past continuous for:

- an unfinished or continuing activity.
  *He **was trying** to turn on his camera.*
  *The lion **was looking** at them.*

- a background situation.
  *It **was raining**, and the trees **were blowing** in the wind.*

Remember that we rarely use the past continuous with stative verbs, such as *like, love, need, own,* or *want*.

We often use the past continuous and the simple past in the same sentence to talk about two things that happened at the same time. We often use *when* and *while* to link the two events in sentences like this.
*They **were driving** home when they **heard** a strange noise.*
*We **got** lost while we **were walking** in the jungle.*

We normally put *when* and *while* in the middle of the sentence. If we want to emphasize the first part of the sentence, *when* and *while* can go at the beginning. Remember to use a comma (,) in the middle of the sentence when this happens.
*While we **were walking** in the jungle, we **got** lost.*

We don't normally use *while* with the simple past, but you can use *when* with the past continuous.
*I was swimming in the sea **when** I saw a dolphin.*
(not *I was swimming in the sea **while** I saw a dolphin.*)
***When** I **was driving** home, I heard a strange noise.*
(or *While I was driving home, …*)

We often make questions in the past continuous to ask about activities at the time of a key event.
***What were you doing** when you first saw the shark?*

We often make questions in the simple past to ask about actions after a key event.
***What did you do** when the shark swam away?*

▶ **Exercises 1, 2, 3, and 4**

Past perfect

We form the past perfect with *had* + past participle.

We use the past perfect simple when we need to make clear that one past action happened before another past action. For the action that happened first, we use the past perfect. For the action that happened second, we use the simple past.
*When they **got** to the station, the train **had left**.*
  2   1

When we're telling a story, we sometimes also use the past perfect to describe events that happened before the start of a story.
*I visited Africa last year. I'd always **wanted** to go there. So I booked a vacation, and …*

We only use the past perfect when we need to make it clear which action happened first. We don't need to use the past perfect when:

- the order of events is the same as the order of the verbs in the sentence.
  *He **looked** down and **saw** a coin on the ground, so he **picked** it up.*
  (not ~~He had looked down and had seen …~~)

- the order of events is clear.
  *They **went** out on the boat after the storm **passed**.*
  (not ~~… the storm had passed~~)

We often use superlatives in sentences with the past perfect and the simple past.
*It was **the biggest** fish she'd ever seen.*

▶ **Exercises 5, 6, and 7**

Exercises

1 Complete the story with the simple past or past continuous form of the verbs in parentheses.

One weekend last summer, I ¹ _____ (decide) to go for a walk in the mountains. It was a perfect day—the sun ² _____ (shine) and it wasn't too hot. But while I ³ _____ (walk), I suddenly ⁴ _____ (see) a huge bear on the path ahead of me. I was terrified! I ⁵ _____ (try) to decide what to do when the bear ⁶ _____ (turn) around and ⁷ _____ (run) away. I ⁸ _____ (not know) I was so scary!

2 Use the prompts to write questions with the tense in parentheses.

1 What / he / do / when / saw the lion? (past continuous)

_____

2 What / he / do / when / the lion walked toward him? (simple past)

_____

3 Who / you / speak to / when / your phone battery died? (past continuous)

_____

4 What / you / do / when / your phone battery died? (simple past)

_____

5 What / they / do / when / the storm started? (past continuous)

_____

3 Match the questions from Exercise 2 with these answers.

1 ☐   2 ☐   3 ☐   4 ☐   5 ☐

a   He ran away!
b   They were swimming in the ocean.
c   I was speaking to my boss.
d   I borrowed my friend's phone.
e   He was sitting on the grass.

4 Complete the sentences with the simple past or past continuous forms of the verbs in parentheses.

1 The sun _____ (shine) when we _____ (go) outside.
2 While I _____ (run) around the park, I _____ (lose) my phone.
3 They _____ (watch) TV when she _____ (get) to their house.
4 Thomas _____ (sleep) when the mailman _____ (ring) the doorbell.

5 Read the sentences and underline the action in bold that happened first.

1 He **sat down** and **watched** TV.
2 They **went out** on the boat after the storm **had passed**.
3 Before we **had** our ice cream, we **went** for a swim.
4 He **didn't have** his phone because he**'d lost** it.
5 The movie **had ended** by the time we **arrived** at the theater.
6 They**'d met** each other many times before they **started** their business.
7 Sophie **felt** very excited because she **hadn't been** to a ballet before.
8 By the time we **found** the store, it **had closed**.

6 Complete the text with the past perfect form of these verbs. Use contractions where possible.

be	be	change	find
go	lose	spend	

Dario and Federica ¹ _____ only _____ married for three days when Federica lost her wedding ring. It happened on the first day of their honeymoon. They ² _____ the whole day on the beach and then they ³ _____ back to the hotel. While Federica was getting ready for dinner, she realized that she ⁴ _____ her ring. She felt terrible because it ⁵ _____ very expensive. The young couple went back to the beach the next day, but they couldn't find the ring. Then Federica remembered something: the day before, she ⁶ _____ her clothes behind a big rock at the end of the beach. So she went back to the rock. Luckily, the ring was still there—she couldn't believe she ⁷ _____ it!

7 Complete the sentences with the simple past or past perfect form of the verbs in parentheses.

1 Tania _____ (not be) to Bangkok before, so she _____ (be) really excited.
2 He _____ (not be) hungry because he _____ (eat) a big breakfast.
3 My cousins _____ (not come) to my birthday party because I _____ (forget) to send them an invitation.
4 The game _____ (already start) when we _____ (get) there.
5 I _____ (not want) to go to the movie theater with my friends because I _____ (already see) the movie.
6 Paco _____ (not know) the time because his watch _____ (stop) working.
7 The restaurant _____ (be) very busy, but luckily we _____ (reserve) a table.

GRAMMAR SUMMARY UNIT 4

Predictions

We use *will*, *may*, and *might* to make predictions.

Form

We use the same form of *will*, *may*, and *might* for all persons (*I*, *you*, *he*/*she*/*it*, etc.) and we don't need to use a form of *do* to make questions or negatives. *Will*, *may*, and *might* are always followed by the base form.

> Robots **will work** in our homes.

Note that *will* is often contracted after pronouns.

> It**'ll rain** tomorrow. (or It **may rain** … and It **might rain** …)

The negative of *will* is *won't*. We never contract *may not*—it always stays as two words.

> It **won't rain** later. (or It **may not rain** … and It **mightn't** / **might not rain** …)

We don't form questions with *may*.

> **Will** it rain later? (or *Might* it rain …)

The most common way to ask somebody to make a prediction is *Do you think* + *will*.

> **Do you think** Jackie **will like** the present?

We don't normally ask questions about predictions using *may*.

Use

will/won't

We use *will* and *won't* when we are confident about a prediction. We often add adverbs like *certainly*, *definitely*, and *probably* to make a prediction sound stronger. Adverbs like these normally come:

- after *will*.
  My job **will definitely** be very different in the future.

- before *won't*.
  Most people at my company **probably won't** have a job next year.

may/might

We use *may* (*not*) or *might* (*not*) when we are less confident about a prediction.

> The company **may** need to close the factory.
> They **might not** give me the job because I don't have much experience.

There is no difference in meaning between *may* and *might*, but *may* is more common in formal, written English.

We use *will* / *won't* / *might* / *might not* + *be able to* to make predictions about ability.

> She probably **won't be able to** come to the meeting.
> We **might be able to** get a discount.

▶ **Exercises 1, 2, and 3**

Future forms

We use different forms to talk about the future.

present continuous

We use the present continuous to talk about a fixed arrangement to do something at a specified (or understood) time in the future. We often use the present continuous when we have agreed to do something with another person, we have bought tickets for something, etc.

> I**'m meeting** my boss at 3:30. (= We both have the meeting in our calendar.)
> She**'s flying** to New York next week. (= She already has her ticket.)

We often use the present continuous to ask people about their plans, especially when we want to make an invitation.

> A: **Are** you **doing** anything tonight?
> B: No, I don't think so.
> A: Would you like to go and see a movie?

will

We use *will* + base form for a decision made at the moment of speaking.

> A: Have you sent Martin the email?
> B: No—I**'ll do** it now.

going to

We use *going to* + infinitive for a plan or intention decided before the moment of speaking.

> I'm **going to look for** a new job. (= This is my intention. I decided this a few days ago.)

The negative of *going to* is *not going to*. We don't normally make the main verb negative.

> He's **not going to** come. (not ~~He's going to not come.~~)

To make questions with *going to*, we use *are you going to* … , *is she going to* … , etc.

> **Are** you **going to** send me the report soon?

We can say *going to go*, but some people prefer to say simply *going*.

> I'm **going to go** to the dentist later.
> (or I'm **going to** the dentist …)

simple present

We use the simple present for an event that follows a regular schedule, like the time of trains, flights, etc.

> My flight **leaves** at 6:34 a.m.
> My class **ends** at 9:30 p.m.

We don't normally use the simple present to talk about an arrangement with other people. We use the present continuous or *going to* instead.

> We**'re** all **meeting** in the square at 8 p.m.
> (not ~~We all meet in the square at 8 p.m.~~)

▶ **Exercises 4, 5, and 6**

Exercises

1 Correct the mistakes in these sentences.

1 They might to go out for a meal later.

2 James definitely will be late to the meeting.

3 Some students mayn't pass their exams.

4 I think you'll to find a new job soon.

2 Put the words in order to make predictions with *will / won't*.

1 snow / it'll / over the weekend
   _____ .

2 be / will / open / the store
   _____ .

3 forget / certainly / their vacation / won't / they
   _____ .

4 be able to / find / she / our house / won't
   _____ .

5 be able to / finish / the report / today / we'll
   _____ .

3 Chiara is starting a new job. Look at her predictions about the job and complete the sentences with *will / won't*, *may / might*, or *may not / mightn't*.

confident	less confident
good things:	good things:
learn new things	good food in restaurant
meet new people	can travel abroad
can speak French	
bad things:	bad things:
can't walk to work	have to work late
anymore	tiring
not know anyone there	
not have many days off	

1 My new job _____ be tiring, but I'm sure
   I _____ learn a lot of new things.
2 I _____ know anyone at first, but
   I _____ meet new people.
3 I _____ speak French, and I
   _____ travel abroad for work.
4 There _____ be good food in the
   restaurant.
5 The office isn't near my home, so I _____
   walk to work anymore.

4 Read the sentences (1–5). Choose the correct option (a–b) to explain each sentence.

1 I'm getting a new computer tomorrow.
   a I plan to buy a new one.
   b I've already chosen and ordered one.
2 I'll have some coffee, please.
   a I'd already decided to have this.
   b I've just decided that I want this.
3 He's going to retake his exam.
   a He's just decided to do this.
   b He plans to do this.
4 We leave at 6:45 tomorrow morning.
   a The train leaves at this time.
   b We plan to leave at this time.
5 He's moving to another country for work.
   a He plans to do this.
   b He already has his contract.

5 Choose the correct options to complete the email.

Hi Rob,
I'm so excited because yesterday I booked a plane ticket for Australia! [1] *I'm moving / I'll move* there for a year! [2] *I'm working / I'm going to work* in Melbourne for the first six months, but I still need to find a job. Then, when I have some money, [3] *I'm going to travel / I'm traveling* around the country for six months. The only annoying thing is the time of my flight— [4] *it's leaving / it leaves* at 4 a.m.! But there are hotels near the airport, so I think [5] *I'm booking / I'll book* a room on the internet. I hope everything's OK with you. [6] *Are you doing / Will you do* anything this weekend? Would you like to meet up?
Anders

6 Complete the conversations with the correct future form. Sometimes more than one form is possible.

1 A: Sorry, Adrien is busy right now.
   B: OK, I _____ (come) back later.
2 A: Do you want to go out tomorrow night?
   B: Sorry, I _____ (go) to the theater. I've
      already bought a ticket.
3 A: What are you doing tonight?
   B: I _____ (study) because I have an
      exam soon.
4 A: Are you hungry? How about going out for
      dinner?
   B: No, it's OK—I _____ (make)
      something to eat.
5 A: When do you need to be at the station?
   B: My train _____ (leave) at 8:23, so I
      need to be there at about 8:15.

GRAMMAR SUMMARY UNIT 5

Modal verbs

Form

We use modal verbs like *must*, *can*, and *should* with the base form of the verb. We use the same form for all persons (*I*, *you*, *he/she/it*, etc.), and we don't need to use a form of *do* to make questions or negatives.

> You **can** leave your bag here.
> You **must not** leave your bag here.

Have to and *be allowed to* have similar meanings to modal verbs, but they do not have the same grammar. We use a form of *do* to make questions and negatives with *have to*.

> **Do** we **have to** sit here?

With *be allowed to*, we make questions and negatives in the same way as other forms with *be*.

> **Are** we **allowed to** come in?

Use

Obligation

To say there is an obligation, we use *must* or *have to*.

> You **have to** leave everything in the oven for two hours.
> Restaurants **must** make their prices clear.

We do not normally ask questions about obligation with *must*. We use *have to* instead.

> **Do** I **have to** take my shoes off?
> (not ~~Must I take my shoes off?~~)

There is no past form of *must* to talk about obligation. We use *had to* to talk about obligation in the past.

> We **had to** be at work at six o'clock this morning!

To say there is no obligation, we use *don't/doesn't have to*.

> We **don't have to** be there until 8 p.m.

Prohibition and permission

To talk about prohibition (to say "don't do it!"), we use *must not*.

> You **must not** talk here.

To give permission, we use *can*.

> You **can** pay for your drinks when you leave.

To say somebody doesn't have permission, we use *can't* or *cannot*.

> You **can't** sit in this part of the restaurant. (or You cannot sit …)

We also use *allowed to* and *not allowed to* talk about permission.

> You**'re not allowed** to park there.

Advice and recommendations

Should doesn't express a rule. We use *should* and *shouldn't* to give advice and recommendations.

> You **should** try to eat some fruit every day.

must and *have to*

The modal verbs *must* and *have to* have very similar meanings. We normally prefer to use *have to* in spoken English to talk about obligation. In formal, written English, we prefer to use *must*. But *must not* and *don't have to* have very different meanings. *Must not* expresses a rule—we use *must not* to say "don't do this." *Don't have to* doesn't express a rule—we use *don't have to* to say "it's not necessary to do this."

> Customers **must not** enter the kitchen. (= Don't do this!)
> The restaurant is huge. You **don't have to** reserve a table. (= This isn't necessary.)

▶ **Exercises 1, 2, and 3**

First conditional

We use the first conditional to talk about future possibility and things that are generally true. The form is usually:

If + simple present, + *will/won't*

> **If** I **have** time, I**'ll call** you tonight. (= future possibility)

Note that we never use a future form in the *if* clause.

> If it**'s** a nice day tomorrow, we'll go for a picnic.
> (not ~~If it will be a nice day …~~)

Conditional sentences have two parts: the *if* clause and the main clause. The main clause describes the result of the situation in the *if* clause.

> If you're late, **we'll go** without you. (we'll go … = main clause = result)

When the *if* clause comes first, we use a comma between the two clauses. When the main clause comes before the *if* clause, we don't add a comma between the two clauses.

> **If** you're late, we'll go without you.
> We'll go without you **if** you're late.

▶ **Exercise 4**

when, as soon as, unless, until, before

We also use *when*, *as soon as*, *unless*, *until*, and *before* to talk about the future. We always use a present tense, not a future form, after these expressions. We often use the expressions in a sentence with *will*.

> **When** I **finish** my work, I'll get something to eat
> I won't eat there again **unless** they **start** using less salt.

As with the first conditional, we put a comma when the clause with the time expression comes first.

▶ **Exercises 5 and 6**

Exercises

1 Correct the mistakes in these sentences.

1 She hasn't to go to work today.

2 I can to make you a sandwich.

3 Do I should come back later?

4 Has he to go to the meeting?

5 We aren't allowed park here.

6 You don't must use your phone here.

2 Read the signs. Complete the sentences with the correct modal form. Write all the possible answers.

1 **TICKETS NEEDED BEFORE ENTRY**
   You _____ / _____ buy a ticket before you enter.

2 **TABLETS AND PHONES ALLOWED ON THIS FLIGHT**
   You _____ turn off your tablets or phones on this flight.

3 **NO PARKING**
   You _____ / _____ / _____ park here.

4 **THIS FILM IS NOT RECOMMENDED FOR CHILDREN**
   Children _____ see this film.

5 **EXAM IN PROGRESS: BE QUIET!**
   You _____ / _____ speak quietly.

3 Complete the text with modal verbs and the verbs in parentheses. Use affirmative and negative forms of the modal verbs.

School lunches are very popular in the US. Most children [1] _____ (pay) for school lunches, but they don't cost a lot. However, poorer families [2] _____ (pay)—the school lunches are free.

There are strict rules about school lunches. For example, every meal [3] _____ (include) meat or fish, fruit and vegetables, and bread, potatoes or other grains. Another rule is that school cafeterias [4] _____ (sell) food and drinks with a lot of sugar and salt.

Children [5] _____ (eat) school lunches if they don't want to. They [6] _____ (bring) a bag lunch from home. There are many rules for the types of food to give children in their bag lunches. For example, children [7] _____ (eat) fruit every day and they [8] _____ (have) junk food like potato chips and candy.

4 Choose the correct option to complete the first conditional sentences.

1 If he *does / will do* more exercise, *he gets / he'll get* fitter.

2 If the train *doesn't / won't* arrive soon, *I'm being / I'll be* late for work.

3 *You feel / You'll feel* better if *you eat / you'll eat* healthier food.

5 Match the beginnings of the sentences (1–6) with the endings (a–f). Then complete the endings of the sentences with the correct form of the verbs in parentheses.

1 If she doesn't leave soon, ____

2 They'll have a picnic in the park next to their house ____

3 You can't go out ____

4 You'll feel sick ____

5 Can you call me ____

6 I think he'll drive to the station ____

a if there _____ too much traffic. (not be)

b until you _____ all your homework. (finish)

c as soon as you _____ this message? (get)

d she _____ her bus. (miss)

e if you _____ all that chocolate! (eat)

f unless it _____ . (rain)

6 Complete the conversation with the correct form of these verbs.

eat	exercise	follow	go
lose	not do	not feel	not lose

A: How are you?

B: I'm fed up! I'm trying to lose weight, but nothing's working!

A: Well, I'm sure if you [1] _____ healthy food, you [2] _____ some weight. And you need to exercise, too.

B: I try to eat healthily, but I never have time to exercise!

A: But you [3] _____ weight if you [4] _____ any exercise.

B: All right! I'll ride on my exercise bike before I [5] _____ to bed tonight.

A: No, that's the worst time to exercise! If you [6] _____ in the evening, you [7] _____ sleepy afterwards. And sleep is also important for losing weight …

B: OK, so I'll go for a run at lunchtime instead.

A: Great. But remember—unless you [8] _____ a regular fitness program, you'll never lose weight.

GRAMMAR SUMMARY UNIT 6

Purpose: *to*, *for*, and *so that*

We use *to*, *for*, and *so that* to explain why people do something or the purpose of an object. Phrases with these words answer the questions *Why?* or *What for?*

the infinitive

We use the infinitive to say why we do something.
> She's taking a class **to improve** her communication skills.
> I used an old piece of plastic **to fix** the hole in the bath tub.

We often use the infinitive to answer questions with *why*.
> A: Why did you call me?
> B: **To ask** if you want to go to the movies.

for + noun

We also use *for* + noun to say why we do something.
> She went there **for a job interview**.
> They stopped at a restaurant **for some lunch**.

We never use *for* with a verb form to say why we do something. Use the infinitive instead.
> I bought this book **to have** something to read on the plane. (not *I bought this book for to have something … / for having something …*)

for + *-ing*

We use *for* + *-ing* to talk about the purpose or function of an object.
> A: What app are you using?
> B: It's a game. It's **for improving** your memory.

so that

We also use *so that* to say why we do something. We often use this:

- with the modal verbs *can*, *could*, *will*, or *would*.
  > I'll call Sam **so that** he'll know where to go.
  > We got to the theater early **so that** we **could** get a good seat.

- when the result is negative.
  > I want to buy an ebook reader **so that** I **don't have to** carry lots of books with me.

We only use *so that* when we do something to get a specific result. To talk about a result on its own, we use *so* without *that*. Note that we use a comma before *so* that introduces a result.
> I didn't wake up on time, **so** I missed my flight.
> (not *… on time so that I missed …*)

We often use *so* instead of *so that* in informal English.
> She drove me to the store **so** (**that**) I didn't have to walk.

▶ **Exercises 1, 2, and 3**

Certainty and possibility

We use the modal verbs *must*, *might (not)*, *may (not)*, *could*, and *can't* to talk about certainty and possibility.

We use *must* when we think that something is probable.
> Her flight was at four in the morning. She **must** be very tired.

We use *might*, *may*, and *could* when we think that something is possible.
> Paul **might** be able to help you.
> Hotel Tourist **may** have a room free.
> There **could** be a problem with the trains.

We can make *might* and *may* negative with this meaning, but not *could*.
> Stephanie **might** not want to eat out.
> (not *Stephanie could not want …*)
> I **may** not have the correct address.
> (not *I could not have …*)

We use *can't* when we think that something is impossible.
> A: Is that Mike in the café?
> B: No, it **can't** be him. He's on vacation in Greece!

When we're talking about things we're totally sure about, we don't use modals at all.
> Stefan lives near here. (= I know this. I've been to his house.)
> Esther doesn't eat meat. (= I know this. She told me.)

▶ **Exercises 4 and 5**

In the present and in the past

We use modal verb + base form to talk about certainty and possibility in the present.
> You **must be** hungry. (= It's probable that you're hungry now.)

We use modal verb + *be* + *-ing* if the action is in progress.
> He's not answering his phone. He **might be driving**.
> (= I think he's driving now.)

We use modal verb + *have* + past participle to talk about certainty and possibility in the past.
> His plane **must have arrived** by now. (= It's probable that his plane has arrived.)

We can also use *couldn't have* instead of *can't have*:
> A: I think I left my phone on the plane.
> B: No, you **couldn't have left** it there—we checked really carefully.

▶ **Exercise 6**

Exercises

1 Match the beginnings of the sentences (1–7) with the endings (a–g). Then complete the endings of the sentences with the infinitives of these words.

ask	buy	catch	get	give	see	watch

1 I've joined a gym _____
2 She's going to the supermarket _____
3 He bought some flowers _____
4 I went to the station _____
5 We opened the box _____
6 I turned on the TV _____
7 Emilia called _____

a _____ what was inside.
b _____ more exercise.
c _____ my train.
d _____ me a question.
e _____ some food for dinner.
f _____ to his wife.
g _____ my favorite series.

2 Rewrite three of the sentences in Exercise 1 with *so that*.

1 _____
2 _____
3 _____

3 Choose the correct options to complete the conversation.

A: You look tired!
B: Well, I'm waking up at 5:30 a.m. these days.
A: Why?
B: [1] *To do / For doing* yoga before I go to work.
A: I'm not surprised you're tired! Well, you should go to bed early [2] *for / so that* a good night's sleep.
B: I'd like to, but I'm always too busy in the evening to have an early night. For example, I've also started an online language course [3] *for improving / to improve* my German! I'm always up until late studying grammar.
A: Maybe you're doing too much. I have a great app on my phone that could help you. It's [4] *for organizing / to organize* my day.
B: Sounds interesting. Can you show it to me [5] *for / so that* I can see how it works?
A: Sure, but I don't have time now. My phone's just told me that I have to take the car to the garage [6] *to / for* a tune up. See you soon. Bye!

4 Read the sentences (1–4). Choose the correct option (a–b) to explain each sentence.

1 John must be asleep.
   a I'm sure John is asleep.
   b It's possible that John is asleep.
2 That can't be my phone. Mine's in my pocket.
   a It's impossible that it's my phone.
   b It's possibly not my phone.
3 Your keys might be in your bag.
   a Your keys are definitely in your bag.
   b It's possible that your keys are in your bag.
4 That woman with Frank could be his wife.
   a I'm certain that she's Frank's wife.
   b I think it's possible that she's Frank's wife.

5 Read the pairs of sentences. Rewrite the first sentence using a present modal verb.

1 It's impossible that that's Martin's car. His car is in the garage.
   That _____ .
2 I'm sure it's cold outside. It's snowing!
   It _____ .
3 It's possible that they aren't at home. Their car isn't outside their house.
   _____ .
4 I'm sure you know each other very well. You've been friends for a long time.
   You _____ .

6 Choose the correct options to complete the conversation.

A: Are we close to the castle ruins yet?
B: I think we [1] *may go / may be going* the wrong way. What did the guidebook say?
A: It said the ruins are near a small lake.
B: Oh—we passed a lake about five minutes ago!
A: So, we [2] *must drive / must have driven* past the road we need to take!
B: OK, oh, look—there's the lake. We [3] *can't be / can't have been* far away now.
B: What's the name of the road we're looking for?
A: Old Hill … Oh, hold on—it [4] *might be / might have been* this one.
B: No, that's Field Lane.
A: Well, we're near the lake, so the road [5] *must be / must have been* close.
B: Look at the top of that hill. I can see something. I'm not sure, but it [6] *might be / must be* part of the ruins. Drive up that way!
B: OK. … Hmm—we [7] *must go / must have gone* the wrong way again. That's a gas station!
A: Maybe the guidebook is wrong! There [8] *can't have been / might have been* a castle here!

GRAMMAR SUMMARY UNIT 7

used to, would, and simple past

used to

We use *used to* to talk about past habits and states.
> We **used to** go on vacation to California every year when I was a kid. (= past habit)
> They **used to** have a really tiny apartment downtown. (= past state)

Used to is always followed by the base form. We use the same form for all persons (*I, you, he/she/it*, etc.). In negatives and questions, we use *use to*, not *used to*.
> **Did** you **use to** live near the coast?

We often use adverbs of frequency and other time phrases with *used to*.
> We used to eat there **every week**.

We often use *used to* to describe past actions and states that aren't true any more.
> I used to live in Germany. (= I don't live there now.)

We sometimes use frequency adverbs with *used to*. They come before *used to*.
> We **always** used to go to the beach in the summer when I was a child.

To talk about habits in the present, we use the simple present with *usually*.
> We **usually** go for a walk in the park every day. (not ~~We use to go for a walk …~~)

We don't normally use *used to* for repeated actions that lasted a short period of time. We use the simple past instead.
> I **walked** to work every day last week. (not ~~I used to walk to work every day last week.~~)

▶ **Exercise 1**

would

We also use *would* + base form to talk about repeated past actions. In spoken English, *would* often becomes *'d*.
> **I'd** spend every day in the summer outside when I was a child.

We only use *would* to talk about repeated actions in the past. We don't use *would* to talk about states.
> We **used to** own a really nice house in the countryside. (not ~~We'd own a house …~~)

We sometimes use frequency adverbs with *would*. They come after *would*.
> I'd **always** do my homework at the last minute when I was in school.

When we talk about the past, we often start with *used to* and then continue with *would*.
> When I first moved to Mexico City, I **used to** go out a lot. I**'d** visit museums and go to concerts.

▶ **Exercises 2 and 3**

Comparative adverbs

more/less + adverb

To make comparative forms of adverbs, we use *more* + adverb (*than*).
> This room gets warm **more quickly** than the rest of the house.
> You can live **more cheaply** in other parts of the city.

The opposite of *more* + adverb is *less* + adverb.
> You clean the apartment **less often** than I do.

Some comparative adverb forms are irregular. They have the same form as the comparative adjective, for example, *well → better, badly → worse, far → farther, fast → faster, high → higher, early → earlier, late → later, soon → sooner*.

▶ **Exercise 4**

(not) as + adverb + as

To make comparisons, we also use *(not) as* + adverb + *as*. *Not* normally goes with the verb.
> Martina can run **as fast as** Silvia. (= Martina and Silvia can run at the same speed.)

▶ **Exercise 5**

Comparative patterns

To say that a situation is changing, we use comparative + *and* + comparative. We can use a comparative adjective or a comparative adverb in this structure.
> It's getting **colder and colder**—it's probably going to snow. (comparative adjective—one syllable)
> Things are becoming **more and more expensive** in this country. (comparative adjective—longer adjective)
> I have so much work that I'm going to bed **later and later**. (comparative adverb)

Remember that we add *-er* to most one-syllable adjectives, and we put *more* before longer adjectives to make the comparative adjective form.

We often use *more and more* + noun.
> **More and more people bike** to work these days.

To say that two things change at the same time, we use *the* + comparative + clause, *the* + comparative + clause.
> The harder you work, the more success you'll have. (= If you work hard, you'll be more successful.)

We sometimes use this structure with only a noun phrase instead of a clause, or with only a comparative form.
> The taller the mountain, the greater the difficulty. (= Tall mountains are more difficult to climb.)

▶ **Exercise 6**

Exercises

1 Complete the sentences with the correct form of *used to* and these verbs.

do	drive	live	love
not be	not feel		

1 I _____ in Lima when I was young.
2 What _____ you _____ on the weekends when you were a child?
3 We _____ going to the theater when we lived in Argentina.
4 There _____ any houses here when I was young—it was all fields.
5 I _____ worried when I had an exam at school.
6 We _____ a lovely house by the water.

2 Circle the sentences in which *used to* can be replaced by *would*.

1 I didn't use to like classical music when I was a teenager, but now I love it.
2 We used to visit Los Angeles often before we had children.
3 When I was younger, I used to believe in UFOs, but I don't any more.
4 Sean used to play basketball every day when he was a teenager.

3 Complete the conversation with *used to*, *would*, or the simple past form of the verbs in parentheses.

A: You've been to Singapore, haven't you?
B: Yes, I [1] _____ (go) there often for work when I was living in Malaysia. Are you going to visit?
A: Yeah, next month. Any recommendations?
B: Well, I [2] _____ (leave) Malaysia in 2012. Things might be different now. But, I remember we [3] _____ (eat) in a great Italian restaurant. It was by the river. I can't remember the name, but they [4] _____ (make) fantastic pizza.
A: OK, I'll look for it. Anything else?
B: Well, I remember I once [5] _____ (visit) the zoo with my company. It was excellent. I think they always [6] _____ (take) visitors there.
A: OK, thanks. Any other advice?
B: Yes—use public transportation! The subway is great. I never [7] _____ (drive) when I was there.

4 Complete the sentences with the correct comparative form of the adverbs in parentheses. Sometimes, you will need to use irregular comparative forms.

1 Jack always wins when they race. Jack runs _____ than John. (fast)
2 Ruth is the most hardworking person in her family. Ruth works _____ than her brothers. (hard)
3 Your motorcycle is really noisy. Your motorcycle runs _____ than mine. (quietly)
4 The last flight is the Fastair flight. The Fastair flight arrives _____ than all the others. (late)
5 Katy is a very slow worker. Sarah doesn't work _____ than Katy. (slowly)

5 Complete the sentences so that they mean the same as the sentences in Exercise 4. Use (*not*) *as … as* and the verbs and adverbs in parentheses.

1 John _____ Jack. (run fast)
2 Ruth's brothers _____ her. (work hard)
3 Your motorcycle _____ mine. (run quietly)
4 The other flights _____ the Fastair flight. (arrive late)
5 Katy _____ Sarah. (work quickly)

6 Match the statements (1–6) with the replies (a–f).

1 I could only find this birthday cake. Is it too big? ____
2 I want to get fit, but jogging is so hard! ____
3 There's so much traffic on the roads these days. ____
4 What time should we go for lunch? ____
5 The price of housing is so high here at the moment. ____
6 Why are you taking another course? ____

a I know—more and more people are driving.
b It's fine—the bigger, the better!
c The earlier the better—I'm already feeling hungry!
d Yes, it's getting harder and harder to find somewhere to live.
e The more qualifications you have, the easier it is to get a job.
f The more you run, the easier it'll get.

Verb patterns: *-ing* form and infinitive

When we put two verbs together in a sentence, the form of the second verb depends on the first. After many verbs we use the *-ing* form.

> I **love** *traveling abroad.*

Other common verbs followed by the *-ing* form: *adore, avoid, can't help, can't stand, describe, don't mind, enjoy, fancy, finish, imagine, keep, mention, miss, practice, recommend, spend (time/money), suggest.*
The negative of the *-ing* form is *not + -ing.*

> I **enjoy not getting** *up early on the weekend.*

After many other verbs, we use a verb in the infinitive form.

> I **hope to see** *you later this year.*

Other common verbs followed by the infinitive form: *agree, arrange, ask, can't afford, choose, decide, expect, fail, hope, intend, learn, manage, need, offer, plan, pretend, promise, refuse, seem, threaten, want, would like, would love, would prefer.*

The negative of infinitive is *not + infinitive.*

> I **promise not to be** *late.*

These verbs can also be followed by both the infinitive and *-ing* form, with no difference in meaning: *begin, continue, hate, like, love, prefer, start.*

> I **began reading** *the book.* (or I **began to read** …)

▶ **Exercises 1 and 2**

Other uses

We use the *-ing* form when we use a verb as the subject of a sentence.

> **Traveling** *can be very educational.*

We also use the *-ing* form when a verb follows a preposition.

> *We often* **think about** *traveling for a year.*

We often use infinitive after an adjective.

> *It was* **amazing to visit** *Chile for the first time.*

▶ **Exercise 3**

Present perfect and present perfect continuous

Form

We form the present perfect with *have/has* + past participle of the main verb. (See the inside of the back cover for a list of common irregular past participles.)

> I've just **got** *back from vacation.*

We form the present perfect continuous with *have/has* + *been* + *-ing* form of the main verb, for example: *I've been waiting, he's been doing, they haven't been reading.*

▶ **Exercise 4**

Use

We use both the present perfect and the present perfect continuous to talk about something that started in the past and continues in the present. We use:

- the present perfect to talk about a state that started in the past and continues in the present.
  I've loved Turkey since I first visited in 2005.

- the present perfect continuous to talk about a long action or a repeated action that started in the past and continues in the present.
  I've been waiting for your email since last week. (long action)
  We've been coming here for years. (repeated action)

We also use both the present perfect and the present perfect continuous to talk about actions in the past that have an effect on the present. We use:

- the present perfect to talk about short actions that are complete and that have an effect on the present.
  Joel has broken his arm. (= it's still broken)

- the present perfect continuous to talk about long actions in the past that have an effect on the present.
  We've been walking in the forest all morning. (= and now we're hungry and tired)

We often use the present perfect continuous to emphasize the duration of a longer past activity and the present perfect to talk about its final result.

> *I've been researching vacations all morning. I think I've found the perfect one for us.* (*researching* = longer activity, *found* = result)

For other uses of the present perfect, see Unit 2.

Remember that we don't normally use stative verbs in the continuous. See Unit 1.

▶ **Exercise 5**

How long?

We make questions with *how long* to ask about duration.

> *How long have you known David?*
> *How long have you been doing conservation work?*
> *How long did you live in Africa?*

We use *for* in answers to questions in all three tenses, but we can't use *since* with the simple past.

> *I lived in Africa for ten years.* (not … ~~since 2002.~~)

▶ **Exercise 6**

Exercises

1 Choose the correct option to complete the sentences. Sometimes, both options are possible.

1 Would you like *going* / *to go* to the movies tonight?
2 He's pretending *being* / *to be* sick so that he doesn't have to go to work.
3 She'd prefer *not speaking* / *not to speak* to anyone at the moment.
4 I love *to swim* / *swimming* in the ocean at night.
5 I hate *to have* / *having* to rush in the morning.
6 I recommend *visiting* / *to visit* the history museum. It's fascinating.

2 Complete the conversation with the correct form of the verbs in parentheses.

A: I'm going on vacation soon!
B: Oh, you're so lucky. I'd really love ¹ _____ (go) away somewhere! Where are you going?
A: To Spain. I'm going to spend all day ² _____ (lie) on the beach! What are you going to do over the summer?
B: Well, I can't afford ³ _____ (travel) very far, but I'm hoping ⁴ _____ (go) camping somewhere near here.
A: At least you won't have to get on a plane. I can't stand ⁵ _____ (fly)!
B: Really? Well, when you're on the plane, just avoid ⁶ _____ (think) about where you are. Just relax and imagine ⁷ _____ (sit) on a beach.
A: I'll try. Well, anyway, I'm going to enjoy ⁸ _____ (not work) for a few weeks!

3 Complete the text with the correct form of these verbs.

drive	eat	get	take	use	visit	walk

If you're interested in ¹ _____ a break from modern life, then La Posada del Inca Eco-Lodge may be the place for you. It's on one of the most beautiful islands on Lake Titicaca, in Bolivia. ² _____ here is impossible because it is a car-free island. This means it's great ³ _____ if you enjoy ⁴ _____ , especially as the views are spectacular. It is possible ⁵ _____ all your meals in the hotel; the food is simple but delicious. The rooms don't have fridges, TVs, or Wi-Fi, but they do have hot water and heating. It is difficult ⁶ _____ an internet connection on the island, so if you really need ⁷ _____ the internet, you'll have to climb up to the restaurants near the top of the hill.

4 Write statements and questions with the present perfect continuous form.

1 I / live / here / since / 2015.
   _____
2 She / not wait / long.
   _____
3 you / work / all day?
   _____
4 They / swim / for / about an hour.
   _____
5 he / play video games / all morning?
   _____

5 Choose the correct option to complete the sentences.

1 I've already *eaten* / *been eating*, so I don't need any dinner.
2 He's *had* / *been having* that car for ages.
3 I haven't *seen* / *been seeing* Jack for three years.
4 She's *studied* / *been studying* all afternoon and now she needs a break.
5 Sorry. Have you *waited* / *been waiting* for long?
6 We haven't *known* / *been knowing* each for long.
7 I travel a lot. I've *visited* / *been visiting* ten countries.

6 Complete the conversation with the present perfect or present perfect continuous of the verbs in parentheses. Sometimes both forms are possible.

A: You look tired. What ¹ _____ (you / do)?
B: I ² _____ (search) on the internet for hours for a vacation destination. And I still ³ _____ (not find) anywhere!
A: What about the usual place you go?
B: Oh, I ⁴ _____ (go) to that resort for the last five years. I'm bored with it!
A: Well, why don't you go on a bicycle trip?
B: A bicycle trip?! I'm not sure … ⁵ _____ (you / go) on one before?
A: Yes. I went on an organized tour around Rajasthan last year. It was the most amazing vacation I ⁶ _____ ever _____ (have)!
B: Really? It sounds very tiring!
A: It was fun! And I made new friends. We ⁷ _____ (stay) in touch since our trip. I ⁸ _____ (already book) my next bike trip with the same company.
B: How long ⁹ _____ (it / do) these tours?
A: Oh, for a long time. They're very good. You should come with me! You'd love it!
B: Well, yes, but I ¹⁰ _____ (not have) much time to exercise recently.
A: That's OK. I'm going in six months. You can start riding your bike tomorrow!

GRAMMAR SUMMARY UNIT 9

Passives

Verbs can be active or passive. We normally use the active form when the focus of the sentence is on the "agent"—the person or thing that does an action.

> **All kinds of people** buy products like these.
> (focus = all kinds of people)

When we use the passive, a sentence isn't about the agent any more. The passive emphasizes the action.

> **Products like these** are bought by all kinds of people.
> (focus = products like these)

Form

When we use the passive, the object of the active sentence becomes the subject of the passive sentence.

> All kinds of people buy <u>products like these</u>.
>   OBJECT
> <u>Products like these</u> **are bought** by all kinds of people.
>   SUBJECT

We form the passive with a form of the auxiliary verb *be* and the past participle of the main verb.

Tense	Active	Passive
Simple present	*buy*	*is/are bought*
Present continuous	*is/are buying*	*is/are being bought*
Simple past	*bought*	*was/were bought*
Past continuous	*was/were buying*	*was/were being bought*
Present perfect	*has/have bought*	*has/have been bought*
Past perfect	*had bought*	*had been bought*
Modal verbs	*can buy*	*can be bought*

We can use *by* + noun to say who does or did the action in a sentence with a passive verb. This makes the information sound new or important.

> The new farmers' market was opened **by a local businessman** last month.

▶ **Exercise 1**

Use

We often use the passive:

- when it's obvious who does an action.
  *The letter **was delivered** this morning.* (= obviously by the mailman)

- when it's unimportant who does an action.
  *When I complained to the company about the camera I bought, I **was sent** a new one.* (= it doesn't matter who sent it)

- when we don't know who does an action.
  *My bag **was stolen**.* (= I don't know who stole it)

- when we don't want to say who does an action.
  *The house **hasn't been cleaned** again.* (= I don't want to say who hasn't cleaned the house.)

▶ **Exercises 2 and 3**

Articles

We use *a/an* the first time we mention something.
> *I just bought **a** new washing machine.*

We use *the* when we mention something that is known (because it has already been mentioned, for example, and when there is only one of something.)
> *I bought a shirt and a tie. **The** shirt was really cheap.*
> *It was warm, and **the** sun was shining.*

We use no article (**zero article**) to talk in general about uncountable or plural nouns.
> ***Tourism** brings a lot of money to the country.*

▶ **Exercise 4**

Quantifiers

We use *a lot of, lots of,* and *plenty of* with uncountable and plural nouns to talk about large quantities. We often use *plenty of* to mean "more than enough."
> *We don't need to go to the supermarket. There's **plenty of** food in the fridge.* (= more than enough food)

We also use *many* + plural noun in more formal, written English to talk about a large quantity.
> *There are **many** ways to save money on your shopping.*

We don't normally use *much* in affirmative sentences. However, we use *too much* with uncountable nouns and *too many* with plural nouns to say there is more than we want.
> *There's **too much** noise here—I can't work.*

We also use *much* and *many* to ask questions about quantities.
> *Were there **many** nice clothes on sale?*

We use *some* to talk about neutral, non-specific quantities with uncountable and plural nouns.
> *I've got **some** food.* (= not a lot, not a little)

We use *several, one or two, a couple of,* and *a few* to talk about smaller quantities with plural nouns. We normally use *several* to refer to larger quantities than *one or two, a couple of,* and *a few*.
> *We have **one or two** questions about the offer.*

We use *a little* to talk about smaller quantities with uncountable nouns.
> *We've got **a little** money left. Let's get some ice cream.*

We use *not any* with plural and uncountable nouns to talk about zero quantity. We also use *any* when we ask questions about uncountable and plural countable nouns.

We use *little* + uncountable noun and *few* + countable noun to say "not much" and "not many" in formal, written English. They have a more negative meaning than *a little* and *a few*.

▶ **Exercises 5 and 6**

Exercises

1 Are the sentences correct? If not, correct any mistakes with the passive.

1 My new book can found online or in bookstores.
2 The hole in the roof still hasn't be repaired!
3 Your order was been sent to you ten days ago.
4 The show is watched from millions of people all over the world.
5 Our friends' food being brought to the table when we arrived.

2 Choose the correct options to complete the text.

Great meal at Rexo!

This new Mexican restaurant [1] *has mentioned / has been mentioned* quite a lot on the radio recently, so I decided to try it. I love Mexican food anyway! We arrived at around 8 p.m. It was really busy, but we [2] *gave / were given* a table after just five minutes. While our table [3] *was prepared / was being prepared*, we [4] *looked / were looked* at the menu. There's a great selection, and the prices are good.

After [5] *we'd ordered / we'd been ordered*, our food [6] *was brought / brought* quickly. Everything was delicious. We only had one complaint. We'd asked for some tap water. But when we paid, we saw that $2 [7] *had added / had been added* for the water. This didn't seem fair—tap water is free in all the other restaurants in town! But overall, I'm sure Rexo will be a success and their delicious food will [8] *enjoy / be enjoyed* by everyone!

---

3 Rewrite the information in the passive. Don't include the agents in parentheses.

1 (The supermarket) has just delivered the shopping.
  The shopping _____ .
2 (The technician) is fixing my computer.
  My computer _____ .
3 Will (you) invite Sonia to the party?
  _____ Sonia _____ to the party?
4 (We) didn't finish the work.
  The work _____ .
5 (You) can't use cell phones here.
  Cell phones _____ here.
6 (The manager) had called the police.
  The police _____ .
7 Do (you) accept credit cards?
  _____ credit cards _____ ?
8 (People) don't use the new shopping center.
  The new shopping center _____ .

4 Complete the text with *the*, *a(n)*, or – (zero article).

[1] _____ cash machine in [2] _____ New York had to be turned off because it was giving out too much money. [3] _____ machine, in one of [4] _____ busiest subway stations, was giving [5] _____ ten-dollar bills instead of [6] _____ five-dollar bills. As soon as [7] _____ people realized what was happening, [8] _____ line developed. Within thirty minutes, news of what was happening appeared on [9] _____ internet, and even more people arrived. But not long after, [10] _____ employee from the bank came to turn it off.

5 Complete the second sentences with these quantifiers so that they mean the same as the first sentences.

a couple of several	a little too much	plenty of

1 There's more traffic than we want in this town.
  There's _____ traffic in this town.
2 There are one or two good stores on this street.
  There are _____ good stores in this street.
3 I have some money left, but not very much.
  I have _____ money left.
4 We won't be late—we have more time than we need.
  We won't be late—we have _____ time.
5 Four or five new restaurants have opened near my apartment.
  _____ restaurants have opened near my apartment.

6 Choose the correct options to complete the conversation.

A: OK, we've spent [1] *a lot of / much* money now. Let's go home.
B: Not yet. I still need to get [2] *a couple of / lots of* things—just a new dress and some shoes.
A: Really? You already have [3] *many / plenty of* pairs of shoes at home—more than you need, in my opinion.
B: Yes, but I [4] *don't have any / have not any* shoes that match my new coat!
A: I see. Well, [5] *how much / how many* time do you need? I'm getting hungry. I only had [6] *a little / a couple of* breakfast.
B: I won't be long—I promise. Why don't you go to the café over there? Then I can have [7] *a little / little* time to myself.
A: All right. I'll see you in [8] *a few / few* minutes.

GRAMMAR SUMMARY UNIT 10

Second conditional

We use the second conditional to talk about unreal situations in the present or future. The form is:
If + simple past + *would* + base form
> *If I **liked** science, I'**d read** more books about space exploration.*
> *If we **had** to live on Mars, it **wouldn't** be easy.*

We can also use *might* in the main clause when we are less sure about the result.
> *If you **saw** the film, you **might** like it.*

We often use *could* in the main clause to talk about ability and possibility.
> *If we lived by the ocean, we **could** go swimming every day.* (= we would be able to go swimming)

When the *if* clause comes first, we use a comma between the two clauses. When the main clause comes before the *if* clause, we don't add a comma between the two clauses.
> *If we wanted to, we could do more to protect the planet.*
> *We could do more to protect the planet **if** we wanted to.*

We don't normally put *would* in the *if* clause. We normally use a past tense.
> *If I **had** more time, I would travel more often.* (not *~~If I would have more time, …~~*)

When we put *be* in the *if* clause, we can use *were* instead of *was*. We normally do this when we use the phrase "If I were you" to give advice.
> *If I **were you**, I wouldn't take the job.*

We also use *were* in this way in other sentences. This normally sounds more formal, but some people consider it more correct.
> *If I **were** richer, I'd become a space tourist.*
> *If he **were** more careful, he wouldn't have so many accidents.*

▶ **Exercises 1, 2, and 3**

Defining relative clauses

We use defining relative clauses to say exactly which person, thing, place, or time we are talking about.
> *That's the doctor **that I saw last month**.* (relative clause tells us which doctor)

that, which, and who

To introduce a relative clause, we use a relative pronoun or relative adverb after a noun. The choice of relative pronoun depends on the type of noun:

- for things, use *that*.
  *This is the finger **that** hurts.*

- for people, use *that* or *who*.
  *The people **that/who** spoke to us are here.*

We can leave out *that* and *who* when they are the object of the verb in the relative clause.
> *She loves **the flowers (that)** you brought.* (*that* = object of *brought*)
> ***The person (that/who)** you know isn't here.*

We can't leave out the relative pronoun if it's the subject of the relative clause.
> *That's **the film that** won five Oscars last year.* (not *~~That's the film won …~~*)

▶ **Exercise 4**

whose, when, and where

We use the relative pronoun *whose* to talk about possession.
> *Sonia has a daughter **whose** dream is to become a doctor.*

We also make relative clauses with the relative adverbs *where* and *when*. They mean the same as preposition + *which*.
> *That's the hospital **where** I was born.* (= the hospital **in which** I was born)
> *Do you remember the moment **when** you decided to become a nurse?* (= the moment **in which** you decided to become a nurse)

▶ **Exercises 5 and 6**

Exercises

1 Match the beginnings of the sentences (1–8) with the endings (a–h).

1 If I were you, ____
2 People wouldn't feel so stressed ____
3 If my sister didn't buy so many things, ____
4 Which sport would you do ____
5 If Paul didn't drink so much coffee, ____
6 If my parents lived closer, ____
7 I wouldn't have to use public transportation ____
8 If space travel were cheaper, ____

a I could visit them more often.
b she'd have more money.
c if you had more free time?
d I'd find another apartment.
e if they didn't work so much.
f he might sleep better at night.
g would more people try it?
h if I had a car.

2 Choose the correct form to complete the sentences.

1 If you *were / would be* a millionaire, what *would / did* you buy first?
2 People would *feel / felt* happier here if it *were / would be* sunnier.
3 If we *lived / would live* in the countryside, *we'll / we'd* be able to see the stars at night.
4 If I *hadn't / didn't have* so much work to do, *I'd go / I went* to bed earlier.
5 I *can / could* buy a new car if *I'd save / I saved* more money.
6 My dad *would have / had* more friends if *he'd be / he was* friendlier.
7 *Would / Did* you take a job for less money if it *was / would be* closer to home?
8 If *I lived / I'd lived* closer to my job, I *could / can* walk there.

3 Complete the sentences to make second conditionals.

1 I don't exercise, so I'm not very fit.
   If I _____ more, I _____ fitter.
2 She doesn't have his number, so she can't call him.
   If she _____ his number, she _____ him.
3 You're tired because you don't get enough sleep.
   You _____ tired if you _____ enough sleep.
4 He doesn't study, so he won't pass his exams.
   If he _____ , he _____ his exams.
5 I'm sick, so I can't go to work.
   If I _____ sick, I _____ to work.

4 Circle the correct relative pronoun or pronouns. Then cross out the relative pronoun(s) that can be omitted.

1 Is that the athlete *what / who* won the gold medal?
2 Those are the books *that / who* I borrowed from the library.
3 This is the website *that / who* has a lot of good recipes.
4 My boss doesn't like the report *that / who* I wrote for him.
5 I've just seen someone *that / who* I know.

5 Complete the sentences with a relative clause.

1 This is a hotel. Leo is staying here.
   This is the hotel _____ .
2 The doctor has already seen those people.
   Those are the people
   _____ .
3 This man is Will. His wife likes running ultramarathons.
   Will is the man _____
   _____ .
4 The first woman won a gold medal at the Olympic Games in 1900.
   1900 was the year _____
   _____ .
5 I got a lovely present from my sister. This is it.
   This is the lovely present _____ .

6 Complete the text with the phrases (a–f) and a relative pronoun or adverb if necessary.

a she grew up
b she was attacked
c story has inspired people
d was based on her life story
e lost her arm
f was living in a hotel nearby

Bethany Hamilton is an American professional surfer [1] _____ in a shark attack at the age of just sixteen and [2] _____ all around the world. On October 31, 2003, Bethany was surfing at a local beach in Hawaii when she was attacked. She lost sixty percent of her blood on the way to hospital, but luckily she was saved by the medical team there, including one doctor [3] _____ . The attack was terrible, but Bethany was surfing again within a month, and in 2005, less then two years after the day [4] _____ , she won her first national surfing competition. Bethany became well known around the world when a film [5] _____ came out. Bethany is now married and has a child. Her wedding was by the ocean on an island in Hawaii [6] _____ .

Reported speech

Statements

We can use direct speech or reported speech to say what someone else said.

> Direct speech: *He said, "I'll see you later."*
> Reported speech: *He said that he'd see me later.*

We can leave out *that*, especially in informal, spoken contexts.

> *She said she'd go.* (or *She said **that** she'd go.*)

When we use reported speech, we normally change the tense of the verb.

Direct speech	Reported speech
Simple present	Simple past
Paul said, "I **want** to give you something."	Paul said (that) he **wanted** to give me something.
Present continuous	Past continuous
Maria said, "**I'm waiting** for the train."	Maria said (that) she **was waiting** for the train.
Simple past	Past perfect
Paul said, "I **sent** you a message."	Paul said (that) he **had sent** me a message.
Present perfect	Past perfect
Maria said, "I **have** just **arrived** home."	Maria said (that) she **had** just **arrived** home.
will, can	would, could
Paul said, "**I'll** call you."	Paul said (that) he **would** call me.
Maria said, "I **can't** come."	Maria said (that) she **couldn't** come.

The modals *might* and *would* don't change in reported speech.

> *"You **might** like it."* → *Paul said I **might** like it.*

When we report words that are still true at the time of reporting, we don't need to change the verb form.

> *"It's a great movie."* → *Nic said it's a great movie.*
> *"I've lost my phone."* → *Max said he's lost his phone.*
> (= *He still hasn't found it.*)

When we report, we normally need to make changes to pronouns and adjectives, and words and expressions about time and place.

pronouns: *I → he/she, we → they*
adjectives: *my → his/her, our → their, this → that*
time: *now → then, today → that day, tomorrow → the next day, yesterday → the previous day*
place: *here → there*

> *Seb said, "We'll see **you here tomorrow**."*
> → *Seb said **they'd see me there the next day**.*

However, if the sentence is reported on the same day it was said, we don't need to change the verb form, the place or the time.

> *Seb said, "We'll see **you here tomorrow**."*
> → *Seb said **they'll see me here tomorrow**.*

▶ **Exercise 1**

Questions

We normally use the verb *ask* to report questions. To report a *wh-* question, we use normal word order (subject before verb). We don't add *do, does,* or *did*.

> *"Where do you work?"* → *She asked where I worked.*

To report a *yes/no* question, we add *if* or *whether* before the subject in the question.

> *"Did you read the article?"* → *She asked **if** I had read the article.* (or *She asked **whether** I had read ...*)

▶ **Exercises 2 and 3**

Reporting verbs

Patterns

To report statements, we use *say* and *tell*. With *tell*, we always use an object before the reported speech. The object is often a pronoun.

> *"I can't help."* → *She told **them** (that) she couldn't help.*

With *say*, we never use an object before the reported speech.

> *"We don't want to come."* → *They said that (they) didn't want to come.* (not ~~They said me ...~~)

We also use many other verbs to report speech and thoughts. We use *ask, tell, remind, invite* with an object + *(not) to* + *base form*. The object is usually a person.

> *"Can you hold my bag?"*
> → *She **asked** me **to hold** her bag.*
> *"Don't sit down."* → *He **told** us **not to sit** down.*

We use *promise* and *offer* + *to* + base form. We do not use an object with these verbs.

> *"I won't be late again."*
> → *He **promised not to be** late again.*
> *"Would you like me to drive you to the station?"*
> → *She **offered to drive** me to the station.*

We can also use *promise* + *(that)* + clause.

> *He **promised that he wouldn't be** late again.*

▶ **Exercise 4**

Thoughts

To report thoughts, we use the verbs *realize, think,* and *know*. They are followed by *that* + subject + verb. We sometimes leave out *that* after these verbs, especially in informal, spoken contexts.

> *I **realized** (that) I had forgotten my wallet.*

We use the verb *wonder* to say "ask yourself." It is followed by *if/whether* or a question word.

> *"Has Julia come home yet?"* → *He **wondered if** Julia had come home yet.* (or *He wondered whether ...*)

▶ **Exercises 5 and 6**

Exercises

1 Choose the correct option to complete the reported speech sentences.

1 "I love the hotel."
He said *he loved* / *he'd loved* the hotel.
2 "We arrived late."
They said *they were arriving* / *they'd arrived* late.
3 "You might not enjoy the film."
She said I *might not enjoy* /
might not have enjoyed the movie.
4 "We're leaving soon."
They said they *were leaving* / *left* soon.
5 "I can't come."
He said he *couldn't come* / *can't came*.

2 Put the words in order to make reported questions. There is one extra word that you don't need.

1 Jo asked (had / seen / if / the movie / been / I)
She asked _____ .
2 Barbara asked (did / lived / I / where)
She asked _____ .
3 Tina asked me (Luke / if / was / had / to / I / spoken)
She asked me _____ .
4 Enzo asked (leaving / why / were / being / we)
He asked _____ .
5 Jaime asked (was / where / hungry / I / if)
He asked _____ .

3 Complete the story with the reported speech form of the direct speech.

I was on the train last week when I saw my old boss. I said "Hi." He asked [1] _____ _____ . I told him that [2] _____ _____ , but that we [3] _____ _____ for years. He said that [4] _____ _____ and asked me [5] _____ _____ . I said [6] _____ , but that [7] _____ . He asked me [8] _____ _____ . I said that [9] _____ _____ , but that [10] _____ _____ . In the end, he gave me a job!

1 "Do I know you?"
2 "We worked together."
3 "We haven't seen each other for years."
4 "I remember."
5 "How are you?"
6 "I'm fine."
7 "I'm looking for a job."
8 "Would you like an interview today?"
9 "I can't."
10 "I'll be free tomorrow."

4 Complete the sentences with these reporting verbs.

asked	invited	offered
reminded	said	told

1 "I can lend you some money."
She _____ to lend me some money.
2 "Would you like to go to the theater?"
He _____ me to go to the theater.
3 "Do you need some help?"
She _____ if I needed some help.
4 "Don't forget to call me later."
I _____ him to call me later.
5 "It's a good movie."
He _____ that it was a good movie.
6 "I don't want to stay."
I _____ her that I didn't want to stay.

5 Choose the correct option to complete the sentences. Both options are possible in one sentence.

1 He asked *me to help* / *I help* to fix his car.
2 They reminded *us to* / *that we* bring our dictionaries.
3 I wondered what *to cause* / *was causing* the delay.
4 He realized *to leave* / *that he'd left* his bag at home.
5 We invited *to go* / *them to go* on vacation with us.
6 She promised *to call* / *that she'd call* right away.

6 The direct speech in these sentences is spoken to you. Complete the reported speech. Use the simple past form of the reporting verbs in parentheses.

1 "Don't leave your bag there." (tell)
She _____ there.
2 "Did I forget my passport?" (wonder)
I _____ passport.
3 "I'll never lie to you again." (promise)
She _____ again.
4 "Oh, dear. We've left the map at home." (realize)
They _____ at home.
5 "Can you give me your email address?" (ask)
He _____ email address.
6 "Would you like me to carry your bag?" (offer)
He _____ bag.
7 "Don't forget to close all the windows." (remind)
She _____ all the windows.
8 "Maria will love the present." (know)
I _____ the present.

GRAMMAR SUMMARY UNIT 12

Third conditional

We use the third conditional to talk about unreal situations in the past. The form is:
If + past perfect + *would* + *have (not)* + past participle

We use a negative verb if the past event happened and a positive verb if the event didn't happen.

> *If you'd worked harder, you wouldn't have failed the exam.* (= You didn't work hard. You failed the exam.)
> *If Tina hadn't helped me, I wouldn't have been able to finish the project.* (= Tina helped me. I finished the project.)

When the *if* clause comes first, we use a comma between the two clauses. When the main clause comes before the *if* clause, we don't add a comma between the two clauses.

> *If you'd invited me, I'd have come to the party.*
> *I'd have come to the party if you'd invited me.*

We use the contraction *'d* in spoken English and more informal writing. It can replace either *had* or *would*.

> *If I'd (= had) had more time, I'd (= would) have visited the castle again.*

We don't normally put *would* or *have* in the *if* clause. We normally use the past perfect.

> *If those people had known the area, they wouldn't have needed a map.*
> (not *If those people would have known ….*)
> *They wouldn't have needed a map if they'd known the area.* (not *… if they'd have known the area.*)

▶ **Exercises 1, 2, and 3**

should have and *could have*

We use *should (not) have* + past participle to talk about regrets about past actions. We use:

- *should have* when something was the right thing to do, but we didn't do it.
  I should have called you to tell you where I was.
  (= I didn't call you. I regret that.)

- *shouldn't have* when something was the wrong thing to do, but we did it.
  I shouldn't have brought such a heavy bag on vacation. (= I brought a heavy bag. I regret it.)

We also use *should/shouldn't have* to criticize people's past actions.

> *You shouldn't have yelled at me. It was very rude.*

▶ **Exercise 4**

We use *could (not) have* + past participle to say whether something that didn't happen was possible or impossible. We use:

- *could have* when something was possible but it didn't happen.
  You could have really hurt yourself! (= You didn't hurt yourself, but it was possible.)

- *couldn't have* when something was impossible and it didn't happen.
  We couldn't have come earlier—the traffic was terrible. (= We didn't come earlier and it wasn't possible because of the traffic.)

We also use *could have* to say something was possible in the past and we're not sure if it happened.

> *He could have gotten lost.* (= It's possible he got lost. But I don't know what happened.)

▶ **Exercises 5 and 6**

Exercises

1 Read the sentences (1–4). Choose the correct option (a–b) to explain each sentence.

1 If you'd called me, I would have helped you.
   a You didn't call me.
   b I helped you.
2 If I hadn't been so rude, we wouldn't have had an argument.
   a We didn't have an argument.
   b I was rude.
3 I wouldn't have gone to Scotland if you hadn't recommended it.
   a I went to Scotland
   b You didn't recommend Scotland.
4 You wouldn't have been so cold if you'd brought a warm coat.
   a You brought a warm coat.
   b You were cold.

2 Match the beginnings of the sentences (1–6) with the endings (a–f). Then complete the main clauses with *would have* or *wouldn't have*.

1 If I'd had my umbrella with me, ____
2 If you hadn't bought that expensive new car, ____
3 If I'd known how boring this job was, ____
4 If you'd been more careful, ____
5 If they hadn't booked such a cheap hotel, ____
6 If we hadn't forgotten to bring the map, ____

a we _____ been able to afford a vacation.
b you _____ broken the window.
c they _____ had a better vacation.
d I _____ got wet.
e I _____ come to work here.
f we _____ got lost.

3 Complete the sentences to make third conditionals. Use contractions where possible.

1 We didn't pay attention and we got lost.
   If we _____
   _____ lost.
2 We didn't take more water because we didn't know how hot it was.
   If we _____
   _____ more water.
3 My phone didn't work, so I couldn't call for help.
   If _____
   _____ for help.
4 I went to Kenya. I met my husband there.
   If _____
   _____ my husband.

4 Complete the sentences with *should have* or *shouldn't have* and these phrases. Use the correct form of the verb.

park more carefully	invite so many people
check it more carefully	stay up so late last night
have a bigger breakfast	tell us earlier

1 Your report was full of mistakes.
   You _____ .
2 Our house is a mess after the party.
   We _____ .
3 John just called to say he can't come.
   He _____ .
4 I was already hungry at 11 a.m.
   I _____ .
5 We all feel exhausted this morning.
   We _____ .
6 I got a parking ticket last week.
   I _____ .

5 Complete the sentences with *could have* or *couldn't have* and the correct form of the verb in parentheses.

1 Why didn't you wear a helmet when you went skiing? You _____ (hurt) yourself.
2 It's normally very hot at this time of year. We _____ (know) it would be so cold.
3 I think he _____ (win) the race, but he hadn't trained hard enough.
4 Thanks for all your help organizing the trip. I _____ (done) it without you.

6 Complete the conversation with *could have, couldn't have, should have,* or *shouldn't have* and the correct form of the verbs in parentheses.

A: Did you read about the woman who survived in the wild for a week after her car broke down?
B: Yes, I saw that. She was twenty kilometers from the nearest town. And she walked into the forest to find help and then got lost. I think it was a mistake to leave the car. She ¹ _____ (stay) there. They ² _____ (find) her more quickly that way.
A: I agree. And I think she ³ _____ (leave) home without telling her friends and relatives where she was going. The article says nobody knew where she was!
B: OK, but she ⁴ _____ (know) her car would break down.
A: I always tell someone if I'm going on a long trip. She ⁵ _____ (tell) at least one person—that's obvious.
B: OK. But even then, it ⁶ _____ (take) a long time to find her. She was really in the middle of nowhere.
A: That's true.

Unit 1

▶ 1

When we look at people and cultures around the world, we find similar things. For example, people need a sense of group identity. Look at this Wanapum girl with her horse. She's taking part in a traditional meeting of Native Americans in the state of Oregon. It's a special occasion that happens every September. Horses are very important in Native American culture, and many children learn to ride a horse before they learn to ride a bike. In the past, they helped people hunt for food and carry things from camp to camp. The girl's clothes are also important. The colors of Native American traditional dress mean different things to different tribes. For example, red can mean Earth or blood, and white can mean winter or death. People around the world wear traditional dress, uniforms, or the colors of our favorite sports team to say the same thing: We belong to this group.

▶ 3

A: Do you want to take this quiz with me?

B: OK. What's it about?

A: Colors and what they mean around the world. For example, look at this photo. Where are the women going?

B: I don't know. To a party?

A: No, they're guests at a wedding in India. The guests and the bride herself wear bright colors. OK, here's your next question. Do you think red means different things in Asian and Western cultures?

B: Yeah, I think it does. I always associate red with strong emotions like love or anger.

A: Let me check the answers … that's right. And in Asian cultures, red often means luck. Oh, and bravery, too. OK, next: Do you know where yellow means knowledge?

B: No, no idea. Where is it?

A: Well, there are two options. Do you think it's China or India?

B: I think it's … oh, China.

A: Let's see … no, you're wrong. It's India. In China, yellow means power.

B: Well, I didn't know that. What's the next question?

A: OK … which color means happiness in some Asian cultures? Orange or pink?

B: Oh, I know this, it's orange.

A: Yes, it is! How did you know that? Amazing! It's happiness and love. OK, the next one's about the color blue. Do people in Mexico wear blue to a funeral?

B: I have no idea. I'd say people in the US usually wear black for funerals, but is it different in Mexico?

A: No, it isn't! The color black is associated with death there too.

B: Are there any more questions?

A: Yeah, the last one is: Who uses green as their symbol? There are two options, but I'm not going to tell you them. It's too easy.

B: Green? Something to do with nature …? Environmentalists and conservationists … that sort of thing. It's everywhere, really.

A: Of course it is! Now, here's a quiz all about the color green. Do you want to try it?

▶ 6

1

K = Keiko C = Colin

K: Good morning! Allow me to introduce myself. I'm Keiko Noguchi.

C: Nice to meet you. My name's Colin Burke.

K: It's a pleasure to meet you, Colin. I see you work for an advertising agency.

C: Yes, um … Keiko. I'm the art director at Arrow Agency. I mostly work on online ads.

K: Do you? That sounds interesting.

C: It is. We're developing some really great ideas for advertising. The internet is vital to an advertising campaign nowadays.

K: Oh, I agree, Colin. I know exactly what you mean—I'm in sales.

C: Oh, are you?

K: Yes, I work for an electronics company. Online sales are very important to our business.

C: Really? Well, Keiko, why don't I give you my card? Here you are.

K: Thanks. It's been good talking to you. Let's stay in touch.

2

L = Lucy, Y = Yuvraj

L: Hello. How are you? I'm Lucy.

Y: I'm very pleased to meet you. I'm Yuvraj Singh. I work for Get Fit—it's a chain of gyms.

L: Oh, yes. My brother goes to Get Fit.

Y: Does he? Great. We're building a big new gym downtown. It's almost ready to open, in fact.

L: Is it? That's great.

Y: Yes, we're all really excited about it. Um, what about you?

L: I'm looking for a new job at the moment, actually.

Y: OK, well, thanks for your time. Let me give you my card. Don't forget to check out our new gym when it opens.

Unit 2

▶ 8

1 I love going to the theater and I especially love seeing new dramas, but I think a lot depends on the director. Sometimes, you can get amazing actors and a great play. But if the director is wrong, then the whole thing can be disappointing. My wife and I usually go a couple of times a month if we can. We take turns choosing what to go and see.

2 I've never been to anything like it before, but I have to say I really enjoyed myself. They recorded it for television, and there were ten different choirs in the competition. The standard of the singers was excellent. Honestly, they were as good as professionals even though they were all amateurs who just sing in their free time. It's on every year, so I am definitely going back next year.

3 I love all the color and movement, and energy and excitement of events like this. When there's a big audience, the atmosphere is amazing. I think it's really important to keep traditional dance alive as well. So it's great when young people join in, like they do here.

▶ 12

Bruce Daley is the owner of a dance studio in Los Angeles. He teaches dance classes for all ages. He spoke to us about his work.

"I adore dancing, and I can't imagine doing anything else with my life. I've taught hundreds of people to dance—it's wonderful. I opened the studio when I retired from dancing professionally. My first students were young kids, but these days it has all changed. Everyone wants to dance. A lot of older people began coming when the big TV shows started. They say it makes them feel young. It's wonderful to watch them. Many people have found a new social life here and have made new friends. Two of my older students even got married last year!

One of the great things about dancing is it can really change your mood. I've seen how dancing can affect people. Traditional ballroom dancing became fashionable a few years ago. It was really popular with young professional people. Once, a very angry and stressed-out young man came to class. After a couple of hours, he left with a smile. The class changed his mood completely.

Dancing has been my life, really. And starting this school was the best thing I've ever done. My injuries ended my career as a dancer ten years ago. But opening the school gave me a new career as a teacher."

▶ 13

Bruce has been my teacher for about two years now. I started coming here during a bad time at work. Bruce's classes are great—I've never had so much fun! I've met all kinds of people here. Some of them have become really good friends. At first, I didn't know how to dance. But I soon realized that you can't get embarrassed—you just have to dance! Everyone here has felt the same way at some point.

▶ 14

1 Bruce has been my teacher for about two years now.
2 Some of them have become really good friends.
3 You just have to dance!
4 Everyone here has felt the same way at some point.

▶ 16

L = Lesley, R = Richard

L: Do you feel like going out tonight?
R: Yeah, why not? We haven't been out in a long time. What's going on?
L: Well, there's a movie about climate change. Do you like the sound of that?
R: Oh, not really. It doesn't really appeal to me. What's it about? Just climate change?
L: I think it's about how climate change affects everyday life. I wonder how they make it entertaining.
R: Well, it sounds really interesting, but I'm not in the mood for anything depressing. What else is happening?
L: There's a flamenco festival downtown.
R: Oh, I love dancing. That sounds great.
L: Apparently it's absolutely amazing. Let's see what it says in the paper: "Aida Gómez leads in a thrilling production of the great Spanish love story Carmen."
R: OK. What time is it at?
L: At 7:30.
R: Well, that's no good. We don't have enough time to get there. Is there anything else?
L: There's a comedy special.
R: Where is it?
L: It's at the City Theater. It's a kind of comedy marathon for charity with lots of different acts. It looks pretty good. The critic in the local paper says it's the funniest thing he's ever seen. It says here: "Roger Whitehead is absolutely hilarious in a night of comedy gold."
R: Hmm, I don't really like him. He's not very funny.
L: Are you sure you want to go out tonight? You're not very enthusiastic!
R: Maybe you're right. OK, let's go and see the flamenco festival but tomorrow, not tonight.
L: Great. I'll go online and book the tickets.

Unit 3

▶ 18

Coming up on today's program, we look at some more active alternatives to lying around on the beach this summer. Jason reports on a kayaking trip around the beautiful Pacific Ocean coastline of Australia—a more relaxing activity than waterskiing or jet-skiing, but just as much fun. Jenna has been to the Red Sea to try diving and snorkeling for the first time, so we'll find out how she did. And we also talk to people here in the US to find out whether windsurfing on a lake is different from windsurfing in the ocean. We'll also ask which are the best rivers to experience the thrill of white-water rafting. But first, the latest travel news from Anya.

▶ 19

1 I live in Zambia, and we have fantastic rivers here. I love rafting on the Zambezi River—it's one of the best white-water runs in the world. On my very first trip, we had a real surprise! We were coming down fast from a section of rapids, and we could see calm water ahead. Then I saw a big hippo near the riverbank. It's best to avoid hippos if you can! We started moving away quickly because it was coming toward us! And then, we were going around a small island in the middle of the river, when suddenly …

2 I began diving when I was about twelve. I actually learned to dive while I was on vacation in Mexico. My parents went there to explore the underground lakes—or cenotes, as they're called here. My brother and I were just sitting around on the beach, getting bored, so we took a diving course. Then we did our first dive in the "easy" cenotes while my parents were exploring the dangerous stuff. It wasn't very deep underground and the sun was shining in through an opening in the roof of the cave. It was really calm and beautiful. I felt like staying there all day! I was concentrating on doing everything right. I didn't notice that …

▶ 20

1 And then, we were going around a small island in the middle of the river, when suddenly we surprised an eight-meter crocodile. It was lying in the sun on the other bank. It jumped into the water about a meter away from our boat—it almost landed in the boat! Fortunately, it didn't take much interest in us, so we got away! Maybe it wasn't hungry!

2 I was concentrating on doing everything right. I didn't notice that I was swimming into an area that was only for advanced divers. There were ropes and signs to stop you from going into some tunnels where it was easy to get lost. Luckily for me, my mom realized pretty quickly that I was missing, and she came after me. I still had no idea where I was going!

▶ 22

1 They tried to get away.
2 We rowed down the river.
3 What happened to you?
4 The crocodile looked dangerous to me.
5 We arrived too late.
6 We walked ten kilometers along the beach yesterday.

▶ 25

1
A: Did I ever tell you about the time my goldfish learned to fly?
B: What? No, I don't think so.
A: Well, we had these two goldfish. They were really huge. And they lived in a fish tank above the kitchen sink. But these two fish were really active. They loved to jump in the air. Especially when someone was doing the dishes.
B: No way!
A: Seriously! After we saw it the first time, we put a lid across the top of the tank. So a couple of weeks later, I came into the kitchen one morning and the tank was empty.
B: Oh, no!
A: Oh, yes! During the night, the fish had jumped out of the tank! They were lying in the sink! Fortunately, there was some water in it!
B: That's incredible!

2
C: I remember once, a couple of years ago, we were taking care of a

friend's parrot when he was on a business trip. Anyway, after a few days, I realized that the parrot knew how to open its cage.

D: Really?

C: Oh, yes! It happened a couple of times. When I left the house, the parrot was in its cage. And when I got back home, it had gotten out. So one day, I was at work and all of a sudden I remembered that I hadn't put food and water in the bird's bowls. I immediately rushed back home … and there it was … the empty cage again. I searched everywhere. I was going around the house calling "Polly! Polly, come here, Polly." But I couldn't find it.

D: What happened then?

C: Well, the next thing was, I started to panic. So I went into the kitchen to make some tea, and guess what! There was the bird. It was taking a bath in my teacup!

D: That's unbelievable!

▶ **26**

1 Especially when someone was doing the dishes.
2 They were lying in the sink!
3 We were taking care of a friend's parrot.
4 I was going around the house calling "Polly"!

Unit 4

▶ **27**

1 When I was little, I wanted to be a superhero, like in my comic books. I wanted to save the world. When I realized that superheroes aren't real people, I decided to be a firefighter. It seemed like a very exciting job. Now, of course, I realize that it's dangerous, dirty, and extremely challenging. So I'm glad I decided to work in an office—it's a very safe job, and I'm not really very brave!

2 When I was a child, my ambition was to drive a train. My uncle was a train engineer and I wanted to be just like him. I liked the idea of being in charge of the train and being responsible for all the passengers. I'm actually an accountant! It's not a very exciting job—but it's not as boring as many people think it is.

3 I was really into sports when I was a kid, especially soccer. My bedroom walls were covered in posters of my favorite players. I wanted to be just like them—the best soccer player in the world. Soccer players were

well-paid and famous. But I'm not likely to be a soccer player now. I'm training to be a nurse—which is not well-paid and is pretty stressful! But in the end, I think nursing will be enjoyable. I hope so!

▶ **29**

1 **Devi is from West Sumatra in Indonesia**

D: I didn't finish school. It's pretty common here for girls to drop out of school early. But then I got this job. I'm the first girl in my family to work outside the home. Since the economic crisis, more women have jobs. I feel very different about my future now. **I'm going to change my job.** I don't want to stay in this one forever. I want to study to be a nurse, so I've applied to college. I hope to get accepted for the next course. **It starts in January. I'm taking the entrance exam next month.** I'm very nervous about it. I haven't told my boss. **I suppose I'll tell him soon.**

2 **Elisabeth is from Portland in the United States**

E: I work in a factory. It's a good job, but the company is laying people off. So I'm going to take the severance package because it's an opportunity to start again. I got married very young and had a family, so I didn't finish my education. But I've just finished evening classes in business studies, and now I'm going to start my own business. It's something I already do as a hobby—I make and sell specialty cheeses. Just a minute, I'll get you some. Here, taste this. Do you like it? Well, I'm meeting the bank manager on Wednesday to discuss my business plan. And hey, maybe I'll take some cheese for him to taste as well!

3 **Sahera is from Kabul in Afghanistan**

S: It's very difficult to go to college here. Many girls get no education at all. But I've managed to finish my degree and graduate from the Department of Language and Literature. Now I'm thinking about the next step. Many of the graduates are going to work as teachers. My friend is going to continue her studies in the United States. I'm going to stay here in the city, because my family is here. I guess I'll take some time off and visit my parents. And I want to spend time with my friend because she's leaving next week.

▶ **31**

R = Rudi, M = Mark

R: This looks interesting—this assistant researcher job for a TV company.

M: I know. The only thing is the experience. They want two years, but I've only worked part-time for a year, really.

R: It says one or two years, experience and you meet the other requirements. You're good under pressure and with deadlines—you always hand your papers in on time at school!

M: That's not the same thing!

R: Of course it is. And you're really well-organized, hardworking, highly motivated …

M: OK, OK, if that's what you think … is it all right if I list you as a reference?

R: Hmm, I'm not sure about that. I don't think you can just put down your friends' names.

M: I know—what a shame! But seriously, do you mind helping me with my resume? I need to make it look a bit more professional.

R: Of course not. Are you going to apply for this job, then?

M: Yeah, I think I will. But I'll need my resume anyway, whichever job I apply for.

R: OK, print it out and I'll take a look at it.

M: Will you be able to do it today?

R: Yes, I will. But what's the hurry?

M: The closing date for applications is in a couple of days. Oh, can you take a look at my cover letter, too?

R: Sure. When can you send it to me?

M: I'll do it this afternoon and then I can send everything off tonight. Hey, they might ask me to come in for an interview this week!

R: Yeah, they might.

M: But I don't have any professional clothes! Would it be OK to borrow your suit?

R: Sure, no problem.

Unit 5

▶ **34**

Really, the first thing to say about food is that everyone has different needs. That means we can't say "a portion should be this size." What you have to do is eat for the size that you are. So children obviously need to eat less than adults, and most women need to eat less than most men. How do you know how much to eat? Use your body as a guide. So for a typical adult woman, the amount of cereal or rice in a portion is the same size as your clenched fist. Notice I say *your* fist, not *a* fist. It's the size of *your* hand that matters. If you're eating a piece of meat, make sure it's no bigger than the palm of *your* hand. For snacks like popcorn, the biggest portion size is two of your own handfuls. And for cake, which we all know we need to be careful with, the portion should no wider than two of your fingers. That doesn't sound like very much? Exactly!

▶ **36**

1

A: I've never tried durian. Have you? Apparently, it tastes much better than it smells.

B: No, I haven't tried it. But I know that it smells so much that you aren't allowed to take it on buses in Singapore.

2

C: What's fugu? F– U– G–U.

D: Oh, I know what it is. It's a kind of fish they eat in Japan. It's actually poisonous, so only qualified chefs are allowed to prepare it in restaurants. If you eat the wrong part, it can kill you!

3

E: Can you eat shark meat?

F: Yes, it's popular in a lot of countries. Sometimes, you have to ferment it first because the fresh meat is bad for you. That's what they do in Iceland. It's called hakarl there.

4

G: Are you going to boil those potatoes like that, without peeling them?

H: Yeah, why? You don't have to peel potatoes before you boil them.

G: Yes, you do. At least that's what we do in my house!

5

I: I love eating oysters, but I can never remember when it's safe to eat them.

J: The rule is you can't eat them in the warm summer months, but I don't know why not.

6

K: I feel a bit sick. I wonder if it was the mayonnaise in my salad.

L: Was it fresh mayonnaise? You should avoid using raw eggs in mayonnaise, you know? It can make you sick.

7

M: Are you making chili con carne?

N: Yes, but the recipe says you must boil red beans for fifteen minutes or they aren't safe to eat. Do you think that's true?

8

O: What's this on the menu? Steak tartare? Is that raw steak?

P: Yes, you can eat steak raw. It's cut into tiny pieces and mixed with onion or garlic. You should try it.

▶ **39**

L = Lin, J = Jack

L: Hi, Jack. Did you read this article on imaginary eating?

J: Hi, Lin. Yes, I saw it this morning. What a load of nonsense! I've never heard anything so ridiculous. It said that if we think about eating food, we'll lose weight.

L: Not exactly. It said if you think about eating food, you stop wanting to eat it so much. So if you don't eat it, you might lose weight. I thought it made sense.

J: No, that's ridiculous. I'll believe it when I see it! You can't "think yourself thin."

L: Well, I'm not so sure. I think willpower is really important, especially where food is concerned. Imagine you are overweight and you want to lose a few kilos. If you don't train your mind, you won't be able to lose weight. I think you can achieve anything if you believe you can do it.

J: You mean like "mind over body"? Well, OK, mental attitude is important when you're trying to change something in your life. But I don't think that's the same as what the news article said. So are you going to do this imaginary eating thing, then? Do you really think it'll work?

L: Yeah, why not? I won't find out unless I try.

J: And what exactly are you going to do?

L: OK, let's think. I eat too many chips and snacks, right? So, when I want to eat a snack, I'll try imagining that I'm eating it. Hey, you know what? This could be amazing. I'll never need to buy chocolate again if this technique works!

J: Well, I'm still not convinced.

L: Hey, as soon as it starts working, I'll let you know. Believing in yourself is what's important.

J: I'm going to buy you some chocolate just in case. I think you'll need it.

▶ **41**

W = waiter

W: Are you ready to order?

A: Um, not quite.

W: No problem. Would you like something to drink while you decide?

A: Yes, please. Water's fine for now.

B: Oh, this menu looks interesting. I love trying new dishes. What are plantain fritters?

A: Well, plantain is a kind of banana and a fritter is a fried dish—in this case, fried, mashed banana balls.

B: Do you mean like a sweet, dessert banana?

A: No, plantain is a type of savory banana. It's quite a bland flavor, really.

B: OK. What about akkra? What's that made from?

A: It's made from a kind of bean called black-eyed peas. They're fritters, too.

B: Hmm. What do they taste like?

A: Well, akkra's usually pretty hot and spicy.

B: Sounds good! I think I'll try that. Now, what's this—ackee and saltfish?

A: Where's that?

B: In the main courses, at the top of the list.

A: Ah, yes. I think ackee's a kind of fruit that's traditionally served with saltfish.

B: And saltfish?

A: That's dried salted cod. You have to soak it in water before you cook it, but then it's kind of like fresh cod. It doesn't taste salty when it's cooked.

B: OK. I might try that. What are you going to have?

A: I can't make up my mind. Oh, here comes the waiter again.

W: Can I take your order now?

A: Yes, please. I'll have the akkra to start with.

B: And I'll have the same.

W: And for your main course?

A: I'd like to try the ackee and saltfish. Does it come with vegetables?

W: Yes, with plantain.

A: And how is that cooked? Is it fried?

W: No, it's boiled.

A: OK, that sounds fine.

W: And what about you, sir?

B: Can I have the goat curry, please?

W: Certainly.

A: I've never had goat.

B: You can try some of mine when it comes. It's like lamb, but the flavor's a bit stronger.

A: OK, great.

Unit 6

▶ **43**

W: What a photo! It's like a dream. Is it real? I mean, do you think the photographer Photoshopped it?

M: No, according to the website, it's totally genuine. It was taken on a really hot day, so maybe that's why it looks a little strange.

W: But I don't really understand where the cows are.

M: They're on a beach. It says here the photographer was driving along a coastal road in Andalusia and saw some cows lying on the empty beach. He couldn't get close in his car, so he had to park and walk along the beach in 35 degrees Celsius heat.

W: That's pretty hot!

M: I know. I'm surprised he didn't frighten them—it's hard to get close to animals.

W: But what's going on in the background? What are the people doing? I can't make it out.

M: It looks like they're parasailing. It's really popular there. It's always windy on that beach.

▶ 44

I have two questions for you today. The first: How good are you at flexible and creative thinking? And the second: Does the promise of a reward make you work harder?

So, let's test your flexible thinking. I'm going to give you a task. You have a candle, a box of thumbtacks, and some matches. The task is to attach the candle to the wall so that the wax doesn't drip on the floor below. How do you do it? Well, clearly the matches are to light the candle with and we know that thumbtacks are for attaching things to other things. But what about the box? Yes, it's for holding the thumbtacks. But you can also use it to hold the candle. And then you attach the box to the wall. Did you get it? Yes? Congratulations! You're a flexible thinker.

Now, let's turn to the second question. Imagine I offer half of you some money to do this task more quickly. Not a lot of money, but a fair amount. It's work—and we all work for money, don't we? And I tell the other half of you that I'm going to see how long it takes you so that we can find out the average time. What do you think will happen? The people with the reward of money will be quicker, right?

Well, I can tell you the results of this experiment. And it's the same result every time. The people in the first group—the ones who are offered some money—need more time to find the answer—usually about three minutes longer, in fact. That's right. It's a mystery. You offer someone a reward, and they work more slowly. What's going on?

▶ 46

The Nasca lines are enormous drawings on the ground, in the Nasca desert in southern Peru. Most of the lines are just shapes, but about seventy are animals such as a spider, different types of birds, a monkey, or a dog. There are human figures as well. And they are huge—the biggest of the drawings is about two hundred meters across. Altogether, there are hundreds of these drawings, and they are in an area that's about eighty kilometers wide.

The lines were made by the Nasca people over a period of time starting about two thousand years ago. They moved the brown stones that cover the desert to show the white ground underneath. You can still see the stones along the edges of the lines.

▶ 47

The mysterious thing about the lines is that they only became clear about one hundred years ago when air travel began. But the Nasca people couldn't have seen the patterns from the air. So the question is how, and indeed why, did they make them?

One of the first people to study the lines was an archeologist named Maria Reiche. She became convinced that the lines must have been a type of calendar. Other people thought they may have been ancient Inca roads. The strangest idea was that they could have guided aliens from space!

One of the other mysterious aspects of the Nasca people is that although this region of Peru is one of the driest places on Earth, they built a successful society there. How could they have done this without water? In fact, there is a river in the mountains. It goes underground for many kilometers before it reappears on the surface. Some people think that this might have seemed mysterious to the Nasca people, so the lines were part of traditional or religious beliefs linked to the water. Whatever the explanation, one thing is for sure: The Nasca people can't have known that the lines would still be visible centuries later.

▶ 51

1

A: Did you hear that story about the sheep?

B: No, I don't think so. What was it about?

A: Apparently, they reflect the sun back into the atmosphere, because they're so white.

B: Oh, yeah?

A: And then the heat from the sun gets trapped, so it makes everything hotter. So they think sheep cause global warming.

B: Come off it!

A: Well, that's what it says in the paper today.

B: You're kidding me!

A: It does—here, look.

B: Hmm, that can't be right! Hang on a minute. What's the date today?

2

C: Let me take a look at those twenty-dollar bills for a minute.

D: Why?

C: The green ones are no good—they're counterfeit.

D: You must be joking! All twenty-dollar bills are green!

C: Not the real ones.

D: Are you sure?

C: I'm absolutely positive. The girl at the travel agency told me. It was on the news last night.

D: They must have made a mistake … oh, no, and we've just changed all this money! What are we going to do?

C: I don't know … but it is April first today …

D: Oh, honestly! I really believed you!

3

D = daughter, F = father

D: Dad, did you see the news about gas prices? They've gone down to almost half the price.

F: Really? How come?

D: I don't know. But anyway, I put gas in the car.

F: Great … hold on … did you say gas?

D: Yeah.

F: Are you serious? The car uses diesel, not gas!

D: I know, but gas is so much cheaper!

F: Yes, but …

D: I'm sorry. Did I do something wrong?

F: Diesel engines don't work with gas. You must know that! Oh, this is going to cost me a fortune.

D: Dad?

F: Yes?

D: How do you think I managed to drive the car home, then? April Fool! It's April first!

Unit 7

▶ 54

1 We're a big family, and we have a pretty small house. I share a bedroom

with my two older brothers. My grandparents live with us, too. It's cramped and noisy, but at least there's always someone around. It's the only house I've ever known. I love living with my family. We all get along so well. I suppose I'll move out when I get married. I don't know when that will be!

2 I had to move to Boston when I started work. I saw an ad in the paper for a room in a shared house. Well, it's an apartment on the first floor of a big house, actually. My roommates are out working a lot, so it's just like living on my own a lot of the time, really … especially during the week. Weekends are different. I have to say that living with friends is more difficult than I thought it would be. For one thing, nobody ever wants to do any housework.

3 I'm in my last year at college, and I'm really looking forward to finishing and traveling or getting out of this town! I can't wait to get away from here and live on my own. It's going to be awesome. My sister and I have shared a room all our lives. My family's great, but I'd like to have the chance of my own space—preferably someplace that's sunny, warm, and beautiful.

▶ 56

1 As an architect, I'm interested in everything about house design. But we can learn so much from traditional buildings and designs. Traditional houses usually survive bad weather conditions better than modern ones, so the question is: What can we copy from those houses when we build new houses? Like the rock homes, for example: They heat up less quickly than brick houses, which is great in hot climates.

2 Well, a shelter is a lot less permanent and more basic than a house. The igloos that people build in the Arctic region are a perfect example of a shelter. A shelter just protects you from the weather, but a home has several spaces with different uses.

3 I'd say a ger is both a shelter and a home. It's organized around a fire in the center with a chimney, and it has separate areas for men and women. A ger isn't as solid as a brick or wooden house, but you can take it down and put it up much faster, which is what nomadic people in Mongolia need.

4 Well, it all depends on the local weather. I mean, if you live in an area that has regular floods, it's a good idea to live in a house on stilts. That way, you can live much more safely above the water, and you don't have to worry every time it rains a lot! The higher the stilts, the safer you are!

5 I think that modern homes are fairly similar wherever they are in the world, which doesn't always mean that they are the best design for every situation. In our crowded cities, modern houses are getting smaller and smaller so that they can be built more cheaply. Unfortunately, sometimes modern houses are also built badly. They don't work as efficiently as traditional houses—they need central heating in winter and air conditioning in summer.

▶ 58

A = real estate agent, C = customer
A: Good morning.
C: Hi. I'm interested in any properties you have in the center of town.
A: OK, and is that to rent or to buy?
C: Oh, it's to rent. I've just started a new job here, so I think I'd rather rent than buy, for now anyway.
A: OK, well, we have quite a few apartments in our system, from one-room studios to four-room apartments.
C: I'd prefer something small, but not too small. I imagine I'll have a lot of friends staying with me. So, two bedrooms, and preferably with an elevator. I ride my bike a lot, and I don't want to carry it up lots of stairs!
A: Well, most of the modern buildings have elevators, but a lot of the properties in the center are pretty old. Would you rather look at new places or older ones?
C: It doesn't matter. At this point I'm just getting an idea of what things are like here.
A: OK … so you're new to the area?
C: Yeah, I lived in a small town up near the mountains until recently.
A: Oh, that sounds nice.
C: To be honest, I prefer cities to towns. The problem with a town is that everyone knows your business. Maybe I'm unfriendly, but I like the way that in a city, you don't know everyone.
A: Ah yes, I've heard a few people say that! To be honest, I prefer living here. I suppose I like my privacy, too. OK. Um. What about parking? Do you need garage space?
C: No, I don't have a car, I prefer to walk or ride my bike. It keeps me fit.
A: Of course, you mentioned your bike!
C: Yeah! And anyway, in my experience, driving in town is a nightmare!
A: I know, and it's getting worse. OK, well, the next thing to consider is your budget and the rental period.

Unit 8

▶ 61

1 A couple of years ago, I went on an around-the-world trip with a friend. What an experience! The best parts were when we took local buses and trains. They stop everywhere, and it takes forever to get to where you're going. On the other hand, we met some really interesting people on the buses in Peru. We learned a lot about the history of the country. But I took way too much luggage with me. I couldn't carry it easily, and I worried about losing it. Just take a small backpack with the essentials, that's my advice.

2 I haven't traveled very much in the last few years. I've been on a few day trips to New York City, and I've taken a couple of weekend trips to Boston this year. I don't go far any more. I'm more interested in the place I'm going to than in the journey. New England has some fascinating towns. But in my experience, the key to a good trip is good planning. Don't leave anything to chance!

3 I work in IT, and I travel a lot—too much—for my job. I spend a lot of time on planes and in my car on the highway, traveling to the projects I'm working on. I don't particularly enjoy it, especially when there are delays, but it's part of my job. I often get a very early flight from O'Hare, and delays can mean I lose a whole working day. I have to go on business trips several times a year. My travel tip? Once the flight starts, take your watch off and relax. You have no control over the time you arrive, so why get stressed?

▶ 63

R = Rose, M = Matt
R: Hi there. I'm Rose.
M: Hi. I'm Matt.
R: Is this your first time in Mexico?
M: No, actually. We come every year. We love staying here.
R: So do we. We keep coming back year after year. It's hard to find somewhere with everything you need for a vacation—great beaches,

fantastic weather, and something for everyone to do.

M: I know. Actually, there's a paragliding class later—I'd like to try that.

R: My friends want to do that, too! To be honest, lying by the pool is my idea of a vacation.

M: Oh, I get kind of bored with doing that after the first day or two. I need to move around and do things.

R: Well, why not? It's a different way of relaxing, I suppose.

M: Yes, that's right. Well, if you decide to go paragliding with your friends, we'll see you there!

▶ 65

When you've walked across half of Africa and you've walked up the west coast of North America, where do you go next? On tomorrow's show, my guest is a man who can give us the answer. I'm talking about the conservationist Mike Fay—a man with a very personal way of saving what he calls the last wild places on Earth. For those of you who don't know Mike Fay, he does some unusual things in his work with the Wildlife Conservation Society. For instance, he's spent more than two years of his life trekking through some of the toughest places on the planet. And he often just takes a T-shirt, a pair of shorts, and a pair of sandals on these treks. Fay says he has slept in a bed only about fifty times in ten years. The last time he was on the show, he'd just finished a survey of giant redwood trees on the west coast of the United States. What has he been doing since then? Well, he hasn't been taking it easy! In fact, recently he's been walking again, this time across Canada. In western Canada, mining companies have been looking for gold and oil. To do this, they've been digging up enormous areas—they've destroyed hundreds of square kilometers of wilderness. You can hear how Mike Fay feels about this on tomorrow's show. And we'll also find out what's been happening to national parks in Gabon since Fay was there. We know that people have been trying to set up mines near the parks and the Gabonese government has stopped at least two mining operations. Hear more tomorrow in my interview with Mike Fay, and find out what he thinks a population of seven billion people might do to our planet.

▶ 67

T = tourist, G = guide

1

T: I wonder if you could help us. Our luggage hasn't arrived.

G: OK. Are you with SunnyTimes tours?

T: Yes. Mr. and Mrs. Kim.

G: And which flight were you on, Mrs. Kim?

T: The Korean Air flight from Seoul. I think it's KE254. We've been talking to some of the other passengers, and their luggage has arrived through, no problem.

G: Ah, yes. It seems some bags have gone to another airport. Flight KE254?

T: Yes, that's right. Do you know where our bags have gone to?

G: Yes, I'm afraid the luggage has gone to Los Angeles.

T: Los Angeles? How did that happen?

G: I'm not sure, but all the missing bags are coming on the next flight.

T: But when's the next flight?

G: It's tomorrow morning. Don't worry, we'll arrange everything. Which hotel are you staying at? Your bags will go straight there.

T: But all our clothes are in the suitcases!

2

G: Hello, Mr. Rodriguez. Is something wrong? Can I help?

T: Well, it's about my wife, actually. She hasn't been feeling well for a couple of days.

G: I'm sorry to hear that. Is it something she's eaten, do you think? Or just travel sickness?

T: I don't know. She's had a temperature all night, but she feels cold.

G: OK, … um, how long has she been feeling like this?

T: A couple of days? Yes, since the boat trip on Tuesday. Is there anything you can do?

G: Well, it's probably nothing to worry about. But I'll ask the hotel to call a doctor, just in case.

T: That's great. Thank you.

Unit 9

▶ 70

R = researcher, S = shopper

1

R: Hi. Do you mind if I ask you some quick questions about your shopping today?

S: Not at all, no.

R: Great. Well, first, can I ask what you've bought?

S: Oh, yes. I bought the latest iPhone.

R: Is it for you?

S: No, for my mom. For Mother's Day, next Sunday. She's really into gadgets and technology.

2

R: Hello. You look happy. Have you bought something nice?

S: Um, I got a couple of nice shirts on sale, actually. That's all I came in for.

R: And who did you buy them for?

S: Just for myself. I buy all my clothes on sale.

R: OK!

3

R: Hi. Do you have time to answer a quick question or two?

S: Yes, I think so. We need a break!

R: Have you been spending a lot of money?

S: No, that's the problem! We're looking for some nice jewelry—earrings, or a gold chain maybe—but we can't find anything we like.

R: And who is it for?

S: It's just for ourselves. We usually buy each other something special for our anniversary every year. It's a little tradition we have.

R: Well, good luck!

▶ 73

D = Dan, S = Samira

D: So, Samira, have you read any interesting articles this week?

S: Yes, I have, Dan. Several websites have articles about impulse buying. They're based on a study by some scientists.

D: And impulse buying is …?

S: OK, have you ever gone to the store to buy just one or two items—like bread and milk—and come back with lots of things you hadn't intended to buy? Well, that's impulse buying. Buying things just because you see them, without really thinking about it.

D: Oh, that sounds like me.

S: Well, don't worry. You're not alone. We've probably all done it at one time or other. And in fact, the study says that about five percent of us have even spent more than $500 on a purchase that wasn't necessary!

D: But sometimes you see special offers or good deals on things. Especially on electronics like TVs or tablets.

If we can save a little money, that's good, isn't it?

S: OK, but as it says in a few of the articles, the fact that something is good value for money doesn't matter if you can't afford it! You should always have a budget—figure out how much you can spend and then stick to that amount. Anyway, there are some points in the research I thought were really interesting. The study divided people into two groups—men and women. If you're female and under twenty-one, you're more likely to buy on impulse. Apparently, many people use shopping as a way of managing their mood when they're unhappy. Also, if you go shopping when you're hungry, you're more likely to buy lots of food.

D: Oh, that explains why I spend too much money at the supermarket! So I just need to make sure I have a snack before I go?

S: Yes, and make a list. Actually, there are plenty of simple things you can do to avoid impulse buying. You just need to take a little time to plan your shopping and you'll save money.

▶ 77

S = Salesperson, C = customer

1

S: Can I help you?

C: Yes. Can I look at this silver chain?

S: This one?

C: Yes, please.

S: It's beautiful, isn't it? Is it for you?

C: No, for my sister.

S: It's on sale, actually—it's twenty percent off.

C: Oh? I like it, but it's kind of heavy. I was looking for something lighter.

S: How about this?

C: Yeah, that's great. That's just right, I think. Um, can she return it if she doesn't like it, though?

S: Yes, she can exchange it within ten days.

C: OK, good.

S: That's as long as she has the receipt, of course.

C: I'll take it, then. Can you gift-wrap it for me?

S: Well, we don't actually do gift-wrapping, but we have some nice gift boxes for sale, over there.

C: OK.

2

C: Excuse me, do you work in this department?

S: Yes. Can I help you?

C: Well, I'm looking for a couch that I saw on your website, but I don't see it here.

S: OK, do you have the reference number or the model name?

C: Yes, it's Byunk. The number is 00 389 276.

S: OK, let me see if it's in stock.

C: The website said "available" this morning …

S: Yes, here we are. Do you want it in red, gray, or blue?

C: Blue, if you have it.

S: Yes, there are plenty in stock. Just give them this reference number at checkout.

C: OK. What about delivery? How much do you charge for delivery?

S: Can you tell me your zip code? The charges go by area.

C: 02718

S: That would be $55.

C: Wow… OK.

S: If you go to the customer service desk, they can take your information and arrange the delivery date.

C: And do I pay here or …?

S: Checkout is by the customer service desk. You can pay by credit card or in cash.

C: OK, thanks for your help. Um, how do I get to checkout, sorry?

S: Just follow the yellow arrows.

Unit 10

▶ 80

This man is Steve Holman. He's 52 years old, and his friends think he's crazy. Why? Because he's running 200 kilometers in the Sahara desert. He has to carry all his food with him, in a backpack that weighs twelve kilos. With the temperature hitting 38 degrees, he struggles up enormous sand dunes, sometimes crawling on his hands and knees. This is the annual *Marathon des Sables*, one of the key events on the ultrarunning calendar. Any race longer than a regular 42-kilometer marathon is called ultrarunning, but there is more to this kind of running than simply the distance. Ultrarunners push the human body to incredible limits and learn that it's stronger than you'd imagine. Another ultrarunner is Leslie Antonis, who ran 160 kilometers in 34 hours at the age of 47. It's amazing what the human body can do!

▶ 82

P = Peter, G = Gail

P: Now, I'm sure most of us are amazed when we watch the Paralympics—the sporting event for people who have a disability. We see athletes who run a marathon on blades, or others who play soccer in a wheelchair. Tonight on Channel 10, there's a documentary that features some famous Paralympians. Gail, you've seen a preview of the program.

G: Yes, Peter. The program is a fascinating look at how medical science is changing people's lives right now. The Paralympians you mentioned use blades and wheelchairs, but these are devices that don't actually give them extra power. We also see some athletes whose devices are bionic.

P: And what's the difference, exactly?

G: I suppose the simplest explanation of a bionic device is one that uses electronics in some way. Sometimes they have their own power. And in sports, this means you can improve your performance.

P: So you mean bionic hands or arms?

G: Yes, and bionic legs, too. Now there are also wheelchairs that are controlled electronically by the user.

P: So bionics is great news for patients who have lost the use of a limb.

G: Absolutely. And the range of bionic devices the program describes is growing all the time. Let me tell you about a woman whose life suddenly changed after a skiing accident. Her name's Amanda Boxtel—she lost the use of her legs and didn't walk for over twenty years. Now she can use a robotic structure that supports her body so that she can walk. The structure she uses is called an exoskeleton. Amanda used to be an athlete, but these days she works with an organization that promotes bionic technology.

P: And I believe there are already devices that help blind people to see and deaf people to hear.

G: That's right. It seems as if there's no limit to the things bionic devices will be able to do. So don't forget to watch the program on Channel 10 tonight at 9:30.

▶ 86

1

A: What happened to you? There's blood all down your leg!

B: Oh, it's nothing. I tripped when I was out running. I fell on a tree branch or something.

A: Let me see. Oh, that looks nasty! It's a pretty deep cut. You'd better clean it right away.

B: Yeah, I will.

A: You know, if I were you, I'd go to the emergency room. I'd get it looked at.

B: It doesn't hurt. It's just a cut, really. I'm not going all the way to the hospital for a cut on my leg.

A: Hmm, it might need stitches, though. I'd keep an eye on it if I were you.

B: OK, if it doesn't stop bleeding, I'll call the doctor and see if a nurse is there.

A: Good, because I don't think we have any bandages big enough!

2

C: Is my neck red? I think I got stung or something.

D: A little, yeah. It looks kind of swollen. Is it itchy?

C: Not exactly. It's painful rather than really itchy. Strange, I don't usually react to insect bites. Oooh, I feel kind of sick, actually.

D: Have you tried putting cream on it? You should put some antihistamine cream on it and see if it gets better.

C: Do you have any?

D: Yes, I'm sure I have some somewhere. You'll have to check the date on the tube, though. I'm not sure how long I've had it.

3

E: Ow!

F: Is your wrist still hurting you?

E: Yeah, actually it is. It hurts when I move it.

F: It might be worth getting it X-rayed. It's been, what, three days now? I wouldn't just ignore it. You might have broken something.

E: No, you're probably right. But I'm sure it's just a sprain, from when I fell against the table …

F: Even so, it's probably best to get it looked at.

E: Hmm.

F: Why don't you go and see Rosana in reception? She's the first-aid person. She'll know.

E: Good idea.

Unit 11

▶ 88

I = interviewer

1

I: Do you follow the news?

M: Yes, most of the time. I get the headlines direct to my phone so that I can keep up with business news. I never buy papers. I just catch up with the news online. Every couple of days, I take a quick look through world news or at the comment and analysis sections, and I bookmark an article if it looks interesting.

2

I: How often do you read or buy a newspaper?

W: Oh! I don't read the paper. I don't have time. I can watch the news on my tablet, but I don't usually click on headlines unless they're about celebrities. If there's a video clip, then I might take a quick look at that. I prefer that to reading.

3

I: What kind of news stories interest you?

M: I like stories about my town, so I follow a couple of local websites. Also, celebrity interviews are always fun to read, but I don't believe everything I read because journalists sometimes change people's words. But when I'm on the bus, I usually read the gossip column rather than the serious news.

4

I: How often do you share news stories you see online?

W: I sometimes send a story to friends if it's something that makes me laugh. I wouldn't share the big headline stories because my friends are probably reading about them, anyway. I mean, we have 24-hour news on TV and live streams of news online all day, don't we?

▶ 90

1

A: I like this Twitter travel idea.

B: What's that?

A: It's this travel journalist, Rita Shaw. She goes to different places and asks her followers on social media to suggest things to do. You know, "I just got off the train in Paris and I'm feeling hungry. Where can I get a good breakfast?" That sort of thing.

B: OK. And then what happens?

A: And then she writes about it. It's like a travel guide by the people who live in places—they're the ones who really know what's good. It's a great idea to use social media for something like that.

B: I didn't realize social media could actually be useful for anything!

2

C: It says here there's an eclipse tomorrow. Did you know?

D: Tomorrow? I thought it was today.

C: No, tomorrow. We should be able to see it from here. I'm just looking at this weather website. It's reminding people not to look at it with telescopes.

D: Yeah, I know.

C: It's a pretty good website, actually. It tells you all kinds of things.

D: I know. I have it bookmarked.

C: Oh, I wondered if you did.

3

E: Wow, that's terrible. Have you seen this? It's bad enough to lose your job, but finding out from a text message would be really bad.

F: I saw that story. The company sent about 200 employees a text message. They told them not to show up for work on Monday.

E: I didn't think that you could do that.

F: Me neither, but the company did it anyway. …

4

G: Oh, that's hilarious!

H: Hmm …?

G: You know that weird politician, the one who believes in UFOs?

H: Oh, yeah, I can't remember his name, but I know who you mean.

G: He posted a video on the internet. He invited all friendly aliens to come to a meeting with the government.

H: No way! I didn't know you followed him online.

G: I don't, but there's an article about it in the paper. Look!

▶ 94

1

A = voicemail, R = Roger

A: The person you are calling is not available. Please leave a message after the tone.

R: Hi. This is a message for Anna Price. It's about the apartment for rent downtown, the one advertised online. OK, um, my name is Roger. My number is 96235601. So, I'll try to call you later if I don't hear from you first. Thanks.

2

R = Roger, S = secretary

S: P and Q Associates, good morning.

R: Oh, hello. Could I speak to Jess Parker, please?

S: I'm afraid she's not in the office at the moment. Can I take a message?

R: Actually, I'm returning her call. She left me a message this morning.

S: OK, I'll let her know that you called. Who's calling?

R: It's Roger Lee. She has my number.

S: OK, well, I'm sure she'll get back to you as soon as she comes in, Mr. Lee.

R: OK, thanks.

▶ 95

1

T = Tony, A = Anna

T: Morning, Anna!

A: Oh, hi, Tony. Oh, someone called about the apartment downtown. He called my number, but it should go to you, really. You're handling those apartments, aren't you? Let me see. His name's Roger and his number is 96235601, but he said he'd call back.

T: OK, thanks. I'll give him a call.

2

J = Jess, S = secretary

J: Hi, I'm back.

S: Hi, Jess. Just a minute. There were a couple of calls for you while you were out. Suzy … she said she would call back … and a guy named Roger said he was returning your call.

J: OK, thanks. Any more?

S: No, that's all.

▶ 96

1 Could I speak to Jess Parker, please?

2 Can you give her a message?

3 I wonder whether I could leave a message.

4 I wonder if you could tell her I called.

Unit 12

▶ 97

I = interviewer, F = farmer

I: I'm here on the Isle of Lewis, in the Hebrides. It takes almost three hours to get here on the ferry from the Scottish mainland, so obviously it's not a journey people do every day. The traditional industries in the Hebrides include fishing and farming—mainly sheep. I'm with Alistair, a Hebridean farmer. Alistair, you were telling me about moving sheep by boat. That sounds like a difficult task! I've never heard of putting sheep in a boat before.

F: Well, it's not as hard as it sounds. It's normal practice for us.

I: Why do you need to move the sheep like this? Where do you take them?

F: We move them over to a small island for the summer, where there's plenty of grass for them to eat. The thing is, we can only fit a few in the boat, so we have to go back and forth a few times.

I: And when do you bring them back?

F: We normally go and get them to bring them back to the main island for the winter. We fetch them before the bad weather starts, usually in September. Do you want to come across to the island with me one day?

I: OK! Why not? It should be interesting.

▶ 99

E = Emma, B = Beth

(The words of Emma Stokes are spoken by an actor.)

E: The first real eye-opener I had of what life was like in the African forest was on my first ever expedition. It was the first day, and we ended up making camp early that evening. I was exhausted, and I fell fast asleep right away.
About four hours later, I was woken up by a lot of screaming and shouting and the words NJOKO, NJOKO! It was the local trackers shouting. Then I heard loud trumpeting and sounds of heavy steps. Basically, we'd put our tent in the middle of a giant elephant path. We couldn't have picked a more inappropriate place! By the time I'd managed to get all my gear and get out of the tent, all of the trackers and all of the local guides had already disappeared into the night. When we came back, three of the tents were completely destroyed. That was my first taste of where not to set up a camp in the forest.

(The words of Beth Shapiro are spoken by an actor.)

B: A couple of summers ago, we went to Siberia. We were looking for mammoth bones and tusks, and even hoping to find some mammoth mummies. We flew in on a small plane. It's pretty remote, and there are no people there. When you land and get out of the plane, you look around and there's nothing there. And you set up your camp and there's still nothing there. And you're sitting there, relaxing, in total silence and there's nothing … Then all of a sudden, you're joined by ten million mosquitoes. I remember we made this kind of rice and fish dish for dinner, and we were sitting there, trying to enjoy this rice and fish meal … being eaten alive by mosquitoes. We had nets over our heads, but they were totally inadequate. The mosquitoes could still bite you. And you had to take the net off in order to eat. Every time

you did that, hundreds of mosquitoes landed all over your face. They got in the food as well. It was just one part rice, one part fish, and one part mosquito! You could go crazy after just a few days of that!

▶ 102

1

A: Is everything OK with your food?

B: Yes, yes, it's fine. But, um, I should have told you that I don't eat meat.

A: Oh! Oh, dear!

B: I'm really sorry you went to all this trouble.

A: There's no need to apologize—it's not a problem.

B: No, I should have said something earlier.

A: It's OK. I should have asked you if there was anything you couldn't eat. It's my fault. I'll make you something else.

B: No, please don't. The vegetables are delicious, and there's plenty to eat.

A: Are you sure?

B: Yes, really. I'm enjoying this. I'll just leave the meat if that's OK with you.

A: OK.

2

C: Oh, my goodness! What was that?

D: I dropped the tray of glasses!

C: Oh, those nice glasses from Italy …

D: I couldn't help it—I slipped.

C: Are you OK? Let me help you up. You are clumsy, though.

D: Don't blame me—this floor is slippery.

C: Yes, but if you'd been more careful …

D: Look, it was an accident! It could have happened to anyone.

C: I know, I know. It's not your fault. Sorry I got upset.

D: It is a shame about those glasses, though. We just got them!

3

E: I'm so sorry I kept you waiting. The bus didn't come!

F: Were you waiting for the number 46?

E: Yes, it was supposed to come at 5:30.

F: Don't worry about it—that bus is terrible. It's always late.

E: I tried to call you, but I couldn't get through.

F: Ah, I think my phone is turned off! Sorry about that!

E: Oh, no! I'm almost an hour late!

F: It's OK. It's just one of those things— buses are unreliable! Anyway, you're here now—that's the main thing.

Life Student's Book 4, 2nd Edition
Helen Stephenson, John Hughes,
Paul Dummett

Vice President, Editorial Director:
  John McHugh

Publisher: Andrew Robinson

Senior Development Editor: Derek Mackrell

Editorial Assistant: Dawne Law

Director of Global Marketing: Ian Martin

Senior Product Marketing Manager:
  Caitlin Thomas

Media Researcher: Rebecca Ray,
  Leila Hishmeh

Senior IP Analyst: Alexandra Ricciardi

IP Project Manager: Carissa Poweleit

Senior Director, Production:
  Michael Burggren

Production Manager: Daisy Sosa

Content Project Manager: Beth McNally

Manufacturing Planner:
  Mary Beth Hennebury

Art Director: Brenda Carmichael

Cover Design: Lisa Trager

Text design: emc design ltd.

Compositor: Doubleodesign Ireland, Ltd

American Adaptation: Kasia McNabb

For product information and technology assistance, contact us at
Cengage Learning Customer & Sales Support, cengage.com/contact
For permission to use material from this text or product,
submit all requests online at **cengage.com/permissions**
Further permissions questions can be emailed to
permissionrequest@cengage.com

Student Book + App: 978-1-337-90565-7
Student Book + App + My Life Online: 978-1-337-90571-8

National Geographic Learning
20 Channel Center Street
Boston, MA 02210
USA

National Geographic Learning, a Cengage Learning Company, has a mission to bring the world to the classroom and the classroom to life. With our English language programs, students learn about their world by experiencing it. Through our partnerships with National Geographic and TED Talks, they develop the language and skills they need to be successful global citizens and leaders.

Locate your local office at **international.cengage.com/region**

Visit National Geographic Learning online at **NGL.Cengage.com/ELT**
Visit our corporate website at **www.cengage.com**

CREDITS
Although every effort has been made to contact copyright holders before publication, this has not always been possible. If notified, the publisher will undertake to rectify any errors or omissions at the earliest opportunity.
Text: p15: source: 'A world together', by Erla Zwingle, National Geographic, August 01, 1999. www.nationalgeographic.com; p36: source: 'Return to Titanic', Titanic: The Final Secret, National Geographic, National Geographic Channel; p39: source: 'Love and death in the sea', by Enric Sala, National Geographic, June 08, 2011. http://newswatch.nationalgeographic.com; p51: source: 'A better life', by Peter Hessler, National Geographic, May 2008. http://ngm.nationalgeographic.com/2008/05/china/whats-next/hessler-text; p58: source: 'Pizza with a pedigree', National Geographic Magazine, August 2008; p60: source: 'Imaginary eating', by Christine Dell'Amore, National Geographic, December 2010. http://news.nationalgeographic.com/news/2010/12/101209-chocolate-obesity-science-mind-diet-weight-loss-eat-food/; p63: source: 'A caffeine-fuelled world', by T.R. Reid, National Geographic. http://science.nationalgeographic.com/science/health-and-human-body/human-body/caffeine-buzz/; p75: source: 'Amelia Earhart Spit Samples to Help Lick Mystery?', by Ker Than, National Geographic, February 18, 2011. http://news.nationalgeographic.com/news/2011/02/110218-amelia-earhart-spit-dna-mystery-disappearance-saliva-science/, and source: 'Where is Amelia Earhart? - Three theories Lost and found', by John Roach, National Geographic, December 15, 2003. http://news.nationalgeographic.com/news/2003/12/1215_031215_ameliaearhart.html; p77: source: 'Georgian woman cuts off web access to whole of Armenia', Guardian News and Media Limited. http://www.guardian.co.uk/world/2011/apr/06/georgian-woman-cuts-web-access; p82: source: 'Before New York', by Peter Miller, National Geographic. http://ngm.nationalgeographic.com/2009/09/manhattan/miller-text; p87: source: 'Sweet songs and strong coffee', by Àitor Garrido Jiménez, allgristthemill.blogspot.co.uk; p94: source: 'Holidays and memories', NG Traveler, National Geographic, April 2013; p96: sources: 'Walking for wildlife', by Mike Fay, National Geographic. http://www.nationalgeographic.com/explorers/bios/michael-fay/, http://kids.nationalgeographic.com/explore/explorers/interview-with-mike-fay/ and http://radio.nationalgeographic.com/radio/ng-weekend-archives/1205/; p111: source: 'The art of the deal', by Andrew McCarthy, National Geographic, January/February 2011, http://travel.nationalgeographic.com/travel/countries/morocco-traveler/; p123: source: 'Diane Van Deren', by Andrea Minarcek, National Geographic, 2009. http://adventure.nationalgeographic.com/, and source: 'John Bul Dau, Humanitarian', National Geographic. www.nationalgeographic.com/; p142: source: 'Want to search for the Northwest Passage like

Printed in Mexico
Print Number: 06   Print Year: 2023

a 19th-century British explorer? Bring your sterling silverware and hubris', by Mary Anne Potts, National Geographic, April 07, 2010. ngadventure. typepad.com/blog/2010/04/want-to-seach-for-the-northwest-passage-like-a-19thcentury-british-explorer-bring-your-sterling-silv.html; p144: source: 'Experts in the wild', by Emma Stokes, National Geographic. http://www.nationalgeographic.com/field/explorers/emma-stokes/, and source 'Experts in the wild', by Beth Shapiro, National Geographic. http://www.nationalgeographic.com/field/explorers/beth-shapiro/; p147: source: 'The Samurai Way', by Tom O'Neill, National Geographic, December 2003, p. 98.

Cover: © Getty Images.

Photos: 6 (t) Andrew Wilson/Alamy Stock Photo; 6 (m) © TebNad/Shutterstock.com; 6 (bl) © NurPhoto/Getty Images; 6 (br) © Cory Richards/ National Geographic Creative; 7 (tl) © NASA; 7 (tr) © Krystle Wright/National Geographic Creative; 7 (bl) © Aaron Huey/National Geographic Creative; 7 (br) © Chris Caldicott/Design Pics/Getty Images; 8 (tl) © Erika Larsen/National Geographic Creative; 8 (tm) © Austin Beahm; 8 (tr) © Kos Picture Source/Getty Images; 8 (mtl) © Robin Van Lonkhuijsen/AFP/Getty Images; 8 (mtm) © Brian Finke c/o Everybody Somebody Inc/ National Geographic Creative; 8 (mtr) © Andrew Lever/4Corners Image Library; 8 (mbl) © Brian Skerry/National Geographic Creative; 8 (mbm) © Jonathan & Angela Scott/AWL Images/Getty Images; 8 (mbr) © Arcansel/Shutterstock.com; 8 (bl) © Pierre Verdy /AFP/Getty Images; 8 (bm) © Chris Rainier; 8 (br) © Jim Richardson/National Geographic Creative; 9 © Erika Larsen/National Geographic Creative; 10 (t) © Passakorn sakulphan/Shutterstock.com; 10 (mt) © Miau/Shutterstock.com; 10 (m) © Joachim Wendler/Shutterstock.com; 10 (mb) © dan_chippendale/Getty Images; 10 (b) chris brignell/Alamy Stock Photo; 12 Keren Su/China Span/Alamy Stock Photo; 13 (t) © Tim Laman/National Geographic Creative; 13 (b) LOOK Die Bildagentur der Fotografen GmbH/Alamy Stock Photo; 15 © Adriana Zehbrauskas/Bloomberg/Getty Images; 16 © Rawpixel. com/Shutterstock.com; 17 © Design Pics Inc/National Geographic Creative; 18 © Chris Caldicott/Design Pics/Getty Images; 20 © sharptoyou/ Shutterstock.com; 21 © Austin Beahm; 22 © Laura Boushnak/AFP/Getty Images; 24 © Tanya Kirnishi; 27 © R.M. Nunes/Shutterstock.com; 29 Photos 12/Alamy Stock Photo; 30 robertharding/Alamy Stock Photo; 32 © Paul Whitton; 33 © Kos Picture Source/Getty Images; 34 (l) © Stuart Westmorland/Getty Images; 34 (r) © Sportstock/Shutterstock.com; 35 © John Stanmeyer/National Geographic Creative; 36 © Emory Kristof/ National Geographic Creative; 37 © Mansell/The LIFE Picture Collection/Getty Images; 38 © hadynyah/iStockphoto; 39 (b) © xavierarnau/Getty Images; 40 © Cesar Badilla/REX Shutterstock; 41 © Jorge Fajl/National Geographic Creative; 42 © Krystle Wright/National Geographic Creative; 44 (l) © Max Earey/Shutterstock.com; 44 (tm) © Catalin Petolea/Shutterstock.com; 44 (tr) © Elena Elisseeva/Shutterstock.com; 44 (bm) © Filipe Frazao/Shutterstock.com; 44 (br) © Andrew Mayovskyy/Shutterstock.com; 45 © Robin Van Lonkhuijsen/AFP/Getty Images; 46 © Monty Rakusen/ Getty Images; 47 © Yoshikazu Tsuno/AFP/Getty Images; 48 (t) ZUMA Press, Inc./Alamy Stock Photo; 48 (m) © Abraham Nowitz/National Geographic Creative; 48 (b) Reuters/Alamy Stock Photo; 51 (t) © Efired/Shutterstock.com; (b) © Fritz Hoffmann/National Geographic Creative; 54 © Aaron Huey/National Geographic Creative; 56 (l) © Fritz Hoffmann/National Geographic Creative; 56 (tm) © Andrey_Popov/Shutterstock.com; 56 (tr) © freedomnaruk/Shutterstock.com; 56 (bm) © gpointstudio/Shutterstock.com; 56 (br) © 135pixels/Shutterstock.com; 57 © Brian Finke c/o Everybody Somebody Inc/National Geographic Creative; 58 © Rebecca Hale/National Geographic Creative; 59 (l) jeremy sutton-hibbert/Alamy Stock Photo; 59 (ml) © mypokcik/Shutterstock.com; 59 (mr) Arctic Images/Alamy Stock Photo; 59 (r) © Bork/Shutterstock.com; 60 © Photography by Fernando de Otto/Getty Images; 63 © TommL/Getty Images; 64 (tl) © Rob White/Getty Images; 64 (tr) © Foodpictures/Shutterstock.com; 64 (bl) Alexander Mychko/Alamy Stock Photo; 64 (br) © Rohit Seth/Shutterstock.com; 66 Malcolm Wray/Alamy Stock Photo; 68 © Abraham Nowitz/ National Geographic Creative; 69 © Andrew Lever/4Corners Image Library; 70 © ThomasVogel/Getty Images; 72–73 © Robert Clark/National Geographic Creative; 75 © Keystone-France/Getty Images; 76 (l) © Ken Welsh/age fotostock/Photo Library; 76 (r) © Paul Chesley/National Geographic Creative; 77 © Sebastian Tomus/Shutterstock.com; 78 Andrew Wilson/Alamy Stock Photo; 80 andrew parker/Alamy Stock Photo; 81 © Brian Skerry/National Geographic Creative; 82–83 (t) © Markley Boyer/National Geographic Creative; 82–83 (b) © Robert Clark/National Geographic Creative; 84 (tl) © Apurva Madia/Shutterstock.com; 84 (tr) © David Edwards/National Geographic Creative; 84 (bl) © Claudiovidri/ Shutterstock.com; 84 (br) © Frans Lanting/National Geographic Creative; 87 © Amy Toensing/National Geographic Creative; 88 Image Source/ Alamy Stock Photo; 90 © TebNad/Shutterstock.com; 92 © Donald Miralle/Getty Images; 93 © Jonathan & Angela Scott/AWL Images/Getty Images; 94 © Sean Gallagher/National Geographic Creative; 96 © Michael Nichols/National Geographic Creative; 99 © Fabi Fliervoet; 100 © koh sze kiat/Shutterstock.com; 101 © 102 © Cory Richards/National Geographic Creative; 104 (l) © Pius Lee/Shutterstock.com; 105 © Arcansel/ Shutterstock.com; 106 (t) keith morris/Alamy Stock Photo; 106 (b) © Chris Ratcliffe/Bloomberg/Getty Images; 107 © Mariana Greif Etchebehere/ Bloomberg/Getty Images; 108 © Matt McClain/The Washington Post/Getty Images; 109 Roger Davies/Alamy Stock Photo; 110 © Chirs Rainer/ National Geographic Creative; 111 © Angiolo Manetti; 112 © pcruciatti/Shutterstock.com; 113 (t) LAMB/Alamy Stock Photo; 113 (b) © topnatthapon/ Shutterstock.com; 114 © Jonathan Knowles/Getty Images; 116 (l) © withGod/Shutterstock.com; 116 (r) © Sylvie Bouchard/Shutterstock.com; 117 © Pierre Verdy /AFP/Getty Images; 118 titoOnz/Alamy Stock Photo; 120 © Michael Buholzer/AFP/Getty Images; 121 © Bryan Christie Design; 123 (t) © Masterfile Royalty Free; 123 (b) © Mark Thiessen/National Geographic Creative; 124 mark phillips/Alamy Stock Photo; 125 © Martin Valigursky/ Shutterstock.com; 126 (inset) ITAR-TASS Photo Agency/Alamy Stock Photo; 126 © NASA; 128 © Jimmy Chin and Lynsey Dyer/National Geographic Creative; 129 © Chris Rainier; 130 © Ricardo Stuckert; 131 © Michael Nichols/National Geographic Creative; 132 © STRDEL/Stringer/Getty Images; 135 © Matthieu Paley/National Geographic Creative; 136 © Dragon Images/Shutterstock.com; 138 © NurPhoto/Getty Images; 139 Eddie Phantana/ Shutterstock.com; 140 Arina Habich/Alamy Stock Photo; 141 © Jim Richardson/National Geographic Creative; 142 © 2011 by Anchor Books, a division of Penguin Random House Group Inc., from "The Man Who Ate His Boots: The Tragic History of the Search for the Northeast Passage" by Anthony Brandt. Used by permission of Alfred A. Knopf, a division of Random House Inc.; 142–143 © Paul Nicklen/National Geographic Creative; 144 (t) © John Goodrich/National Geographic Creative; 144 (b) © Beth Shapiro/National Geographic Creative; 145 © Lynn Johnson/National Geographic Creative; 147 © Ira Block/National Geographic Creative; 148 © Birgid Allig/Getty Images; 149 © Image Source/Getty Images; 150 Danita Delimont/Alamy Stock Photo; 152 © Steve Winter/National Geographic Creative.

Illustrations: 6–7 DATA SOURCES: Shaded relief and bathymetry: GTOPO30, USGS EROS Data Center, 2000. ETOPO1/Amante and Eakins, 2009. Land cover: Natural Earth. naturalearthdata.com. Population Density: LandScan 2012 Global Population Database. Developed by Oak Ridge National Laboratory (ORNL), July 2013. Distributed by East View Geospatial: geospatial.com and East View Information Services: eastview.com/ online/landscan. Original copyright year: 2015; 28 (l, r) Matthew Hams; 28 (m) emc design; 70 Laszlo Veres/Beehive Illustration.

ACKNOWLEDGEMENTS

The *Life* publishing team would like to thank the following teachers and students who provided invaluable and detailed feedback on the first edition:

Armik Adamians, Colombo Americano, Cali; Carlos Alberto Aguirre, Universidad Madero, Puebla; Anabel Aikin, La Escuela Oficial de Idiomas de Coslada, Madrid, Spain; Pamela Alvarez, Colegio Eccleston, Lanús; Manuel Antonio, CEL – Unicamp, São Paolo; Bob Ashcroft, Shonan Koka University; Linda Azzopardi, Clubclass; Éricka Bauchwitz, Universidad Madero, Puebla, Mexico; Paola Biancolini, Università Cattolica del Sacro

Cuore, Milan; Lisa Blazevic, Moraine Valley Community College; Laura Bottiglieri, Universidad Nacional de Salta; Richard Brookes, Brookes Talen, Aalsmeer; Alan Broomhead, Approach International Student Center; Maria Cante, Universidad Madero, Puebla; Carmín Castillo, Universidad Madero, Puebla; Ana Laura Chacón, Universidad Madero, Puebla; Somchao Chatnaridom, Suratthani Rajabhat University, Surat Thani; Adrian Cini, British Study Centres, London; Andrew Clarke, Centre of English Studies, Dublin; Mariano Cordoni, Centro Universitario de Idiomas, Buenos Aires; Kevin Coughlan, Westgate Corporation; Monica Cuellar, Universidad La Gran Colombia, Colombia; Jacqui Davis-Bowen, St Giles International; Maria del Vecchio, Nihon University; Nuria Mendoza Dominguez, Universidad Nebrija, Madrid; Robin Duncan, ITC London; Christine Eade, Libera Università Internazionale degli Studi Sociali Guido Carli, Rome; Colegios de Alto Rendimiento, Ministry of Education of Peru; Leopoldo Pinzon Escobar, Universidad Catolica; Joanne Evans, Linguarama, Berlin; Scott Ferry, UC San Diego ELI; Juan David Figueroa, Colombo Americano, Cali; Emmanuel Flores, Universidad del Valle de Puebla; Bridget Flynn, Centro Colombo Americano Medellin; Sally Fryer, University of Sheffield, Sheffield; Antonio David Berbel García, Escuela Oficial de Idiomas de Almería, Spain; Lia Gargioni, Feltrinelli Secondary School, Milan; Roberta Giugni, Galileo Galilei Secondary School, Legnano; Monica Gomez, Universidad Pontificia Bolivariana; Doctor Erwin Gonzales, Centro de Idiomas Universidad Nacional San Agustin, Peru; Ivonne Gonzalez, Universidad de La Sabana; J Gouman, Pieter Zandt Scholengemeenschap, Kampen; Cherryll Harrison, UNINT, Rome; Lottie Harrison, International House Recoleta; Marjo Heij, CSG Prins Maurits, Middelharnis; María del Pilar Hernández, Universidad Madero, Puebla; Luz Stella Hernandez, Universidad de La Sabana, Colombia; Rogelio Herrera, Colombo Americano, Cali; Amy Huang, Language Canada, Taipei; Huang Huei-Jiun, Pu Tai Senior High School; Carol Humme, Moraine Valley Community College; Nelson Jaramillo, Colombo Americano, Cali; Jacek Kaczmarek, Xiehe YouDe High School, Taipei; Thurgadevi Kalay, Kaplan, Singapore; Noreen Kane, Centre of English Studies, Dublin; Billy Kao, Jinwen University of Science and Technology; Shih-Fan Kao, Jinwen University of Science and Technology, Taipei; Youmay Kao, Mackay Junior College of Medicine, Nursing, and Management, Taipei; Fleur Kelder, Vechtstede College, Weesp; Waseem Khan, YBM; Dr Sarinya Khattiya, Chiang Mai University; Lucy Khoo, Kaplan; Karen Koh, Kaplan, Singapore; Susan Langerfeld, Liceo Scientifico Statale Augusto Righi, Rome; Hilary Lawler, Centre of English Studies, Dublin; Jon Leachtenauer, Ritsumeikan University; Eva Lendi, Kantonsschule Zürich Nord, Zürich; Michael Ryan Lesser, Busan University of Foreign Studies; Evon Lo, Jinwen University of Science and Technology; Peter Loftus, Centre of English Studies, Dublin; José Luiz, Inglês com Tecnologia, Cruzeiro; Christopher MacGuire, UC Language Center, Chile; Eric Maher, Centre of English Studies, Dublin; Nick Malewski, ITC London; Claudia Maribell Loo, Universidad Madero, Puebla; Malcolm Marr, ITC London; Graciela Martin, ICANA (Belgrano); Michael McCollister, Feng Chia University; Erik Meek, CS Vincent van Gogh, Assen; Marlene Merkt, Kantonsschule Zürich Nord, Zürich; Jason Montgomery, YBM; David Moran, Qatar University, Doha; Rosella Morini, Feltrinelli Secondary School, Milan; Christopher Mulligan, Ritsumeikan University; Judith Mundell, Quarenghi Adult Learning Centre, Milan; Cinthya Nestor, Universidad Madero, Puebla; Nguyen Dang Lang, Duong Minh Language School; Peter O'Connor, Musashino University, Tokyo; Cliona O'Neill, Trinity School, Rome; María José Colón Orellana, Escola Oficial d'Idiomes de Terrassa, Barcelona; Viviana Ortega, Universidad Mayor, Santiago; Luc Peeters, Kyoto Sangyo University, Kyoto; Sanja Brekalo Pelin, La Escuela Oficial de Idiomas de Coslada, Madrid; Itzel Carolina Pérez, Universidad Madero, Puebla, Mexico; Sutthima Peung, Rajamangala University of Technology Rattanakosin; Marina Pezzuoli, Liceo Scientifico Amedeo Avogadro, Rome; Andrew Pharis, Aichi Gakuin University, Nagoya; Hugh Podmore, St Giles International, UK; Carolina Porras, Universidad de La Sabana; Brigit Portilla, Colombo Americano, Cali; Soudaben Pradeep, Kaplan; Judith Puertas, Colombo Americano, Cali; Takako Ramsden, Kyoto Sangyo University, Kyoto; Sophie Rebel-Dijkstra, Aeres Hogeschool; Zita Reszler, Nottingham Language Academy, Nottingham; Sophia Rizzo, St Giles International; Gloria Stella Quintero Riveros, Universidad Catolica; Cecilia Rosas, Euroidiomas; Eleonora Salas, IICANA Centro, Córdoba; Victoria Samaniego, La Escuela Oficial de Idiomas de Pozuelo de Alarcón, Madrid; Jeanette Sandre, Universidad Madero, Puebla; Bruno Scafati, ARICANA; Anya Shaw, International House Belgrano, Argentina; Anne Smith, UNINT, Rome & University of Rome Tor Vergata, Italy; Courtney Smith, US Ling Institute; Suzannah Spencer-George, British Study Centres, Bournemouth; Students of Cultura Inglesa, São Paulo; Makiko Takeda, Aichi Gakuin University, Nagoya; Jilly Taylor, British Study Centres, London; Caroline S. Tornatore, Austin Community College; Juliana Trisno, Kaplan, Singapore; Ruey Miin Tsao, National Cheng Kung University, Tainan City; Michelle Uitterhoeve, Vechtstede College, Weesp; Anna Maria Usai, Liceo Spallanzani, Rome; Carolina Valdiri, Colombo Americano, Cali, Colombia; Keith Vargo, Westgate Corporation; Gina Vasquez, Colombo Americano, Cali; Andreas Vikran, NET School of English, Milan; Helen Ward, Oxford, UK; Mimi Watts, Università Cattolica del Sacro Cuore, Milan; Yvonne Wee, Kaplan Higher Education Academy; Christopher Wood, Meijo University; Kevin Wu, Hangzhou No.14 High School; Yanina Zagarrio, ARICANA.